KU-497-932

THE ECONOMICS OF HOUSEHOLD GARBAGE AND RECYCLING BEHAVIOR

NEW HORIZONS IN ENVIRONMENTAL ECONOMICS

Series Editors: Wallace E. Oates, *Professor of Economics, University of Maryland, USA* and Henk Folmer, *Professor of General Economics, Wageningen University and Professor of Environmental Economics, Tilburg University, The Netherlands*

This important series is designed to make a significant contribution to the development of the principles and practices of environmental economics. It includes both theoretical and empirical work. International in scope, it addresses issues of current and future concern in both East and West and in developed and developing countries.

The main purpose of the series is to create a forum for the publication of high quality work and to show how economic analysis can make a contribution to understanding and resolving the environmental problems confronting the world in the twenty-first century.

Recent titles in the series include:

Economic Theory for the Environment
Essays in Honour of Karl-Göran Mäler
Edited by Bengt Kriström, Partha Dasgupta and Karl-Gustaf Löfgren

Instruments for Climate Policy
Limited versus Unlimited Flexibility
Edited by Johan Albrecht

Environmental Co-operation and Institutional Change
Theories and Policies for European Agriculture
Edited by Konrad Hagedorn

Valuing Environmental and Natural Resources
The Econometrics of Non-Market Valuation
Timothy C. Haab and Kenneth E. McConnell

The Economics of Household Garbage and Recycling Behavior
Edited by Don Fullerton and Thomas C. Kinnaman

Controlling Global Warming
Perspectives from Economics, Game Theory and Public Choice
Edited by Christoph Böhringer, Michael Finus and Carsten Vogt

Environmental Regulation in a Federal System
Framing Environmental Policy in the European Union
Tim Jeppesen

The International Yearbook of Environmental and Resource Economics 2002/2003
A Survey of Current Issues
Edited by Tom Tietenberg and Henk Folmer

International Climate Policy to Combat Global Warming
An Analysis of the Ancillary Benefites of Reducing Carbon Emissions
Dirk T.G. Rübbelke

Pollution, Property and Prices
An Essay in Policy-making & Economics
J.H. Dales

The Contingent Valuation of Natural Parks
Assessing the Warmglow Propensity Factor
Paulo A.L.D. Nunes

The Economics of Household Garbage and Recycling Behavior

Edited by

Don Fullerton

Department of Economics, University of Texas at Austin

Thomas C. Kinnaman

Department of Economics, Bucknell University

Foreword by

Tom Tietenberg

NEW HORIZONS IN ENVIRONMENTAL ECONOMICS

Edward Elgar

Cheltenham, UK • Northampton, MA, USA

© Don Fullerton and Thomas C. Kinnaman 2002.

All rights reserved. No part of this publication may be reproduced, stored in a retrieval system or transmitted in any form or by any means, electronic, mechanical or photocopying, recording, or otherwise without the prior permission of the publisher.

Published by
Edward Elgar Publishing Limited
Glensanda House
Montpellier Parade
Cheltenham
Glos GL50 1UA
UK

Edward Elgar Publishing, Inc.
136 West Street
Suite 202
Northampton
Massachusetts 01060
USA

A catalogue record for this book
is available from the British Library

ISBN 1 84064 718 3

Printed and bound in Great Britain by MPG Books Ltd, Bodmin, Cornwall

Contents

Acknowledgements

The Editors and publisher wish to thank the following who have kindly given permission for the use of copyright material.

Academic Press for 'Garbage, Recycling, and Illicit Burning or Dumping', *Journal of Environmental Economics and Management*, **29** (1), July 1995, 78–91; 'Policies for Green Design', D. Fullerton and W. Wu, *Journal of Environmental Economics and Management*, **36** (2), September 1998, 131–48; 'Garbage and Recycling with Endogenous Local Policy', *Journal of Urban Economics*, **48**, November 2000, 419–42.

American Economic Association for 'Household Responses to Pricing Garbage by the Bag', *American Economic Review*, **86** (4), September 1996, 971–84; 'Environmental Levies and Distortionary Taxation: Comment', D. Fullerton, *American Economic Review*, **87** (1), March 1997, 245–51.

Kluwer Academic Publishers for 'How a Fee Per-Unit Garbage Affects Aggregate Recycling in a Model with Heterogeneous Households', in A.L. Bovenberg and S. Cnossen (eds), *Public Economics and the Environment in an Imperfect World*, 1995, 135–59.

Sage Publications for 'Explaining the Growth in Municipal Recycling Programs: The Role of Market and Nonmarket Factors', T. Kinnaman, *Public Works Management and Policy*, **5** (1), July 2000, 37–51.

The editors wish to thank the U.S. National Science Foundation for funding much of the research in this book. They are also grateful to many colleagues for helpful comments and suggestions.

Every effort has been made to trace all the copyright holders but if any have been inadvertently overlooked the publishers will be pleased to make the necessary arrangements at the first opportunity.

Foreword

Environmental economists have long been frustrated about how little policy makers take economic analysis into account. The laments began in the 1970s with the publication of Allen V. Kneese and Charles L. Schultze's *Pollution, Prices and Public Policy* (1975), but continued to flourish into the 1990s (Hanley *et al.*, 1990).

Recently, however, the tide has been changing. Economic principles and analysis have been having more influence on environmental policy. Some examples of policies that are based at least in part on economic principles include:

- Tradable sulfur dioxide allowances, which encourage utilities to find least cost strategies for controlling acid rain (Ellerman, Joskow *et al.*, 2000)
- Basing air emission permit fees on the quantity of emissions and charging for the disposal of industrial effluents in water treatment plants (Anderson, 2000)
- Imposing liability for natural resource damages caused by oil spills, an incentive to encourage precaution (Alberini and Austin, 1999)
- Subsidizing farmers and others to conserve habitat and control pollution (Smith, 1995)
- Encouraging reductions in pollution by broadly disseminating information about emissions to local communities (Tietenberg and Wheeler, 2001)

One of the most obvious areas where economic incentives have played a major role in reforming environmental policy is in solid waste. The original motivation for the reform was quite simple. The most common existing pricing strategy, charging fees that were unrelated to the volume of waste, resulted in a situation where the marginal cost of disposal was zero. Recognizing this aspect of the pricing system immediately implied that the amount of waste disposed was inefficiently high. This finding in turn seemed to imply that the recycling rate was inefficiently low and so reliance on virgin materials was inefficiently high. Add in the possibility that the combination of reduced waste, coupled with increased revenues from recycled material, could (and in some cases, did) lower waste disposal cost to the reforming community and the reform movement took off.

As with most policies based upon simple principles, however, implementing an efficient policy proved to be somewhat more complex than it initially seemed. How should the disposal fees be set? Does the answer depend on whether illegal disposal is possible? What is an efficient set of waste disposal policies? Can the higher cost associated with curbside recycling be justified by the additional benefits? How much recycling is efficient?

The articles in this volume go a long way to providing a much greater understanding of the sometimes complex issues surrounding solid waste policy. The volume collects the substantial body of work of two economists, Don Fullerton and Tom Kinnaman. Their collaboration began when Kinnaman was a graduate student working with Fullerton at the University of Virginia.

The contributions in this volume include new analytical models, careful empirical work that is based upon original data sets, a benefit–cost analysis of solid waste policies and a comprehensive survey of the broad literature that now exists on this topic.

The analytical models developed in these essays allow us not only to think more systematically about how we would define efficient policy instruments, but they also spawn a wealth of testable hypotheses. One of the most interesting aspects of the derivation of optimal policy instruments in these essays is the crucial role played by the possibility of illegal disposal. In general, if illegal disposal is a possibility (and the evidence presented in these essays suggests that it frequently is), then the traditional approach to volume pricing may be quite inefficient. A theoretically superior alternative, involving a two-part tariff, is also developed in one of the essays in this volume.

The empirical research in these essays not only is based on some unusually rich data sets, but it also takes seriously the problems of dealing with policy endogeneity. The evidence on which the empirical studies are based includes a rich micro-data set on household behavior as well as another data set involving waste disposal practices and results from over 700 communities.

It turns out that moving beyond simple estimating procedures has an important effect on the conclusions of the analysis. For example, the authors discover that correcting for endogenous policy increases the estimated effects of both volume pricing and curbside collection.

One essay in this volume also conducts a detailed benefit–cost analysis of a recycling program in one city (Lewisburg, Pennsylvania). The results suggest that conventionally measured benefits fell short of costs, but when the nonmarket value of recycling was assessed via a contingent valuation study, the benefits comfortably exceeded the costs.

This is a wide-ranging, careful use of economic analysis to shed light on an important environmental problem. Its value stems not only from its contribution to the specific policy issue it addresses, but also as a broader illustration of how good economic research can inform policy. Readers will be rewarded with a host of intriguing (and sometimes provocative) new insights.

Tom Tietenberg
Mitchell Family Professor of Economics
Colby College
Waterville Maine

References

Alberini, A. and D. Austin (1999), 'Strict Liability as a Deterrent in Toxic Waste Management: Empirical Evidence from Accident and Spill Data', *Journal of Environmental Economics and Management*, **38** (1), 20–48.

Anderson, R. (2000), The United States Experience with Economic Incentives for Protecting the Environment (EPA#-240-R-10-001).

Ellerman, A.D., P.L. Joskow, *et al.* (2000), *Markets for Clean Air: The U.S. Acid Rain Program*, Cambridge, UK: Cambridge University Press.

Hanley, N., S. Hallett, *et al.* (1990), 'Research Policy Review 33: Why is More Notice not taken of Economists Prescriptions for the Control of Pollution?', *Environment and Planning A*, **22** (11), 1421–39.

Kneese, A.V. and C.L. Schultze (1975), *Pollution, Prices and Public Policy*, Washington, DC: The Brookings Institution.

Smith, R.B.W. (1995), 'The Conservation Reserve Program as a Least-Cost Land Retirement Mechanism', *American Journal of Agricultural Economics*, **77** (1), 93–105.

Tietenberg, T. and D. Wheeler (2001), 'Empowering the Community: Information Strategies for Pollution Control', *Frontiers of Environmental Economics*, H. Folmer, H.L. Gabel, S. Gerking and A. Rose, Cheltenham, UK: Edward Elgar, 85–120.

[1]

The economics of residential solid waste management

Thomas C. Kinnaman and Don Fullerton

1 INTRODUCTION

The market for residential solid waste management and disposal has experienced dramatic changes over the past 20 years. In the early to mid 1970s, most towns used local garbage dumps. Even though recycling was well known and utilized by the commercial and industrial sectors of the economy, residential recycling was limited to spontaneous collection drives by charitable organizations for old newspapers and aluminium cans. Today, 46 per cent of Americans have access to municipal curbside recycling programmes, many other Americans have local access to drop-off recycling facilities, and garbage is often transported tens, hundreds or even thousands of miles for disposal in a large regional landfill. Recycling has also become more popular in Europe and in other parts of the world.

These market shifts have attracted the attention of economists who have devoted significant attention to understanding the causes and impacts of these events. Economists have also participated in discussions aimed at shaping efficient solid waste policy strategies. This survey article summarizes the economic literature devoted to household solid waste collection and disposal. The next section provides a brief historical introduction to these markets. Section 3 surveys the theoretical literature devoted to suggesting the best way to regulate garbage collection and disposal. Section 4 follows with a summary of solid waste policies in place, and it surveys the empirical studies devoted to those policies. Since household disposal choices determine garbage and recycling totals, section 5 develops a model of household behaviour that generates hypotheses that are subsequently tested by the empirical economics literature.

100

1

2   RECENT TRENDS IN RESIDENTIAL SOLID WASTE

The editors of *Biocycle* magazine (Glenn, 1998) began an annual survey of the 50 states in 1989. Included in these surveys were state estimates of the quantity of solid waste landfilled, incinerated, and recycled in that state. Figure 3.1 summarizes the total use of these three methods of waste removal over the past decade. Although the percentage of household solid waste incinerated remained near 10 per cent over the last decade, the percentage disposed in a landfill decreased from roughly 85 per cent in 1989 to just over 60 per cent in 1997. This decrease was associated primarily with the simultaneous increase in recycling. As illustrated in Figure 3.1, the United States recycled nearly 30 per cent of waste in 1997, up from just 10 per cent in 1989.

How were the states able to increase the recycling rate so dramatically over this time period? The *Biocycle* surveys also show that the number of curbside collection programmes in operation nationwide increased monotonically from

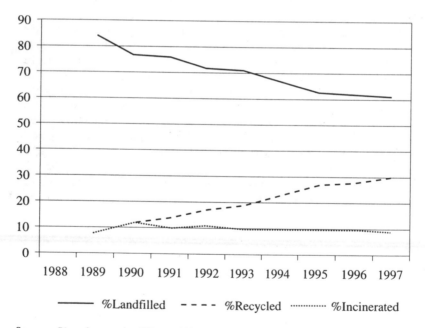

Source: *Biocycle* magazine (Glenn, 1998).

Figure 3.1   Disposal trends (per cent)

just 1000 programmes in 1989 to nearly 9000 programmes in 1997. Local governments administer all of these programmes either by collecting the material directly or by contracting with a single private firm. Growth in the number of programmes has steadied of late.

Economists have debated the extent to which the growth in curbside recycling can be attributed to economic factors such as increases in disposal costs or to non-economic factors. Although this debate is explored more thoroughly below, we now introduce two important economic variables at play. Figure 3.2 presents average tipping fees in several states, and Figure 3.3 presents average prices of recycled materials in the United States over the past ten years. Tipping fee data were obtained from *Biocycle*'s annual survey of the 50 states (Glenn, 1998). Rather than presenting the average for each state, Figure 3.2 illustrates the past ten years' nominal tipping fee for one state from each region of the country. Two lessons can be drawn from this figure. First, the overall trend for tipping fees is weakly positive. But accounting for increases in the general price level, the real tipping fee may not have changed

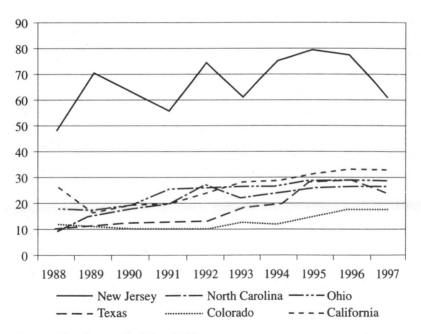

Source: *Biocycle* magazine (Glenn, 1998).

Figure 3.2   Tipping fees (per cent)

much over the past decade. Therefore, attributing the national rise in curbside recycling to increases in the tipping fee is difficult to support with such casual use of data. However, tipping fees in the northeastern region (New Jersey) are greater than in other regions of the country. And, indeed, curbside recycling programmes have become popular in the northeast. Perhaps, then, tipping fees have played an indirect role in encouraging recycling.

The second variable of interest to economists is the price paid for recycled materials. The Bureau of Labor Statistics' data on the prices of corrugated cardboard, old newspaper waste, and scrap aluminium appear in Figure 3.3. Two lessons can also be learned from Figure 3.3. First, when accounting for increases in the general price level, the prices of recycled materials have remained rather constant over the past decade (Ackerman, 1997). Second, prices of recycled materials are highly variable over time. For old newspaper, six spikes have appeared over the past 30 years (not all are illustrated in

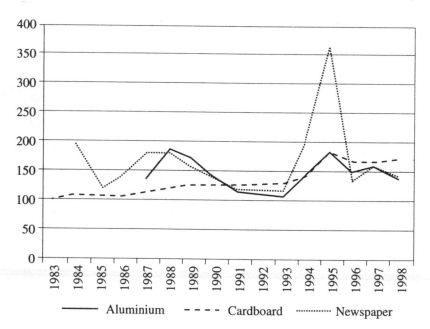

Note: 1982 = 100

Source: Bureau of Labor Statistics (http://stats.bls.gov/blshome.html).

Figure 3.3   Price index of recyclable materials

Figure 3.3). The most recent spike was in 1995 when the price for old newspaper (and many other materials) hit all-time highs. This latest spike has been attributed to new recycled-content laws passed by several state governments (Ackerman, 1997). But overall, these trends do not appear to support the argument that economic forces are responsible for the growth in curbside recycling. This debate is conducted more systematically in the economic papers reviewed below.

The dramatic increase in the number of curbside recycling programmes in operation in the United States could instead be a function of non-economic influences such as changes in voter tastes for the environment or purely political concerns. Misinformation may have contributed to the public's perception of a shortage of landfill space. This perception may have emerged in 1987, when the barge 'Mobro', loaded with Long Island garbage, was unable to unload its cargo after repeated attempts (see Bailey, 1995 for a discussion of the incident). A wave of state and local legislation encouraging or mandating recycling was passed soon after this incident.

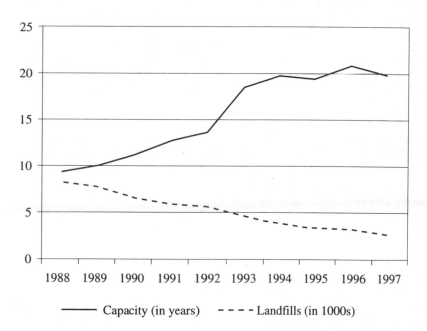

——— Capacity (in years)   – – – Landfills (in 1000s)

Source: *Biocycle* magazine (Glenn, 1998).

Figure 3.4   Landfill crisis?

Is the United States running out of landfill space? Available landfill capacity is difficult to quantify, but the *number* of landfills in operation can be ascertained and reported quite easily. Figure 3.4 illustrates the number of landfills (in thousands) operating each year in the United States over the past decade. This number has been steadily decreasing by about 500 landfills each year. Voters could have confused these data with a national shortage in landfill space (Bailey, 1995). While the *number* of landfills has been steadily decreasing over the past ten years, the estimated *capacity* of remaining landfills has been steadily rising. Based on state-reported estimates (also illustrated in Figure 3.4), the remaining capacity of landfill space has doubled from roughly ten years of remaining capacity in 1988 to 20 years in 1997.

The reason for these dual trends has been the replacement of small local town dumps with large regional sanitary landfills. This trend is due mostly to Subtitle D of the Resource Conservation and Recovery Act (RCRA) of 1976. This law was designed to reduce the negative externalities associated with garbage disposal. This law imposed technology-based standards on the construction, operation, and closure of solid waste landfills. Landfills are now required to install thick plastic linings along the base, collect and treat leachate, monitor groundwater and cover garbage within hours of disposal. Because the fixed costs of constructing and operating a landfill have increased, cost-minimizing landfill sizes increased and fewer landfills have been built. The trend towards large regional landfills may also have been brought on by heightened public awareness over the siting of a landfill in their 'back yard'. Expanding an existing landfill could be politically more feasible than constructing a new one.

A final general development over the past decade has been the slight increase and subsequent decline of incineration as a method of garbage disposal. Figure 3.5 illustrates the number of incinerators in operation in the United States over the past decade. Incineration, once considered a dual solution to the solid waste and energy crises, reached a peak in 1991 when 170 incinerators operated nationally. Since then, the number of incinerators in operation has gradually decreased. This decline has been attributed to a number of factors, but most notably the quantity of garbage available to incinerators became lower than expected. If fixed costs are high, then average costs can be reduced with an increase in garbage throughput. But incinerators could not lower tipping fees to levels necessary to encourage more garbage without incurring financial losses. Therefore, many local governments passed laws requiring all local garbage to be brought to the incinerator, effectively giving the incinerator monopsony power over local garbage. But the Supreme Court struck down these laws, exposing the incineration industry to competition from cheaper landfills. The Supreme Court dealt a second blow to the incineration industry when it ruled that incinerator ash is toxic and must be

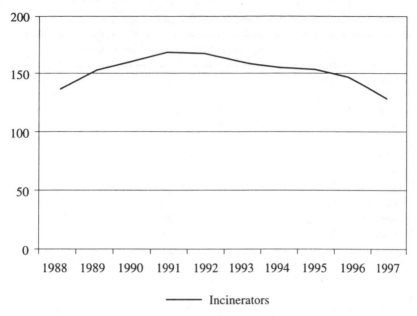

— Incinerators

Source: *Biocycle* magazine (Glenn, 1998).

Figure 3.5   Number of incinerators

disposed of in an expensive toxic waste landfill. The increased use of recycling in the early 1990s further reduced the quantity of garbage available to incinerators, adding to their financial dilemmas. Finally, policymakers were not eager to rescue the industry once the public began to oppose the resulting air pollution emitted by incinerators.

Where land is scarce, however, incineration has become a more viable option. The northeastern portion of the United States incinerates 40 per cent of its waste. Incineration is also popular in Japan and several European countries where population densities and land values are high. Table 3.1 indicates the percentage of waste that was landfilled in several European countries in the mid 1980s (the remaining portion was incinerated). Greece, Ireland and the UK relied almost exclusively on landfills. But Switzerland, Sweden and Denmark relied on incineration to manage the bulk of their garbage. Facing less competition from land-intensive landfills, incinerators in these countries as well as in the northeast region of the United States could capture the economies of scale necessary to keep the average costs of incin-

Table 3.1   Use of landfills for waste disposal in Europe

Country	Per cent landfilled (net of recycling)
Denmark	44
France	54
Greece	100
Ireland	100
Italy	85
The Netherlands	56–61
Sweden	35–49
Switzerland	22–25
United Kingdom	90
United States	90
West Germany	66–74

Source: Jenkins (1993), based on data gathered by US Congress, Office of Technology Assessment (1989).

eration down (Halstead and Park, 1996). But even though many countries relied heavily on incineration, Brisson (1997) finds the private and full external costs of incineration exceed those associated with landfill disposal in most European countries.

3   THE OPTIMAL POLICY IN THE THEORETICAL LITERATURE

This section reviews the economic literature devoted to designing solid waste management policies to achieve the efficient quantity of garbage and recycling. A skeletal model is developed here to frame discussion of optimal policy design. Notation developed for this model will be used throughout this review.

Assume that N identical households each maximizes utility that is defined over consumption (c). Consumption produces waste that must either be disposed of as garbage for collection at the curb (g) or recycled (r). We use $c = c(g,r)$ to represent the various combinations of g and r that are consistent with any particular level of consumption. Given prices paid for consumption (p_c), and garbage collection (p_g), and received for recycled materials (p_r), the household with income (y) will make disposal decisions to maximize utility (u)

$$u = u(c) = u[c(g,r)]$$

subject to the budget constraint

$$y = p_c c(g,r) + p_g g - p_r r.$$

Producers in the model choose virgin (v) and recycled (r) inputs to produce c according to the production function $c = f(v, r)$. Given input prices p_r and p_v (for recycled and virgin materials, respectively), the producer chooses inputs to maximize profit

$$\pi = p_c f(v,r) - p_v v - p_r r.$$

Firms in this model would employ virgin and recycled materials so that the ratio of input prices equals the ratio of marginal products. Households would choose between garbage and recycling in a similar manner. In fact, it is easy to show that since agents in this simple model internalize all of the costs and benefits of their choices, resources are allocated efficiently and the optimal quantities of garbage and recycling are produced. But the total amount of solid waste disposed of ($G = Ng$) could emit foul odour, pollute groundwater, create an eyesore, or contribute to climate change.[1] Household utility could be impacted by these effects, so assume now that $u = u(c, G)$, where $u_G < 0$. Under this assumption, households fail to internalize the full social costs of their disposal decisions. Too much garbage and too little recycling is produced by a decentralized economy.

In order to internalize disposal costs, economists have suggested several tax and subsidy schemes. This section will review the economic literature devoted to designing the tax/subsidy policy that can achieve the efficient allocation of resources in the presence of external costs from garbage disposal. Households could be taxed on each unit of garbage disposed of (at rate t_g) or subsidized for their recycling effort (at rate s_{hr}). Households could also be required to pay an advanced disposal fee at the time of purchase (t_c). Under these policy schemes, households maximize utility

$$u = u[c(g,r), G]$$

subject to the amended budget constraint

$$y = (p_c + t_c)c(g,r) + (p_g + t_g)g - (p_r + s_{hr})r.$$

The producer's use of virgin material could be taxed (t_v), or use of recycled materials could be subsidized (s_{fr}), resulting in the profit function

$$\pi = p_c f(v,r) - (p_v + t_v)v - (p_r - s_{fr})r.$$

Economic research reviewed below has found that various combinations of these policies (t_c, t_g, s_{hr}, s_{fr}, t_v) can encourage a decentralized economy to achieve an efficient allocation of resources. Command and control policies, such as mandatory household recycling ordinances and minimum recycled-content standards on producers, can also achieve efficient outcomes in theory. But economists rarely support such forms of policy because the information required to achieve efficient outcomes is not likely to be available to policymakers. The literature devoted to the study of command and control policies is not rich.

The most direct approach to internalizing the external costs of garbage disposal is to tax each bag of garbage presented by the household (t_g). Most households have traditionally either paid for garbage removal with a flat monthly or quarterly fee, or through local property or income taxes. House-holds that contribute large quantities of garbage therefore pay the same as households that contribute smaller quantities, so the cost per bag ($p_g + t_g$) is zero, even though the social marginal cost of that extra bag is greater than zero. The implementation of a tax (also called a user fee) on each bag of garbage can require households to internalize the social marginal collection and disposal costs.

Using a panel of 12 cities with direct pricing, Jenkins (1993) estimates that pricing garbage according to its social marginal cost would reduce the quantity of garbage produced by households and therefore improve social welfare by as much as $650 million per year, roughly $3 per person per year. Fullerton and Kinnaman (1996) use household data and also estimate the potential benefits of marginal cost pricing to be in the neighbourhood of $3 per person per year. Podolsky and Spiegel (1998) study a cross-section of towns in New Jersey and estimate the economic benefits of charging per unit of garbage to be as great as $12.80 per person per year.

One particular advantage of taxing garbage directly (employing a user fee) is that other tax instruments discussed above are unnecessary for achieving the efficient allocation of resources (Fullerton and Kinnaman, 1995; and Palmer and Walls, 1994). Households may recycle, compost or engage in source reduction according to the private costs they face. As long as house-holds face the full social cost of their disposal decisions, they will make those decisions efficiently. Any increase in recycling can reduce the price of recy-cled materials, making these materials more attractive to manufacturers without a direct tax on virgin materials or subsidy to recycling. In fact, Dinan (1993) finds that a tax on virgin materials (t_v) in combination with a user fee would not be efficient, since the same material is effectively taxed twice. Another advantage of taxing garbage directly is that the only information needed by the local policymaker is the full social cost of each bag of garbage. Repetto *et al.* (1992) estimate this cost to be $1.43–$1.83 per bag, depending on local private and social disposal costs.[2] Finally, Fullerton and Wu (1998) show that pricing garbage according to its social marginal costs can also encourage firms to produce the optimal amount of packaging per unit and to engage in the optimal amount of green design.[3]

Perhaps in response to these arguments, an estimated 4000 communities in the United States have started to price garbage directly (Miranda and Bynum, 1999). These programmes levy a fee on each bag of garbage collected from each household. Garbage collectors can exclude non-payers by utilizing some method of identifying who has paid, such as requiring households to purchase specially marked bags, tags, or stickers.

Several arguments against the use of direct marginal cost pricing of garbage have also appeared in the economics literature. First, taxing garbage may be problematic if illicit or illegal dumping on the part of households is encouraged.[4] Second, the administrative costs of implementing the programme may exceed the social benefits estimated above. Fullerton and Kinnaman (1996) estimate that the administrative costs of printing, distributing and accounting for garbage stickers in Charlottesville, Virginia could exceed the $3 per person per year benefits mentioned above. Third, a uniform tax on all types of garbage may be inefficient if materials within the waste stream produce different social costs (Dinan, 1993). If, for example, the social cost of disposing of flashlight batteries is greater than that of old newspapers, then the disposal tax on flashlight batteries should exceed that on old newspapers. But such a precise tax scheme is costly to administer.

To respond to these problems, Dobbs (1991) and Fullerton and Kinnaman (1995) develop models that suggest that if households have the option to litter or dump their garbage, and if the external costs of littered garbage exceeds that of legally disposed garbage, then the optimal tax on legal garbage disposal (t_g) could be negative. That is, legal garbage disposal should be subsidized. In fact, if the administrative costs of levying a tax on each bag of garbage are significant, then the optimal policy may involve subsidizing garbage at its full price (set $p_g + t_g = 0$). Policymakers can instead implement other policies defined below to achieve efficient disposal choices.

If taxing or even pricing garbage directly is problematic, economists have studied whether the implementation of a tax on virgin materials (t_v) can achieve the efficient allocation of resources in a world where garbage disposal produces external costs. Such a tax could increase producer's demand for recycled inputs, drive up the price paid for recycled materials, and thus increase the economic benefits to households that deliver recyclable materials to secondary markets. Miedema (1983) finds that a tax on virgin materials (t_v) set equal to the social marginal cost of disposing of any resulting waste material produces welfare gains greater than would result from a subsidy on producer's use of recycled materials (s_{fr}), a direct tax on household solid waste (t_g), or an advanced disposal fee (t_c). The main advantage of virgin materials tax is that it both discourages the economy's use of virgin materials (resulting in less subsequent solid waste) and encourages the development of the market for recycled materials.

Other studies have questioned the use of a tax on virgin materials. Dinan (1993) finds that, although a tax on virgin materials encourages the use of recycled materials in industries where the recycled input is a substitute for the taxed virgin input, other industries that do not use the taxed virgin input will not increase demand for recycled materials. For example, farmers could use old newspapers for animal bedding, but a tax on paper manufacturer's use of virgin wood pulp will not encourage this form of recycling. Dinan (1993) also suggests that a domestic tax on virgin materials does not encourage exporters to purchase recycled materials. Significant portions of recyclable paper are currently exported.

Palmer and Walls (1994) develop a model that suggests that, although a tax on virgin materials can encourage the efficient mix of inputs, it can discourage production and consumption in the overall economy. The result is an inefficiently low quantity of garbage. Therefore, the virgin materials tax is only efficient when combined with a subsidy on the sales of final goods. Only for the special case where the marginal product of recycled materials is exactly one (1) can a tax on virgin materials lead to the efficient input mix and output level. Finally, both Fullerton and Kinnaman (1995) and Walls and Palmer (1997) find that as long as other policy options are available (namely a deposit/refund system discussed below), then a tax on virgin materials is only necessary to correct for any external costs associated with cutting or extracting the virgin material. The tax is not needed to correct for the external costs associated with garbage disposal.

Palmer and Walls (1994) find that a recycling subsidy (s_{hr} or s_{fr}) by itself can indeed provide the efficient input mix (between virgin and recycled inputs), but it leads to excess production, consumption and waste. Therefore, the subsidy to recycling must be combined with a tax on consumption (t_c). But the implementation of an advanced disposal fee (t_c) by itself only encourages source reduction, not recycling. Only the combination of an advanced disposal fee and a subsidy to recycling encourages both source reduction at the time of production and recycling at the time of disposal (Palmer, Sigman and Walls, 1997). This policy is essentially a deposit/refund system.[5]

Several economic studies have favoured the use of deposit/refund systems to correct for the external costs associated with garbage disposal, including Dinan (1993), Dobbs (1991), Fullerton and Kinnaman (1995), Palmer and Walls (1994), Palmer, Sigman and Walls (1997), Fullerton and Wu (1998), and Atri and Schellberg (1995). To achieve the efficient allocation, the deposit is set equal to the social marginal cost of disposing of the resulting material, and the optimal refund is set equal to the difference between the marginal external cost of garbage and the marginal external cost of recycling. If the external costs of recycling are zero, then the refund matches the deposit. The deposit could be levied either on the production or the sale of goods. As long as transaction costs are low, the refund can be given either to the households that recycle the materials or to the producers that use the recycled materials in production. If the refund is given to the households, then the supply increase will drive down the price of recycled materials to firms. If the refund is given to firms, firms will increase demand for recycled materials and drive up the price received by households (Atri and Schellberg, 1995). In addition, Fullerton and Wu (1998) find that the refund given under a deposit/refund system will encourage firms optimally to engineer products that are easier to recycle. Households will demand such products in order to recycle and receive the refund. This result is important since directly encouraging the recyclability of product design can be administratively difficult.

Economists have also discussed some implementation issues related to a deposit/refund system. Palmer and Walls (1994) argue that a deposit/refund system would be easier to implement than a tax on virgin materials with a subsidy to consumption (an alternative policy combination that could also achieve the efficient outcome). Firms could organize a strong defence against the implementation of a tax on virgin materials. Households may lack this political organization. Furthermore, the subsidy to recycling may earn the support of households with strong tastes for the environment. Also, less information is necessary to implement the deposit/refund system efficiently. The policymaker only needs to know the marginal social cost of waste disposal. The optimal deposit and refund need only be set equal to this value. The application of a virgin materials tax on the other hand requires information on each firm's technical rate of substitution between recycled and virgin inputs. This type of information is normally not available to the policymaker (Palmer and Walls, 1994). If the administrative costs associated with operating the deposit/refund programmes are high, then Dinan (1993) suggests that policymakers could single out products that comprise a large segment of the waste stream (newspaper) or that involve very high social marginal disposal costs (batteries). Palmer and Walls (1999) argue that a tax on produced intermediate goods combined with a subsidy paid to collectors of recycling would preserve the efficiency effects of a deposit/refund system but would be less costly to administer.

One 'command and control' policy to receive the attention of environmental economists is a recycled content standard; a law requiring firms to employ a minimum portion of recycled materials in their products. Several states have passed such a law. Palmer and Walls (1997) point out the problems associated with a recycled content standard. First, recycled content standards can only achieve efficiency if carefully implemented with other policies. If recyclable materials are highly productive at the margin, but are not used because of their high price, then a recycled-content standard could increase production and therefore solid waste. A tax on consumption is also necessary. If recycled materials are unproductive on the margin, standards will decrease output (and solid waste) and will therefore require a subsidy to consumption to achieve efficiency. Their model also requires a tax on labour (the other input to production). Finally, the efficient implementation of a recycled-content standard requires information not ordinarily available to policymakers.

This section provided an overview of the economic literature on the best policy approaches to respond to the external costs of traditional garbage disposal. Although a direct tax on garbage disposal (t_g) and a tax on virgin materials (t_v) have been supported by some, the combination of an advanced disposal fee (t_c) and a subsidy to recycling $(s_{fr}$ or $s_{hr})$ is supported by the majority of studies. The next section provides a survey of the current set of policies implemented by local, state, and the federal governments in the United States and across the world, and it discusses empirical lessons from the vast array of policies currently in place.

4   SOLID WASTE POLICIES – A SUMMARY OF EMPIRICAL STUDIES

This section provides a broad review of the various solid waste management policies implemented in the United States and abroad. The reader will quickly see that actual approaches used by policymakers often differ from the theoretical policy prescriptions detailed in the last section. The results of empirical economic papers related to each policy are discussed where available.

Policy Directives in the United States

Federal government
The most influential disposal regulation passed by the Federal Government of the United States was the Resource Conservation and Recovery Act (RCRA) of 1976. Subtitle D of RCRA imposed technology-based standards on the construction, operation, and closure of solid waste landfills. Prior to RCRA, almost every town in the United States had a local dump. These dumps were often formed near the edge of town, perhaps on a flood plain near a river.

Today's regulated landfills are constructed with a base of several inches of various grades of plastic lining to prevent leachate from seeping. Underground plumbing systems capture and treat leachate, and local groundwater supplies are continuously monitored. In terms of operation, garbage must be covered with soil within hours of disposal to reduce foul odour, discourage pests, and reduce the risk of health hazards. Many landfills capture and burn methane to produce electricity. Access roads must be watered several times each day to prevent dust from heavy truck traffic from rising. These regulations have decreased substantially the external costs associated with garbage disposal, but have also increased average disposal costs from an estimated $9 per ton to $20 per ton (Beede and Bloom, 1995).

Even with the recent advances in the technology of landfill construction and operation, local environmental activist groups still often oppose the creation or expansion of landfills in their region. Landfills depress property values. Housing values have been estimated to rise by 6.2 per cent for each mile (up to two miles) away from a landfill (Nelson, Genereux and Genereux, 1992, as cited in Beede and Bloom, 1995). Roberts, Douglas and Park (1991) interviewed 150 households in Tennessee and estimated households were willing to pay $227 per year to avoid having a landfill nearby. Reported amounts increase with income, education, and dependency on well water for water consumption.

A second Federal Government initiative that has influenced the market for the collection and disposal of household solid waste is the subsidy of virgin material extraction in the United States. First, income earned by the timber industry has been taxed at the capital gains rate instead of the corporate income tax rate. Second, the depletion of minerals extracted can be deducted from earned income as a form of depreciation. Third, mineral exploration has traditionally been encouraged on public lands. Fourth, freight rates charged for recycled materials have often been higher than for their virgin counterparts. These various forms of favourable tax treatments may have, on the margin, encouraged firms to utilize virgin inputs over recycled inputs, perhaps resulting in the current underdevelopment of the market for recycled materials.

Through a variety of papers, economists have learned a great deal about the market for recyclable materials. For example, Nestor (1992) reports that firms that could purchase recyclable materials are often capital intensive. Most of the existing capital stock is suitable for the use of virgin material in production. Retooling these industries to accept recycled inputs could be expensive. She also estimates the paper industry's price elasticity of demand for old newspapers. The short-run price elasticity of demand is estimated at only –0.0475. This elasticity increases to –0.0732 (1 year), –0.1009 (3 years), –0.1128 (5 years), and to –0.1216 in the 'long run'. These estimates are inelastic because the newsprint industry in many countries is equipped for the use of virgin fibre. The short-run marginal cost to the firm of using substitute

LIVERPOOL UNIVERSITY
JOHN MOORES UNIVERSITY
AVRIL ROBARTS LRC
TITHEBARN STREET
LIVERPOOL L2 2ER
TEL. 0151 231 4022

inputs is high. The implication of an inelastic demand is that policies aimed at increasing the supply of old newspapers could indeed reduce their price but will not effectively increase the quantity of newspapers recycled. Furthermore, the elimination of existing tax subsidies on virgin inputs in the United States, Nestor (1992) reports, will also have little impact on the quantity of old newspapers recycled. The more effective approach would involve subsidizing the firm's purchases of capital equipment that would allow for the substitute use of both virgin and recycled inputs.

Anderson and Spiegelman (1977) also find the price elasticity of demand for scrap steel and old newspaper to be inelastic (−0.64 and −0.08, respectively). The elimination of tax advantages for virgin inputs is estimated to increase newspaper recycling by only 0.04 per cent and scrap steel recycling by only 0.37 per cent.[6] Anderson and Spiegelman (1977) also forecast that a subsidy to the suppliers of scrap iron (a 15 per cent depletion deduction) would decrease the price of scrap steel by 7.2 per cent and increase its quantity demanded by 2.9 per cent. A similar subsidy to wastepaper suppliers (of 18 per cent) would decrease the price of old newspapers by 8.6 per cent but increase the quantity recycled by only 0.57 per cent. A $10 per ton subsidy to the purchasers of old newspaper is forecasted to increase the quantity of newspaper recycled by only 2 per cent. The common theme found throughout these empirical studies is the relative unresponsiveness of quantity demanded for recycled inputs to its price. Policies designed to increase the supply of recycled materials may have little impact on the quantity of recycled materials used in production.

One explanation given for the resistance on the part of many firms to make capital improvements to allow for the use of recycled materials has been the uncertainty over obtaining a steady supply of recycled materials. Prior to the widespread use of municipal recycling programmes, the market's supply of recycled materials was highly variable. To determine whether tax or subsidy policies could stimulate the supply of recycled materials, several economists have estimated the effect of price on the quantity supplied. Most of these studies found the supply of recycled materials also to be inelastic. For example, Bingham, Youngblood, and Cooley (1983) estimate the price elasticity of supply of glass (0.165), steel (0.372), and aluminium (0.730). Miedema (1976 – cited in Edwards and Pearce, 1978) also finds the price elasticity of supply of wastepaper to be inelastic (0.09). Van der Kuil (1976 – cited in Edwards and Pearce, 1978) finds evidence that increases in the price of recycled materials simply shifts the source of the supplied materials from municipalities to volunteer scout groups.[7] But now that municipal governments supply the industry with a steady and predictable stream of recycled materials, firms may find the environment more conducive to investment in capital equipment suitable for recycled inputs.

State governments

RCRA also assigned to the states the responsibility of regulating the market for household solid waste collection and recycling. The logic behind this action was based on the inherent differences in industry practices and environmental conditions across the states (Callan and Thomas, 1997). Delegating disposal authority to the states has resulted in a wide variety of policy approaches. Table 3.2 provides a glance at the policies enacted by each of the 50 states and the District of Columbia to increase recycling. The most common state action is to set a goal for recycling as a percentage of the solid waste stream. These goals range from 20 per cent in Maryland to 70 per cent in Rhode Island. The laws are ceremonious, for the most part, since they rarely state the consequences of falling short. In fact, the strategy employed by many states facing a failure to achieve the goal is to delay the deadline. Kinnaman and Fullerton (1997) find no significant impact of these goals on recycling quantities.

States have also passed laws that set recycling guidelines for municipalities within the state. The strongest law requires all municipalities to implement curbside recycling programmes *and* to pass local ordinances making household participation in the recycling programme mandatory. Seven states, including Pennsylvania and New Jersey, have passed such laws. Seven other states have passed similar laws requiring municipalities to offer recycling programmes to households, but do not require the implementation of mandatory ordinances. Finally, eight states have set recycling goals for each town or county to satisfy, but allow each town or county to decide how to go about achieving the goal.

In exchange for these various mandates, 34 states provide grants to localities to help finance the costs of recycling expenses. For example, in Pennsylvania, each municipality receives a state grant that is based on the total quantity of materials recycled. Although economists have not devoted attention to estimating the incidence of these various forms of state recycling mandates, anecdotal evidence indicates the laws are costly but have had a dramatic impact on the number of municipal recycling programmes operating within these states.

An approach taken by 23 states to regulate household solid waste is to prevent yard waste from being disposed in landfills. Large composting facilities are usually established to accommodate yard waste more cheaply than disposal in landfills. Several other states have passed laws preventing materials such as automobile tyres, batteries, motor oil and old appliances from entering landfills (not presented in Table 3.2). In one highly publicized example, the state of Maine banned the disposal of aseptic packaging (drink boxes) in landfills. The ban was repealed after a Tellus Institute study found them to be environmentally friendly relative to other drink containers (Ackerman, 1997).

Table 3.2   US state policies designed to increase recycling

Policy	Number of states implemented
Pass a recycling goal	45
Require all municipalities to implement curbside recycling programmes and pass local ordinances making household and commercial recycling mandatory	7
Require all municipalities to implement curbside or drop-off recycling programmes but not a mandatory ordinance	7
Require all municipalities and counties to satisfy a minimum recycling quota without designating the method to achieve it	8
Provide grants to municipalities to help finance recycling programmes	34
Ban yard waste from being disposed of in landfills	23
Implement a deposit/refund system for beverage containers	9
Provide tax credits for new recycling facilities	29
Provide low-interest loans for new recycling facilities	15
Require all state government offices to purchase recycled materials	29

Source: Glenn (1998).

The oldest policy implemented at the state level is deposit/refund systems for empty beverage containers. The state of Oregon was the first to pass this form of legislation in 1983. Eight other states have followed suit, though no state has implemented a new deposit/refund system since the early 1980s.

States quickly learned that their policies aimed at stimulating the supply of recyclable materials produced a glut of recycled materials (see a review of economic research on this topic above). To help balance the market, states began to implement policies designed to stimulate the demand for recycled materials. Twenty-nine states provide tax credits to encourage the production of new recycling plants, 15 states provide low-interest loans for the same, and 29 states require government offices and in some cases private firms to purchase a minimum of their inputs from recycled products. As mentioned above, Palmer and Walls (1997) find recycled-content standards to be a difficult policy to implement and administer.

A final area of state intervention involves the use of restrictions on shipments of solid waste imported from other states. The transition from local dumps to regional landfills also brought an increase in the amount of solid waste transported across state and national boundaries. Today, an estimated 8 per cent of all waste generated in the United States is disposed of in another state. A few states, especially Pennsylvania, Virginia, and those in the Midwest, have recently attempted to restrict the quantity of solid waste imported. Repeated attempts by these states to restrict the importation of garbage were struck down by the Supreme Court, which ruled that import restrictions violate the free flow of interstate commerce.[8] More recently, several governors have petitioned Congress to pass Federal legislation imposing import restrictions on interstate garbage shipments. Congress has yet to pass such legislation.

The top importer of solid waste in the United States is Pennsylvania, followed by Ohio, Virginia, Illinois, and Indiana. In 1996, Pennsylvania received its waste from New York (3 300 000 tons), New Jersey (3 100 000 tons), Maryland (819 000 tons), Delaware (261 000 tons), and Connecticut (141 000 tons). Overall garbage imports to Pennsylvania have increased from 3.8 million tons in 1993 to 7.9 million tons in 1996. Similar growth rates have emerged in other importing states.

One reason state governments are frustrated with imported garbage is that their states have devoted significant public resources to reducing the quantity of solid waste generated within the state. As discussed above, resources have been devoted to implementing curbside recycling programmes, banning certain materials from being disposed of in landfills, providing tax advantages and/or subsidized loans to commercial recycling activities and distributing grants to help run local recycling services. State officials may wonder what the state has gained by these efforts if the saved landfill space is filled by imports from other states. For example, in 1996 the state of Pennsylvania recycled 1.9 million tons of solid waste, but imported 7.9 million tons.

Traditional economic theory suggests free trading of garbage is efficient since those states with a comparative advantage in garbage disposal can specialize in garbage disposal. Any policy that interferes with the free flow of garbage would therefore be socially costly. Ley, Macauley and Salant (1997) estimate the loss in total surplus resulting from various restrictions on the flow of garbage considered by Congress. First, a $1 per ton surcharge on imported garbage would result in a 4 per cent decrease in the quantity of garbage traded and a loss of total surplus of only $0.02 per person. The implementation of caps on the quantity of garbage traded across state lines (caps consistent with a Senate bill passed in 1995 that would require a reduction in garbage imports to 65 per cent of their 1993 levels after a prolonged introductory phase) results in a surplus loss of $10 per person.

Finally, a law that restricted all trading of garbage would result in a $18 per person loss in surplus. This study assumes that all external costs associated with garbage disposal are internalized through the tipping fee.

Other economic arguments can be made that flow controls improve welfare. Copeland (1991) provides two arguments in favour of restrictions of garbage imports. First, governments in some states (or countries) may not adequately regulate the industry to ensure that the external costs of garbage disposal are internalized. Total welfare can improve if exports from a highly regulated country are prevented from entering a weakly regulated country. Since landfill regulations across the United States are uniform, this rationale is probably more appropriate to inter-country shipments of solid waste. Second, even if regulations are uniform across trading partners, Copeland argues that restricting garbage trade can still improve welfare if evading the regulations is easier in one area than another. Also, Macauley *et al.* (1993) explain that allowing landfills the option to practice third-degree price discrimination (for example, charging a greater fee on imported garbage relative to local garbage) can be welfare improving if these landfills operate in imperfectly competitive markets. A landfill that can lower prices to local customers (with relatively elastic demand curves for garbage disposal) without having to lower prices to importers (with more inelastic demand curves) can make the local landfill and local residents better off without making the rest of the world worse off.[9]

Interestingly, while many state governments have attempted to restrict out-of-state garbage, other local governments have attempted to prevent local garbage from being exported from the area. As discussed above, such restrictions on garbage flow were designed to help support local incinerators that levy tipping fees that often exceed those of neighbouring landfills. The Supreme Court recently struck down the use of such export restrictions. Tawil (1999) estimated that this event did not impact the profit levels of the participating incinerators or waste-hauling firms. Perhaps entry into the waste management industry is easy, eroding any profits that could have followed the Supreme Court's ruling. Finally, Podolsky and Spiegel (1999) argue that the existence of economies of scale in garbage disposal practices could in some cases merit restrictions on garbage exports. The local reduction in average disposal costs attributed to the increase in garbage brought on by the export restriction could exceed the increase in average disposal costs experienced by a distant site.

Public and academic attention devoted to the issue of flow controls may increase when the Fresh Kills Landfill on Staten Island closes in 2002. New York City currently disposes of 13 000 tons per day (4.7 million tons per year) in the Fresh Kills Landfill, the largest landfill in the country. Given the recent 38 per cent cut in New York City's recycling budget, all signs indicate that New York City's garbage will be exported to other states.

Local governments
Markets for household solid waste collection and disposal were once decentralized. As cities began to develop, dumps often formed near the outskirts of each town, and households were typically responsible for transporting their own waste to this dump. To ensure that all garbage was removed from neighbourhoods, and to help capture economies of density, many communities designated a single collector for household solid waste.

In the United States, this intervention has typically taken one of two forms. First, direct government provision meant that municipalities would purchase trucks, hire drivers, and define collection routes. The cost of this local service was typically financed out of general tax revenue or the issuing of monthly or quarterly bills to each household. Second, the local government could regulate a single private collector. The town could contract with a single firm to collect all garbage or it could award a franchise permission to collect garbage to a single private garbage collector. The main difference between these two latter forms is that under a franchise agreement the private collector bills the households rather than the town.

Town governments could also pass local ordinances requiring households to hire their own company. Although such competitive garbage systems still operate today, the single collector model is the norm. Dubin and Navarro (1988) estimate that 43 per cent of communities in the United States rely upon contract or franchise agreements, 26 per cent of municipalities operate municipal collection programmes, and 30 per cent rely on the competitive market.[10]

Economies of density suggest that a single collector could reduce the overall collection costs. Dubin and Navarro (1988) find that an increase in the population density by 100 persons per square mile decreases the average cost per ton of collected materials by $1.62. Kemper and Quigly (1976) estimate that competitive markets are 25 per cent to 36 per cent more expensive than a single collector, and that contract or franchise agreements reduce costs over municipal collections by another 13 to 30 per cent (depending on the level of service). Stevens (1978) estimates that the contract or franchise agreements are 26 per cent to 48 per cent cheaper than a competitive private market and 27 to 37 per cent cheaper than municipal provision (for cities over 50 000 population). Savas (1977) finds that municipal collection is 14 per cent more costly than that by a single private firm. Bohm, Folz and Podolsky (1999) estimates that municipally run curbside recycling programmes are on average $82 000 more costly per year than private recycling programmes. Finally, McDavid (1985) finds in Canada that public collection is 41 per cent more costly than private collection. This difference is identified (by McDavid) as arising from the fact that workers in private firms receive productivity bonuses and private collectors are more likely to use larger trucks with smaller crew sizes.

Why don't all communities employ the most efficient contract or franchise method? Dubin and Navarro (1988) find that the community's choice of method depends upon the power of rent-seeking interest groups (such as labour unions) and the ideological preferences of the community. Conservative towns are more likely to rely on the free market than liberal towns, but liberal towns are more likely to use municipal collection rather than contract or franchise agreements.

Beyond the mere collection of household garbage, local governments have also attempted to influence the decisions of households to reduce the quantity of garbage collected and disposed. Drop-off and curbside recycling programmes, unit-based pricing programmes, and mandatory recycling ordinances have been passed. Although precise year-to-year data are unavailable, recent estimates indicate that over 9000 curbside recycling programmes and 4000 unit-based pricing programmes are currently in operation in the United States. Economic studies of the impact of these policies are summarized in section 5 below.

At first, towns began to offer drop-off recycling services. Towns would usually purchase (or rent) a few large trailers, and would leave those trailers on municipal property, usually a parking lot or near the entrance of a park or other municipal property. Residents would voluntarily transport certain materials (usually newspaper, aluminium cans and perhaps glass). Jakus, Tiller and Park (1996) estimate that rural households devote an average of 90 seconds to recycle one unit of glass and one unit of old newspaper. Given the opportunity cost of household time, households paid $1.29 to recycle one pound of each material. Based on quantities recycled, Jakus, Tiller and Park (1996) estimate that these households value local access to drop-off facilities at $5.78 per month.

As municipal governments gained expertise in the area of marketing recycled products, they began to implement curbside recycling programmes. Curbside recycling programmes decrease the household's time and effort devoted to recycling. Households are expected to respond by recycling more, while municipal governments collect more, save disposal costs, and earn greater revenues from the sale of materials. The external costs of garbage collection and disposal could also decrease. Powell *et al.* (1996) find that the costs associated with vehicle emissions, traffic accidents and road congestion are much less for curbside programmes (£4.99 per ton recycled) than for drop-off programmes (£22.95 per ton recycled). Direct estimates of the impact of the implementation of curbside recycling programmes on household disposal choices are presented in section 5 below, where the disposal choices of the household are carefully modelled.

Are economic or non-economic forces responsible for the recent increase in the number of municipal curbside recycling programmes? The answer is probably both. Tawil (1995) and Kinnaman and Fullerton (1997) estimate the probability of implementing a curbside recycling programme. Tawil (1995) employs a cross-sectional database of 80 towns in Massachusetts to estimate that every $1000 that can be saved by curbside recycling increases the probability of adoption by 11 per cent. But Tawil (1995) also finds that a 1 per cent increase in the percentage of households belonging to an environmental interest group increases the probability of adoption by 4 per cent. Kinnaman and Fullerton (1997) also uncover economic reasons for implementing a recycling programme. The likelihood increases by 0.78 per cent with a $1 increase in the tipping fee (from the average tipping fee of $26) and by 0.39 per cent with a 100–person increase per square mile (from the average density of 2,600) since average collection costs could decrease with the population density (Bohm, Folz and Podolsky, 1999). However, non-economic variables also partly explain the move towards recycling. A 1 per cent increase in the percentage of the population with a college degree (from the average of 23.6 per cent) increases the likelihood that a town implements curbside recycling by 0.77 per cent.

Several economic studies have estimated directly the benefits and costs of curbside recycling programmes. Most suggest that the costs of operating a curbside programme exceed the benefits resulting from the subsequent decrease in garbage disposal costs and sale of collected materials. Franklin Associates (1994) use national cost averages to estimate that recycling costs the municipality $9.52 to $16.53 per ton more than the cost of landfill disposal. Other studies suggest recycling is much more costly. The Solid Waste Association of North America (SWANA, 1995) estimates it costs an extra $74 per ton to recycle in a sample of six communities. Kinnaman (1998) estimates that a recycling programme costs an extra $55.45 per ton recycled. This estimate includes costs to firms that are required by local ordinance to recycle. Carroll (1997) uses cross-section data from Wisconsin to estimate that recycling costs over $140 per ton, roughly $100 more than the cost of disposing the material. Only Hanley and Slark (1994) estimate recycling to be economically beneficial for the recycling of newspaper in Scotland. Palmer, Sigman and Walls (1997) estimate the benefits of recycling exceed the costs if the recycling rate is less than 7.5 per cent of total waste. Recycling beyond this threshold is costly.

Kinnaman (1998) and Jakus, Tiller and Park (1996) estimate the political/ environmental benefits of curbside recycling through use of contingent valuation surveys. In a survey of 100 households, Kinnaman (1998) finds that households are on average willing to pay about $86 per year to keep curbside recycling of newspaper, glass and aluminium. Jakus, Tiller and Park (1996) estimate that households are willing to pay $69.36 per year for curbside collection of newspaper and glass. In addition, Tiller, Jakus and Park (1997) estimate that suburban households that classify themselves as recyclers are willing to pay $11.74 per month for drop-off recycling facilities. If such preferences influence the decisions of local officials, then some of the trend towards greater recycling may in fact be attributable to political or environmental forces.

Other studies have estimated the costs of curbside recycling programmes. Judge and Becker (1993) estimate that such costs increase with the addition of weekly collection (as opposed to monthly) of commingled (rather than separated) material collected from the porch of households (rather than the curb). Carroll (1997) uses self-reported cost figures from 1103 programmes in the state of Wisconsin to estimate that the costs of curbside recycling programmes increase with the population, the tons recycled and the number of materials collected. Interestingly, Carroll does not find a relationship between population density and collection costs. Bohm, Folz and Podolsky (1999) estimate the costs of recycling with data based on a national survey of 1021 municipal recycling programmes in the United States. They find that the average costs of recycling decrease with the quantity collected, indicating economies of scale in collection. The total costs of recycling are estimated to increase with the cost of labour, the cost of capital and if the municipality collects the material rather than a private company. Butterfield and Kubursi (1993) also find that recycling is costly. Laws that require or encourage recycling in Canada are found to decrease employment levels in several industries.

Huhtala (1997) and Brisson (1997) break down the private and external costs of recycling by type of material. Huhtala develops a dynamic model of waste accumulation with recycling as a backstop technology. The model is simulated using 1993 data from the Helsinki region. Results show that the social benefits of recycling paper, cardboard and metal exceed the social costs. Glass and plastic do not pass the benefit/cost criterion. Brisson (1997) finds that the recycling of aluminium produces the greatest social benefits, followed by glass, ferrous metals, paper board and rigid plastic.

As described above, several states in America have implemented recycling goals. England has also set a 50 per cent recycling goal and The Netherlands set a goal for plastics of 42 per cent. Palmer, Sigman and Walls (1997) and Huhtala (1997) estimate the optimal recycling rate. Using the lowest cost policy to encourage recycling (a deposit/refund of $45 per ton), Palmer, Sigman and Walls (1997) find that only 7 per cent of solid waste should be recycled in the United States (where the social marginal cost of garbage disposal is estimated to be $33 per ton). Huhtala (1997) find the optimal recycling rate to be between 31 per cent and 52 per cent in Finland (where the *private* marginal cost of garbage disposal is estimated at $101 per ton). In addition, Huhtala (1997) adds a contingent valuation estimate of the nonmarket benefits of recycling to the analysis. Such benefits include the value of less air pollution from solid waste incinerators plus an estimate of the 'environmental friendliness of recycling'.

To ensure participation in the curbside recycling programme, some local governments have passed a local ordinance making it illegal to include recyclable waste with regular garbage. As mentioned above, several states have passed laws requiring all towns to implement such mandatory ordinances. Kinnaman and Fullerton (1997) find mandatory recycling ordinances have little significant impact on recycling or garbage quantities. A plausible reason for this non-result is that municipalities do not adequately enforce their mandatory ordinances. Garbage collectors rarely inspect household garbage carefully. Any found violators usually just receive a written warning (Kinnaman, 1998). Duggal, Saltman and Williams (1991) find that communities that enforce mandatory recycling laws with fines experience no more recycling than towns without such enforcement.

Four thousand local governments have also implemented unit-based pricing programmes. Most empirical papers devoted to user fees for garbage collection estimate the impact of the programmes on household garbage and recycling behaviour. These studies are discussed in section 5 below. In addition to estimating the incidence of the programmes, a few studies have estimated the likelihood of such programmes being implemented, the change in illegal dumping, and the benefits and costs of implementing a price per bag. Miranda and Aldy (1998) provide an in-depth analysis of the experiences of nine communities in the United States that implemented a price per bag.

Kinnaman and Fullerton (1997) and Callan and Thomas (1999) estimate the likelihood that a community will implement a unit-based pricing programme. Kinnaman and Fullerton (1997) use data representing a national cross-section of 909 communities with and without unit-based pricing programmes. They find that the likelihood increases with the local tipping fee, with the use of municipal (rather than private) resources to collect garbage, and with the education level of the community. Callan and Thomas (1999) find that the likelihood increases with household income, housing value, the age of the population, and whether the regional landfill is due to close within the next two years. They use data representing 317 communities in Massachusetts.

Available data rarely allow for direct comparisons between illegal dumping quantities before and after the implementation of unit pricing. Many economists have requested town officials to provide their opinion over whether they believe illegal dumping has increased. Many local officials have stated that it has, though many more have stated otherwise. Reschovsky and Stone (1994) and Fullerton and Kinnaman (1996) asked individual households whether they observed any change. In the former study, 51 per cent of respondents reported an increase in dumping. The most popular method was household use of commercial dumpsters (skips). For the 20 per cent who admitted to burning trash, the authors were unable to confirm whether these burners did so in response to the programme. Roughly 40 per cent of the respondents to the Fullerton and Kinnaman (1996) survey indicated that illegal dumping had increased in response to the unit-pricing programme. Many of these lived in the more densely populated urban areas of the city. Fullerton and Kinnaman (1996) also use survey responses with direct household garbage observations to estimate that 28 per cent of the reduction of garbage observed at the curb was redirected to illicit forms of disposal. See note 4 for a list of other papers that study the dumping issue.

Two types of unit-based programmes have been implemented in the United States. Traditional bag or tag programmes require households to pay for each additional bag of garbage presented at the curb for collection. The second programme type requires households to pre-commit or 'subscribe' to the collection of a specific number of containers each week. The household pays for the subscribed number, whether these containers are filled with garbage or not. Many communities in California and Oregon have utilized subscription programmes since early in the century. One advantage of subscription programmes is that their direct billing systems may reduce administrative costs. Yet, economists believe the first type of user fee more truly represents marginal cost pricing. Kinnaman and Fullerton (1997) use city-wide data from over 700 communities to estimate that subscription programmes have less of an impact than bag/tag programmes on garbage and recycling quantities. Miranda and Aldy (1998) find that subscription programmes can be effective if pricing applies to smaller trash containers. Nestor and Podolsky (1998) employ self-reported household data to estimate that subscription programmes are about as effective as bag/tag programmes at reducing garbage. Neither programme is found to encourage source reduction in the presence of a curbside recycling programme, since such programmes subsidize recycling households' overall disposal practices.

Policy Directives in Europe

Many of the approaches taken above in the United States have also been pursued, to a greater or lesser extent, in other countries. For example, the United Kingdom has established a 50 per cent recycling goal to be achieved by 2000. Powell *et al.* (1996) reported a recycling rate in the UK of just 5 per cent. To increase the recycling rate, the UK implemented credits for recycling and has been considering a tax on the disposal of solid waste in landfills. Seven other EC countries (Belgium, Finland, France, Germany, Italy, Luxembourg and The Netherlands) have implemented some variation of user fees for garbage collection. The UK rejected the idea of user fees due to the uncertainty of their effects. Also, deposit/refund systems for beverage containers have been implemented in Australia, Canada, France, Germany and Switzerland. Germany has also implemented deposit/refund programmes for detergent and paint containers.

Germany implemented a unique policy in 1991 called the 'Law on Waste Management' that is designed to internalize the external costs of packaging choices by industry. This law requires the original product manufacturers to pay to recycle the packaging it produces even after the product is sold to retail firms or directly to consumers. The law also set an original recycling target of 80 per cent. That is, firms would be required to recycle 80 per cent of all packaging they produce. Amendments to the original legislation are expected to ease these targets to 60–70 per cent.

Over 400 retail and packaging firms have combined with the large waste-hauling firms to create the Duales System of Deutschland (DSD). The purpose of this syndicate is to reduce the administrative costs associated with satisfying the minimum recycling standards. Rather than requiring that each bottle be delivered back to its original manufacturer, local waste management firms agree to collect for recycling *all* bottles of member organizations in exchange for payment from the DSD. Participating manufacturers identify their membership in the DSD by affixing a green dot on their packaging. In essence, the programme becomes a national recycling effort operated by the DSD rather than by independent municipal governments, as is common in the United States.[11]

The collection, sorting, and marketing costs incurred by the waste management firms are paid by the DSD. The DSD then charges manufacturers according to the quantity and type of packaging used. For example, manufacturers pay the DSD $.82 for each pound of plastic packaging produced, $.27 per pound for aluminium, and only $.04 for each pound of glass. These charges represent the marginal cost to the DSD of collecting and sorting each type of material. The cost of glass is low because consumers traditionally separate and transport glass bottles themselves; these costs are paid by consumers and are therefore not internalized by the DSD or product manufacturers. Fullerton and Wu (1998) find that if the charges to manufacturers are set optimally, then the German Green Dot programme can encourage firms to produce the optimal amount and type of packaging. The quantity of packaging consumed by households decreased by 4 per cent following the implementation of the Green Dot programme (Rousso and Shah, 1994).

The success of the Green Dot programme in achieving the efficient quantities of garbage and recycling rests on two critical issues (Fenton and Hanley, 1995). First, households must be willing to separate materials for recycling.

A mandatory deposit on non-refillable beverage containers gives consumers the incentive to return these forms of packaging. But lacking such incentives for other types of packaging, the household cannot be expected to recycle efficiently. Second, private collectors must recycle the materials. But, in the absence of other regulations, the private collectors face private rather than social disposal costs. Thus, the collectors of recyclable material may find disposal in other countries cheaper than negotiating with a recycler to take the material.[12] Palmer and Walls (1999) argue that replacing Extended Producer Responsibility programmes (like the Green Dot programme) with a combined tax on intermediate goods and a subsidy paid to the collectors of recycled materials could alleviate these problems while preserving the more desirable outcomes.

Countries within the European Union have implemented other versions of producer responsibility programmes, but few have set recycling goals as lofty as Germany's 60–70 per cent target. Austria, Denmark, France, Italy, The Netherlands and Sweden have made manufacturers at least partly responsible for the management of their packaging materials. The European Union itself has set a recycling target of between 50 per cent and 75 per cent to be met by the year 2000, and is watching the German experience carefully. The UK has dropped its national eco-labelling programme but is cooperating with all other EU policy guidelines.

Developing Nations

This paper is concerned predominantly with residential solid waste in industrialized countries, but we discuss briefly some events in less-developed countries. Solid waste management is a different story in developing countries. First, only 50–70 per cent of the solid waste generated is actually collected (Cointreau-Levine, 1994). Second, the collection that does take place is very labour intensive. Households bring garbage to transfer stations, or collectors (scavengers) agree to carry garbage to a transfer station in exchange for any recyclable material found in the garbage. The World Bank estimates that 7000 such workers operate in Manila, 8000 in Jakarta, and 10 000 in Mexico City. In poorer sections of Egypt, India, Indonesia and the Philippines, individuals using handcarts collect garbage door-to-door (Beede and Bloom, 1995).

The experiences in developing countries have allowed economists to estimate the relationship between per capita income and garbage generation rates. Beede and Bloom (1995) find that per day garbage generation rates vary between 0.5 kilograms per capita in underdeveloped Mozambique to 1.9 kilograms per capita in developed Australia. These cross-national data are used to estimate that the income elasticity of supply of garbage is 0.34,

quite similar to estimates based on data sets gathered entirely
oped countries (described below). On the policy front, Cyprus
Lebanon and Syria have implemented deposit/refund sys
containers.

5   A MODEL OF HOUSEHOLD BEHAVIOUR WITH EMPIRICAL IMPLICATIONS

The household is at centre stage in the market for solid waste collection and
disposal because the household chooses among various abatement options,
including whether to devote resources to the separation and storage of recyclable materials. Every policy discussed above – from a tax on virgin materials
to a per-bag user fee on garbage disposal or the German Green Dot programme – depends crucially on household behaviour to influence disposal
quantities.

The model of household disposal decisions developed in section 3 derived
normative propositions about the optimal pricing of garbage, recycling, and
virgin material. The model developed in this section can be used to derive
empirical propositions for testing and estimation. This model is quite simple,
but demonstrates the main forces influencing the disposal decisions of households. Specific functional forms are assigned to the equations to simplify the
interpretation of results. Some of the comparative statics generated from the
model are tested in the available economics literature.

Assume the household consumes a single composite commodity good c
that generates waste material m, according to

$$m = (1/\alpha)c, \qquad (3.1)$$

where $1/\alpha$ is the portion of consumption that forms waste material. Assume
$(1/\alpha) < 1$. Material m can either be presented at the curb for garbage collection (g) or recycled (r)

$$m = g + r. \qquad (3.2)$$

Since these two equations imply that $c = \alpha(g + r)$, they are just a more
restrictive version of the expression $c = c(g, r)$ given in section 3 above.

Household utility is a function of its own consumption of the composite
commodity good

$$u = u(c), \qquad (3.3)$$

where $u_C > 0$ and $u_{CC} < 0$. The impact of aggregate garbage (G) on household utility is suppressed here for ease of presentation. Households do not notice a change in aggregate garbage attributable to their own disposal when making such choices.

Instead of having fixed income as in section 3 above, the household here is endowed with $\bar{k}$ units of a resource such as time that can be exchanged in a labour market k^m for a wage p_k. Therefore, $y = p_k k^m$. The household resource can also be used to prepare waste material for recycling (k^r). The resource is fully employed ($k^m + k^r = \bar{k}$).

The amount of recycling generated by the household (r) is a function of the time allocated to recycling (k^r),

$$r = r(k^r), \tag{3.4}$$

where the marginal product of labour in recycling is positive ($r_k > 0$) and labour devoted to recycling experiences diminishing marginal returns ($r_{kk} < 0$). Equation (3.4) can be solved for k^r to give the cost of recycling

$$k^r = k(r), \tag{3.5}$$

where $k_r > 0$ and $k_{rr} > 0$. For simplification, we specify

$$k(r) = 0.5\delta r^2 \tag{3.6}$$

where the first derivative $k_r = \delta r$ and the second derivative $k_{rr} = \delta$. Thus δ is the rate at which the marginal cost rises with r. A decrease in the parameter δ implies less household effort is required for recycling.

Household income ($p_k \bar{k} - p_k k^r$) can either be used to purchase the composite commodity good (for a price p_c), or to pay for each bag of garbage (at cost p_g) presented at the curb for collection. Using (3.6) to substitute for k^r in the above resource constraint, the household's budget constraint is

$$p_k \bar{k} - p_k (0.5\delta r^2) = p_c c + p_g g. \tag{3.7}$$

Each household maximizes utility (3.3) subject to technological constraints (3.1) and (3.2) and the budget constraint (3.7), by choosing the quantity of material to discard (g) and to recycle (r). The Lagrange Function from this maximization problem is

$$L = u[\alpha(g + r)] + \lambda[p_k \bar{k} - \alpha(g + r)p_c + p_g g - p_k (0.5\delta r^2)]. \tag{3.8}$$

Assuming the existence of interior solutions for g and r, first-order conditions are

$$\alpha u_c / \lambda = [\alpha p_c + p_g] \tag{3.9a}$$

$$\alpha u_c / \lambda = [\alpha p_c + p_k \delta r] \tag{3.9b}$$

$$p_k \bar{k} - \alpha(g+r)p_c - p_g g - p_k k(r) = 0, \tag{3.9c}$$

where λ is the marginal utility of income. At the utility-maximizing choices, condition (3.9a) requires the marginal benefit of acquiring an additional unit of material (measured in dollars) to equal the purchase price of the material plus the price of discarding the material at the curb. Condition (3.9b) has a similar interpretation, except the marginal cost of acquiring an additional unit of material is comprised of the purchase price plus the resource cost of recycling it ($p_k \delta r = p_k k_r$). Solving conditions (3.9a) and (3.9b) provides the relationship $p_g = p_k \delta r$ at the utility-maximizing choices of g and r. The household increases recycling to the point where the marginal cost of recycling another unit of the material ($p_k \delta r^*$) equals the marginal cost of discarding the material (p_g).

Utility-maximizing solutions for the choice variables take the form

$$g^* = g^*(\alpha, \bar{k}, p_c, p_g, p_k, \delta), \tag{3.10a}$$

$$r^* = r^*(\alpha, \bar{k}, p_c, p_g, p_k, \delta). \tag{3.10b}$$

Equations (3.1) and (3.2) can be used to solve for the utility-maximizing consumption level

$$c^* = \alpha(g^* + r^*). \tag{3.11}$$

How would the equilibrium values of g^* and r^* be affected by an exogenous change in the values of p_g, δ, p_k, or α? The comparative statics reported below are obtained by first substituting the solutions (3.10) into the first-order conditions (3.9), then differentiating with respect to the exogenous variable of interest, and finally solving the system of differential equations for the comparative static terms (as in Silberberg, 1990, p. 323).[13]

A Change in the User Fee (p_g)

If the town has implemented a unit pricing programme, the representative household in the model is required to pay for each bag of garbage collection

(p_g). How will the household respond to an increase in the per-bag fee? Comparative static analysis indicates that the change in recycling attributable to a change in the value of the user fee is[14]

$$\frac{\partial r^*}{\partial p_g} \equiv \frac{1}{p_k \delta} > 0, \tag{3.12}$$

which is unambiguously positive. A household will respond to an increase in the user fee by increasing recycling. This increase varies across households with different wage levels (p_k), and would be the greatest for households with the lowest wage. The increase also varies across households with different recycling production functions (value of δ in equation 6). The change in recycling would be greater for a household that experiences less-rapidly diminishing marginal product of time in recycling (a low value of δ). Proxies for δ could include household size, age composition, and other demographic variables.

An increase in the price per bag of garbage collection also changes the utility-maximizing quantity of garbage discarded:[15]

$$\frac{\partial g^*}{\partial p_g} \equiv -\frac{\partial r^*}{\partial p_g} - \frac{g^*}{\alpha u_c / \lambda^*} < 0, \tag{3.13}$$

which is unambiguously negative. Households are predicted to respond to an increase in the value of the user fee by decreasing the quantity of garbage presented at the curb. The first component of the right-hand side might be called the 'substitution' effect since it represents the change in garbage directly attributable to the increase in recycling. The second component of this comparative static might be called the 'income' effect since it represents the decrease in garbage brought about by the reduction in material generated from less consumption. The increase in the price per bag reduces the amount of income available to purchase other goods, decreasing the quantity of waste material. To see this more formally, note that

$$\frac{\partial m^*}{\partial p_g} \equiv \frac{\partial g^*}{\partial p_g} + -\frac{\partial r^*}{\partial p_g} \equiv -\left[\frac{g^*}{\alpha u_c / \lambda^*}\right] < 0. \tag{3.14}$$

Relative to the average household, this 'income' effect is greatest for households that generate more garbage (high g^*), generate more waste material from consumption (low α), exhibit a low marginal utility of consumption (low u_c, perhaps because of a large c^*), or possess a high marginal utility of income (λ^*). The denominator of (3.14) is identical to the left-hand side of the first-order condition in (3.9a). A household that experiences a low mar-

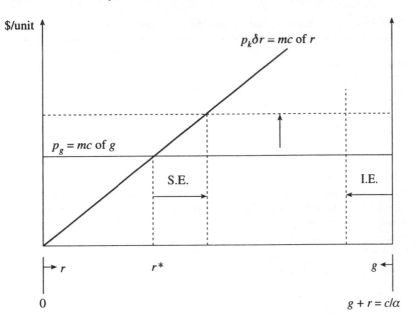

Note: An increase in p_g raises the flat marginal cost of garbage disposal (*mc* of *g*). It thus moves r^* to the right by a substitution effect (S.E.), and it moves the right-hand origin (c/α) to the left by an income effect (I.E.). Both effects reduce garbage *g*.

Figure 3.6   The choice of garbage g and recycling r

ginal benefit of generating an additional unit of waste material ($\alpha u_c/\lambda^*$) will react to the user fee by reducing garbage more than other households.

To see why the income effect only reduces *g* and not *r* in this simple model, consider Figure 3.6. Total waste ($g + r$) on the horizontal axis is divided between r^* and g^* at the point where the flat marginal cost of *g* (equal to p_g) intersects the rising marginal cost of *r* (equal to $p_k\delta r$). When the income effect reduces consumption *c* (and thus the sum $g + r$), the right vertical axis shifts to the left, reducing *g* but leaving *r* unchanged.

Several economic papers have estimated these comparative static relationships. A brief overview of some of these studies appears in Table 3.3. One element common to every study mentioned in Table 3.3 is the use of original data. Data collection techniques include interviews with local solid waste officials, direct phoning of households and actual measurement of household waste.

Table 3.3   Empirical estimates of the effect of unit-pricing

Study	Data	Model	Change in garbage	Change in recycling
Wertz (1976)	Compares subscription programme in San Francisco with flat fees imposed by 'all urban areas'	Comparison of means	ε = –0.15	
Jenkins (1993)	Panel of 14 cities (10 with user fees) over 1980–88		ε = –0.12	
Hong, Adams, and Love (1993)	1990 survey of 4306 . households in and around Portland, Oregon	Ordered probit and 2SLS	No significant impact	Unspecified positive relationship
Reschovsky and Stone (1994)	1992 mail survey of 1422 households in and around Ithaca, NY.	Probit		No significant impact
Miranda et al. (1994)	Panel of 21 cities over 18 months beginning in 1990	Comparison of means	17%–74% reduction in garbage	Average increase of 128%
Callan and Thomas (1997)	1994 cross-section of 324 towns in MA, 55 with unit-pricing programmes	OLS		6.6%–12.1% increase
Fullerton and Kinnaman (1996)	Two-period panel of 75 households in 1992	OLS	ε = –0.076 (weight) ε = –0.226 (volume)	Cross-price elasticity is 0.073
Podolsky and Spiegel (1998)	1992 cross-section of 159 municipalities in NJ, 12 with unit-pricing	OLS	ε = –0.39	
Kinnaman and Fullerton (1997)	1991 cross-section of 959 towns across the US, 114 with unit-pricing	OLS 2SLS	ε = –0.19 ε = –0.28	ε = 0.23 ε = 0.22
Strathman, Rufolo and Mildner (1995)	Seven year (1984–91) time series in Portland, OR	OLS	ε = –0.11	
Seguino, Criner and Suarez (1995)	1993–94 cross section of 60 towns in Maine, 29 with unit-pricing	Comparison of means	56% decrease	

Note: ε = price elasticity of demand, OLS = ordinary least squares, 2SLS = two stage least squares.

Wertz (1976) was the first to derive the impact of a user fee on garbage quantities. By simply comparing the average quantity of garbage collected in San Francisco, a town with a user fee, with the average town in the United States, Wertz calculates a price elasticity of demand equal to –0.15.

Jenkins (1993) expanded the understanding of the impact of user fees on garbage totals by gathering monthly data from 14 towns (ten with unit-pricing) over several years. Jenkins also found inelastic demand for garbage collection services; a 1 per cent increase in the user fee is estimated to lead to a 0.12 per cent decrease in the quantity of garbage.

Two studies rely on self-reported garbage quantities from individual households (rather than as reported by municipal governments). Hong, Adams and Love (1993) utilize data based on 4306 surveys. Households indicate whether they recycle and how much they pay for garbage collection. Results indicate that a user fee increases the probability that a household recycles, but does not appreciably affect the quantity of garbage produced at the curb. Reschovsky and Stone (1994) mailed questionnaires to 3040 households and received 1422 replies. Each household reported its recycling behaviour and income and demographic information. The price of garbage was estimated to have no significant impact on the probability that a household recycles. When combined with a curbside recycling programme, recycling rates increase by 27–58 per cent, depending on type of material.

Miranda *et al.* (1994) gather data from 21 communities with unit-pricing programmes and compare the quantity of garbage and recycling over the year preceding the implementation of unit-pricing with the year following it. Results indicate that these towns reduce garbage by between 17 per cent and 74 per cent and increase recycling by 128 per cent. These large estimates cannot be attributed directly to pricing garbage, since in every programme curbside recycling programmes were implemented during the same year as the unit-pricing programme. Callan and Thomas (1997) predict that the implementation of a user fee increases the portion of waste recycled by 6.6 percentage points. This impact increases to 12.1 percentage points when the user fee is accompanied by a curbside recycling programme.

Only Fullerton and Kinnaman (1996) use household data that are not based on self-reported surveys. The weight and volume of the garbage and recycling of 75 households were measured by hand over four weeks prior to, and following, the implementation of a price-per-bag programme in Charlottesville, VA. A curbside recycling programme had already been in operation for over one year. Results indicate that the weight of garbage decreased slightly, but the volume of garbage (number of bags or cans) decreased by more. Indeed, the density of garbage increased from 15 pounds per bag to just over 20 pounds per bag.

Two studies expanded on the work of Jenkins (1993) by increasing the number of communities in the sample. Podolsky and Spiegel (1998) employ a 1992 cross-section of 159 towns clustered in New Jersey, 12 with unit-based pricing programmes. They estimate the largest price elasticity of demand in the literature (−0.39). The authors attribute this estimate to the fact that no towns in their sample had implemented subscription programmes (as was the case for Wertz and Jenkins) and had mature recycling programmes in place. Kinnaman and Fullerton (1997) use a 1991 national cross-section of 959 towns, 114 that implemented user fees (none with subscription programmes). The estimated demand elasticities are also higher than Jenkins, but not as large as Podolsky and Spiegel (1998). The Kinnaman and Fullerton estimates account for possible endogeneity of the policy variables. They find that towns with high garbage totals and low recycling totals are more likely to introduce a user fee. Previous estimates may have underreported this elasticity by assuming that these policy variables are exogenous.

Strathman, Rufolo and Mildner (1995) employ data obtained by officials near Portland, Oregon, and they find that a 10 per cent increase in the tipping fee decreases garbage disposed at the landfill by 1.1 per cent.[16] Seguino, Criner and Suarez (1995) find that the implementation of user fee programmes in 29 towns in Maine decrease solid waste by 8.73 pounds per person per week (a 56 per cent decrease). Regarding illegal dumping, almost half of the towns reported initial increases in roadside dumping, and over half reported increases in backyard burning (30 per cent say it is a continuing problem). Backyard burning is permitted in the state of Maine.

Only Klein and Robison (1993) and Jenkins estimate the impact of disposal fees on commercial behaviour. Firms are estimated to reduce solid waste generation when faced with higher disposal rates.

What can be learned from all of these empirical studies? First, demand for garbage collection services is inelastic. Substitutes are not readily available. Advocates of unit-based pricing suggest demand may become more elastic in the long run as households learn of available substitutes for garbage disposal. The empirical economics literature has yet to address this point.

A Change in Ease of Recycling (δ)

Recall that household resources are required to recycle materials. According to the cost function given in (6), the implementation of a curbside recycling programme can be modelled by a decrease in the value of δ. Many expect the ease of curbside recycling to increase the quantity of recycling chosen by the household. Comparative static results of the model make a similar prediction[17]

$$\frac{\partial r^*}{\partial \delta} \equiv \frac{-r^*}{\delta} < 0. \tag{3.15}$$

Kinnaman and Fullerton (1997) confirm that this effect is positive. The implementation of a curbside recycling programme is estimated to increase the annual quantity of recycling by 195 pounds per person (this estimate corrects for policy endogeneity). Reschovsky and Stone (1994) also find that a recycling programme, especially when combined with a mandatory ordinance, increases recycling rates. Callan and Thomas (1997) find that a curbside recycling programme increases by 4.15 per cent the ratio of material recycled to all materials disposed of. This impact increases to 9.67 per cent when the curbside recycling programme is accompanied with a unit-based pricing programme.

The comparative static result in (3.15) predicts a greater than average increase in recycling for households that already recycle (a high r^*) and households that are very efficient recyclers (have a low value of δ). Reschovsky and Stone (1994) find that households reporting adequate storage space are much more likely to report that they recycle (using self-reported data). Judge and Becker (1993) study the recycling habits of 1000 households in towns of Minnesota (with different programme attributes). They estimate that recycling totals are increased by allowing households to commingle recyclable materials, offering weekly collections (rather than biweekly), and not requiring households to put materials on the curb. They also find that special information about the recycling programme did not increase recycling when controlling for other factors. Once a curbside recycling programme has been implemented, Duggal, Saltzman, and Williams (1991) estimate that recycling totals increase with the age of the programme, the frequency of collection, and the number of items collected.

The model does not provide a refutable hypothesis regarding the change in garbage attributable to the implementation of a curbside recycling programme,

$$\frac{\partial g^*}{\partial \delta} = \frac{\partial r^*}{\partial \delta} - \frac{p_k k(r^*)}{\delta \left(\frac{\alpha u_c}{\lambda} \right)} > \text{or} < 0. \tag{3.16}$$

The implementation of a municipal recycling programme diverts some material from the garbage pile to the recycling pile (thus the first component of the comparative static is positive), but it frees up additional household resources for consumption, which may result in more material (the second term is negative). In order for the overall effect to be negative, the first component must exceed the second in absolute value. Most policymakers believe the direction of the comparative static in (3.16) to be positive. That is, the implementation of a curbside recycling programme (a decrease in δ) reduces garbage.

The empirical evidence testing that assumption is inconclusive. Only Kinnaman and Fullerton (1997) estimate the impact of curbside recycling on household garbage totals, but they find the impact on garbage is not statistically significant.

A Change in the Wage (p_k)

Households may also change their utility-maximizing disposal choices with a change in their wage. As the wage rises, households face a higher opportunity cost of recycling and thus may recycle less. The comparative static result verifies this claim

$$\frac{\partial r^*}{\partial p_k} \equiv -\frac{r^*}{p_k} < 0. \tag{3.17}$$

Relative to the average household, this negative effect is greater for households that recycle more (r) or earn low wages (p_k). Thus, poorer households are expected to respond to an increase in wage by decreasing recycling by a greater amount than richer households, *ceteris paribus*.

Hong, Adams and Love (1993) test the relationship in (3.17). They regress the probability of recycling on the wage rate of the female member of the household and find that as the wage rate increases, the probability of recycling decreases. Kinnaman (1994) also finds that recycling decreases with the number of full-time workers in the household.

A change in the wage is also predicted to affect the optimal quantity of garbage

$$\frac{\partial g^*}{\partial p_k} \equiv -\frac{\partial r^*}{\partial p_k} + \frac{k^m}{\alpha u_c / \lambda^*} > 0, \tag{3.18}$$

which is unambiguously positive. Again, this comparative static can be partitioned into an 'income' and 'substitution' effect. Part of the increase in garbage is a direct result of the decrease in recycling. The remaining portion arises from the fact that more material is being generated by the household with the higher wage. In Figure 3.6, the marginal cost of recycling ($p_k \delta r$) would rotate upward with the increase in p_k, so r falls. Garbage is increased both by the decrease in recycling and by the *rightward* shift of the right vertical axis. This can be expressed more formally by

$$\frac{\partial m^*}{\partial p_k} \equiv \frac{\partial g^*}{\partial p_k} + \frac{\partial r^*}{p_k} \equiv \frac{k^m}{\alpha u_c / \lambda^*} > 0. \tag{3.19}$$

The increase in total waste material is particularly high for households that devote more time to working (high k^m) since these households will enjoy the greatest boost to income for an increase in p_k. *Ceteris paribus*, households that experience a low marginal benefit of consumption $(\alpha u_c/\lambda^*)$ will generate more additional material than the average household (following a boost in p_k).

Though Hong, Adams and Love (1993) find a positive relationship between garbage and the wage rate, the estimate is statistically insignificant. Podolsky and Spiegel (1998) estimate that an increase in the ratio of employees to household members increases garbage. Kinnaman (1994) also finds that an increase in the portion of the household that are full-time workers increases garbage.

A Change in α

The portion of consumption that becomes waste material $(1/\alpha)$ is exogenous to the household.[18] This exogenous value of α could change if firms reduce the quantity of material used to package their products.[19] How would households respond to an exogenous change in α? The comparative static results are[20]

$$\frac{\partial r^*}{\partial \alpha} \equiv 0 \tag{3.20}$$

$$\frac{\partial g^*}{\partial \alpha} \equiv -\frac{p_c m^*}{\alpha u_c / \lambda^*} < 0. \tag{3.21}$$

An increase in the value of α is interpreted as a decrease in the portion of consumption that becomes waste material. Households respond to this increase by decreasing garbage, but do not change recycling. The change in garbage is especially large for households that discard a high amount of material (m^*), face high prices for goods and services (p_c), or experience a low marginal benefit of acquiring an additional unit of material $(\alpha u_c/\lambda^*)$. No empirical evidence has been found to test these predictions.

Other Considerations

Many of the empirical studies mentioned above control for income and demographic variables in the regression when estimating the quantity of garbage and recycling produced by households. The estimated coefficients on these variables could assist local governments to forecast future garbage disposal needs.

A change in the wage rate, as modelled above, has both an income effect and a price effect (on the cost of recycling). The pure income effect of a change in non-labour income on household garbage has been estimated in several empirical studies. This relationship could be expected to be positive if additional income implies more consumption and garbage. However, if increases in income are spent on dining out and longer vacations, household garbage totals could decrease with income. The empirical literature finds more evidence supporting the former prediction. In fact, Podolsky and Spiegel (1998) find the strongest relationship between garbage quantities and income by estimating the income elasticity of demand for garbage collection to be 0.55. Other studies also find a positive but weaker relationship between income and garbage. Jenkins (1993) estimates an income elasticity of demand equal to 0.41, Wertz (1976) at 0.279 and 0.272 using two sets of data, Kinnaman and Fullerton (1997) at 0.262, Richardson and Havlicek (1978) at 0.242, 0.22 by Reschovsky and Stone (1994), 0.2 by Petrovic and Jaffee (1978) and finally 0.049 by Hong, Adams and Love (1993). Strathman, Rufolo and Mildner (1995) find that garbage disposed of at landfill sites decreases with the average manufacturing income of the city.

The effect of non-labour income on recycling is not as well understood. (The simple model in Figure 3.6 would predict no effect.) Callan and Thomas (1997) and Duggal, Saltzmane and Williams (1991) find that income increases household recycling quantities, but Hong, Adams and Love (1993) find income does not impact self-reported recycling participation. Jakus, Tiller and Park (1996) find income increases the recycling of paper but not glass. Saltzman, Duggal and Williams (1993) find that additional income increases the recycling of newspaper but decreases the recycling of glass.

Economists have also estimated the relationship between education and household garbage totals. Educated households could be more aware of recycling opportunities. Educated households may also have greater tastes for the environment. Indeed, Hong, Adams and Love (1993), Callan and Thomas (1997), Judge and Becker (1993), Reschovsky and Stone (1994) and Duggal, Saltzman and Williams (1991) find education increases recycling. Using household data, Kinnaman (1994) estimates that educated households produce less garbage. Using a cross-section of 959 communities, Kinnaman and Fullerton (1997) find a similar result. Though Judge and Becker (1993) find no impact from publicity efforts to increase the awareness of municipal recycling opportunities, Callan and Thomas (1997) find that an extra dollar spent per household on such efforts increases the recycling rate by 2.55 per cent.

The effects of other demographic variables have also been estimated. Jenkins (1993), Kinnaman (1994), and Podolsky and Spiegel (1998) find that increases in the size of the household decrease the per capita quantity of garbage disposed. Larger families could share meals in a way that produces less waste than the same number of people eating separately. Hong, Adams and Love (1993) find that larger households also are more likely to report participation in recycling. Regarding the age of the household and its impact on garbage totals, Podolsky and Spiegel (1998) find that an increase in median age decreases garbage. Jenkins (1993) finds that an increase in the portion of population between 18 and 49 increases garbage. Jakus, Tiller and Park (1996) find that older individuals are more likely to recycle glass. Kinnaman (1994) estimates that households with married couples produce less per capita garbage and recycling. Reschovsky and Stone (1994) find that married households produce more total recycling (not controlling for household size). Finally, Kinnaman (1994) estimates that homeowners produce more garbage and recycling than renters do.

CONCLUSION

The solid waste collection and disposal industry has undergone dramatic changes over the past two decades. First, the structure of landfills has changed from local town dumps to large regional landfills equipped to reduce the negative externalities associated with garbage disposal. Second, Japan, much of Europe, and the northeast regions of the United States have turned to incineration to manage residential solid waste since the 1970s. Financially, incineration has been most successful where land is scarce (and hence the costs of landfills are high). Some still question the environmental benefits of incineration. Third, the portion of solid waste that is recycled has risen sharply over the past decade. This growth has been facilitated by greater government involvement designed to encourage households to separate waste. The growth in the supply of recycled materials has resulted in a short-run glut of materials, and governments have been active in finding markets for these materials. Several states in the US have passed an assortment of policies with this goal in mind. Finally, roughly 4000 local communities in the US have begun to price garbage by the bag. These local programmes have helped to pay the rising costs of disposal in some areas, and they provide an incentive for households to recycle more. The extent to which these programmes produce positive net benefits is still debated in the economics literature.

As residential solid waste became a more important issue to policymakers, intellectual attention from economists increased. The number of economic papers devoted to residential solid waste and recycling has risen sharply over the past ten years. The bulk of these papers provide empirical estimates of the effects of government policies on household disposal behaviour. Another portion is devoted to prescribing the efficient policy approach. Most models support the use of some form of a 'deposit/refund' system. The deposit or advanced disposal fee could be applied at either the point of production or purchase. The refund or subsidy to recycling could be given to households that recycle or to firms that purchase recycled materials. Other economic models support a tax on virgin material or a direct tax on the household's disposal choices.

Even though the economics literature has reached some consensus over the choice of policy directives, very few of these recommendations have been pursued explicitly by the policymaking community. Advanced disposal fees exist only for some products in some countries. Explicit recycling subsidies are also few and far between. Deposit/refund systems have been implemented only for beverage containers and have only been implemented in some countries. Perhaps additional work could design structures for these policies to help minimize the administrative costs. Palmer and Walls (1999) have begun work in this area. On the other hand, many jurisdictions already have *implicit* deposit/refund systems on all goods, to the extent that they impose a general sales tax on all purchases and use some of the money to pay for free curbside recycling collection.

Many economic predictions have been confirmed by empirical work: a higher price per bag of garbage is found to reduce demand for garbage collection, and higher incomes are found to increase waste for disposal. Other behaviours are not yet well understood, however, such as observed amounts of recycling even when households have no incentive to recycle.

NOTES

1. An estimated 6 per cent of the world's emissions of methane (a greenhouse gas) are released from landfills (Beede and Bloom, 1995).
2. This estimate is comprised of private and external collection and disposal costs (including a depletion allowance). The external costs are based somewhat on the work of Stone and Ashford (1991) and the Tellus Institute (1991).
3. Kennedy and Laplante (1994) also develop a model that suggests garbage should be priced at its social marginal cost. But, if governments must balance the disposal *portion* of their budget (and lump-sum taxes are not available), then the optimal policy may change. In particular, if the social marginal cost of waste disposal is greater than the household's marginal cost of dumping, then the user fee should be set just equal to the household's private marginal cost of dumping, and the subsidy for recycling should be lowered.
4. Fullerton and Kinnaman (1996) estimate that 28 per cent of the reduction in garbage resulting from pricing garbage at the curb may have been dumped. Jenkins (1993), Blume (1991), and Miranda and Aldy (1998) also find evidence of increased dumping. A number of other studies find minimal changes in dumping, including Podolsky and Spiegel (1998), Strathman, Rufolo and Mildner (1995), Miranda *et al.* (1994), Miranda and Bauer (1996) and Nestor and Podolsky (1998).
5. Palmer, Sigman and Walls (1997) find that a 10 per cent reduction in solid waste can be achieved with a $45 per ton deposit/refund system, an $85 per ton advanced disposal fee by itself or a $98 per ton recycling subsidy by itself. The latter amounts are larger because

these policies must 'work harder' to achieve the reduction in garbage since they do not encourage both source reduction at time of production and recycling at the time of disposal. For example, Starreveld and Van Ierland (1994) estimate that using only a disposal fee of $.30 per kilogram (roughly $272 per ton) of plastic will result in the recycling of 25 per cent of disposed plastic in The Netherlands.

6. If, in the long run, virgin and recycled inputs are perfect substitutes, then the elimination of tax advantages for virgin input would still only increase newspaper recycling by 1.68 per cent and scrap steel by 3.4 per cent.

7. Many of these empirical studies also uncover a negative relationship between a previous period's prices and current supply quantities. This relationship is explained by the use of stockpiling. If prices of recycled materials were low in a previous period, then firms may build up their inventories rather than sell at the low price. An increased inventory then increases supply in the current period. The assumption that suppliers stockpile materials to wait for higher prices has not been tested by the economics literature.

8. As an exception, US courts have often applied the Market Participant doctrine that allows local governments to restrict out-of-state garbage from government-owned disposal sites. See Podolsky and Spiegel (1999) for a thorough review of the case law related to inter-state garbage shipments.

9. This conclusion is an application of more general findings related to the efficiency of Ramsey pricing.

10. In Canada, McDavid (1985) estimates that only 20.6 per cent of cities with populations in excess of 10 000 use municipal collection, though another 37.3 per cent rely partly on the municipality to collect household garbage at the curb and partly on private firms to compete for collection from commercial establishments and apartment buildings.

11. Michaelis (1995) and Rousso and Shah (1994) provide further background on Germany's Green Dot programme.

12. Such concerns arose after several packages with green dots were found in French landfills. In response, the European Union recently banned the export of recyclable materials headed for foreign landfills or incinerators. Reliable data are not available to characterize the quantity of residential solid waste that is shipped between European countries. Europe has been exporting solid waste to Africa.

13. One implication of the model presented here is that if the price of garbage is zero, then the household has no incentive to engage in recycling since garbage is free and recycling requires scarce household resources. This result is clearly inconsistent with the available data. In fact, Fullerton and Kinnaman (1996) find that 73.3 per cent of households recycled even in the absence of any legal or economic incentive. Why do these households recycle? Even if households value the quality of the environment (a public good) and their recycling efforts improve the quality of the environment, households cannot be expected to provide this public good at their own cost. Perhaps households simply enjoy recycling or feel a civic duty to participate in the recycling programme. Understanding why households have been willing to participate in municipal recycling programmes remains an interesting question to economists and policymakers.

14. A simple way to see this result is to solve (3.9a) and (3.9b) to get $r = p_g/\delta p_k$ and then differentiate that with respect to p_g.

15. This result requires the use of all equations (3.9) and (3.10).

16. Nestor and Podolsky (1996) published a comment suggesting that the changes in tipping fees may not have been passed on to households – the generators of garbage.

17. From (3.9a,b) we get $r = p_g/\delta p_k$, so differentiation yields $\partial r/\partial \delta = -p_g/\delta^2 p_k = -r/\delta$.

18. An extension of the model would allow α to be a choice variable. Households could choose the mix of consumption goods to include less waste-intensive goods. Additional constraints would have to be imposed on the current model, or households here would simply choose α to be 0.

19. See Fullerton and Wu (1998) for a further discussion of the packaging decisions of firms.

20. Again, the first result follows directly from differentiating $r = p_g/\delta p_k$.

REFERENCES

Ackerman, Frank (1997), *Why Do We Recycle?*, Washington, DC: Island Press.

Anderson, Robert C. and Richard D. Spiegelman (1977), 'Tax policy and secondary material use', *Journal of Environmental Economics and Management*, **4**, 68–82.

Atri, Said and Thomas Schellberg (1995), 'Efficient management of household solid waste: a general equilibrium model', *Public Finance Quarterly*, **23**(1), January, 3–39.

Bailey, Jeff (1995), 'Waste of a sort: curbside recycling comforts the soul, but benefits are scant', *The Wall Street Journal*, January 19, A1.

Beede, David N. and David E. Bloom (1995), 'The economics of municipal solid waste', *The World Bank Research Observer*, **10**(2), August, 113–50.

Bingham, Tayler H., Curtis E. Youngblood and Philip C. Cooley (1983), 'Conditionally predictive supply elasticity estimates: secondary materials obtained from municipal residuals', *Journal of Environmental Economics and Management*, **10**(2), June, 166–79.

Blume, Daniel R. (1991), 'Under what conditions should cities adopt volume-based pricing for residential solid waste collection?', Unpublished manuscript, The Office of Management and Budget, Office of Information and Regulatory Affairs, Natural Resources Branch, May.

Bohm, Robert A., David H. Folz and Michael J. Podolsky (1999), 'Cost and economies of scale in the provision of recycling services', Working Paper, University of Tennessee, January.

Brisson, Inger E. (1997), 'Assessing the "waste hierarchy" a social cost–benefit analysis of MSW management in the European Union', Samfund, Okonomi and Miljo Publication Number 19.

Butterfield, David W. and Atif A. Kubursi (1993), 'Regional economic effects of recycling in Ontario', *Canadian Journal of Regional Science*, **16**(3), Autumn, 413–31.

Callan, Scott J. and Janet M. Thomas (1997), 'The impact of state and local policies on the recycling effort', *Eastern Economic Journal*, **23**(4), Fall, 411–23.

Callan, Scott J. and Janet M. Thomas (1999), 'Adopting a unit-pricing system for municipal solid waste: policy and socio-economic determinants', *Environmental and Resource Economics*, forthcoming.

Carroll, Wayne (1997), 'The costs and performance of residential recycling programs: evidence from Wisconsin', Working Paper, University of Wisconsin.

Cointreau-Levine, Sandra J. (1994), 'Private sector participation in municipal solid waste services in developing countries', *The Formal Sector*, vol. I, Washington, DC: World Bank.

Copeland, Brian R. (1991), 'International trade in waste products in the presence of illegal disposal', *Journal of Environmental Economics and Management*, **20** (2), March, 143–62.

Dinan, Terry M. (1993), 'Economic efficiency effects of alternative policies for reducing waste disposal', *Journal of Environmental Economics and Management*, **25**(3), November, 242–56.

Dobbs, Ian M. (1991), 'Litter and waste management: disposal taxes versus user charges', *Canadian Journal of Economics*, **24**(1), February, 221–7.

Dubin, Jeffrey A. and Peter Navarro (1988), 'How markets for impure public goods organize: the case of household refuse collection', *Journal of Law, Economics, and Organization*, **4**(2), Fall, 217–41.

Duggal, Vijaya G., Cynthia Saltzman and Mary L. Williams (1991), 'Recycling: an economic analysis', *Eastern Economic Journal*, **17**(3), July–September, 351–8.

Edwards, Ron and David Pearce (1978), 'The effect of prices on the recycling of waste materials', *Resources Policy*, December, 242–8.

Fenton, R. and N. Hanley (1995), 'Economic instruments and waste minimization: the need for discard-relevant and purchase-relevant instruments', *Environment and Planning*, **27**(8), August, 1317–28.

Franklin Associates (1994), 'The role of recycling in integrated solid waste management to the year 2000', report prepared for Keep America Beautiful, Inc., Stamford, CT, September, Chapter 6, appendix I.

Fullerton, Don and Thomas C. Kinnaman (1995), 'Garbage, recycling, and illicit burning or dumping', *Journal of Environmental Economics and Management*, **29**(1), July, 78–91.

Fullerton, Don and Thomas C. Kinnaman (1996), 'Household responses to pricing garbage by the bag', *American Economic Review*, **86**(4), September, 971–84.

Fullerton, Don and Wenbo Wu (1998), 'Policies for green design', *Journal of Environmental Economics and Management*, **36**(2), September, 131–48.

Glenn, Jim (1998), 'The state of garbage in America', *Biocycle*, April, 32–43.

Halstead, John M. and William M. Park (1996), 'The role of economic analysis in local government decisions: the case of solid waste management', *Agricultural and Resource Economics Review*, April, 76–82.

Hanley, Nick and Rick Slark (1994), 'Cost–benefit analysis of paper recycling: a case study and some general principles', *Journal of Environmental Planning and Management* **37**(2), 189–97.

Hong, Seonghoon, Richard M. Adams and H. Alan Love (1993), 'An economic analysis of household recycling of solid wastes: the case of Portland, Oregon', *Journal of Environmental Economics and Management*, **25**(2), September, 136–46.

Huhtala, Anni (1997), 'A post-consumer waste management model for determining optimal levels of recycling and landfilling', *Environmental and Resource Economics*, **10**(3), October, 301–14.

Jakus, Paul M., Kelly H. Tiller and William M. Park (1996), 'Generation of recyclables by rural households', *Journal of Agricultural and Resource Economics*, **21**(1), July, 96–108.

Jenkins, Robin R. (1993), *The Economics of Solid Waste Reduction*, Aldershot, UK: Edward Elgar.

Judge, Rebecca and Anthony Becker (1993), 'Motivating recycling: a marginal cost analysis', *Contemporary Policy Issues*, **11**(3), July, 58–68.

Kemper, Peter and John M. Quigly (1976), *The Economics of Refuse Collection*, Cambridge, MA: Ballinger Publishing Company.

Kennedy, Peter W. and Benoit Laplante (1994), 'Municipal solid waste management: the optimal pricing of garbage and recyclables collection', Working Paper, Department of Economics, University of Victoria.

Kinnaman, Thomas C. (1994), 'On user fees for refuse collection', Dissertation, Department of Economics, University of Virginia.

Kinnaman, Thomas C. (1998), 'The efficiency of curbside recycling: a benefit-cost analysis', Working Paper, Department of Economics, Bucknell University.

Kinnaman, Thomas C. and Don Fullerton (1997), 'Garbage and recycling in communities with curbside recycling and unit-based pricing', NBER Working Paper Series, 6021, May.

Klein, Yehuda L. and H. David Robison (1993), 'Solid waste disposal costs, product prices, and incentives for waste reduction', *Atlantic Economic Journal*, **21**(1), March, 56–65.

Ley, Eduardo, Molly K. Macauley and Stephen W. Salant (1997), 'Spatially and intertemporally efficient waste management: the costs of interstate flow control', Working Paper, December: Resources for the Future.

Macauley, Molly K., Stephen W. Salant, Margaret A. Walls and David Edelstein (1993), 'Managing municipal solid waste: advantages of the discriminating monopolist', Discussion Paper ENR93–05, Resources for the Future, Washington, DC, January.

McDavid, James C. (1985), 'The Canadian experience with privatizing residential solid waste collection services', *Public Administration Review*, September/October, 602–8.

Michaelis, Peter (1995), 'Product stewardship, waste minimization and economic efficiency: lessons from Germany' *Journal of Environmental Planning and Management*, **38**(2), June, 231–43.

Miedema, Allen K. (1976), 'The case for virgin material charges: a theoretical and empirical evaluation in the paper industry', prepared for the US Environmental Protection Agency by the Research Triangle Institute, North Carolina.

Miedema, Allen K. (1983), 'Fundamental economic comparisons of solid waste policy options', *Resources and Energy*, **5**, 21–43.

Miranda, M.L. and J.E. Aldy (1998), 'Unit pricing of residential municipal solid waste: lessons from nine case study communities', *Journal of Environmental Management*, **52**(1), January, 79–93.

Miranda, Marie Lynn and Scott Bauer (1996), 'An analysis of variable rates for residential garbage collection in urban areas', Working Paper, Nicholas School of the Environment, Duke University.

Miranda, Maria Lynn and David Z. Bynum (1999), 'Unit based pricing in the United States: a tally of communities', Working Paper, Nicholas School of the Environment, Duke University.

Miranda, Marie Lynn, Jess W. Everett, Daniel Blume and Barbeau A. Roy, Jr. (1994), 'Market-based incentives and residential municipal solid waste', *Journal of Policy Analysis and Management*, **13**(4), Fall, 681–98.

Nelson, Arthur C., John Genereux and Michelle Genereux (1992), 'Price effects of landfills on house values', *Land Economics*, **68**(4), November, 359–65.

Nestor, Deborah Vaughn (1992), 'Partial static equilibrium model of newsprint recycling', *Applied Economics*, **24**(4), April, 411–17.

Nestor, Deborah Vaughn and Michael J. Podolsky (1996), 'The demand for solid waste disposal: comment', *Land Economics*, **72**(1), February, 129–31.

Nestor, Deborah Vaughn and Michael J. Podolsky (1998), 'Assessing incentive-based environmental policies for reducing household waste disposal', *Contemporary Economic Policy*, **16**(4), 401–11.

Palmer, Karen, Hilary Sigman and Margaret Walls (1997), 'The cost of reducing municipal solid waste', *Journal of Environmental Economics and Management*, **33**(2), June, 128–50.

Palmer, Karen and Margaret Walls (1994), 'Materials use and solid waste: an evaluation of policies', Discussion Paper 95–02, Resources for the Future, Washington, DC, October.

Palmer, Karen and Margaret Walls (1997), 'Optimal policies for solid waste disposal: taxes, subsidies, and standards', *Journal of Public Economics*, **65**(2), August, 193–205.

Palmer, Karen and Margaret Walls (1999), 'Extended product responsibility: an economic assessment of alternative policies', Discussion Paper 99–12, Resources for the Future, Washington, DC, January.

Petrovic, W.M. and B.L. Jaffee (1978), 'Measuring the generation and collection of solid waste in cities', *Urban Affairs Quarterly*, **14**, December, 229–44.

Podolsky, Michael J. and Menahem Spiegel (1998), 'Municipal waste disposal: unit-pricing and recycling opportunities', *Public Works Management and Policy*, **3**(1), December, 27–39.

Podolsky, Michael J. and Menahem Spiegel (1999), 'When interstate transportation of municipal solid waste makes sense and when it does not', Working Paper, February, US Environmental Protection Agency, *Public Administration Review*, forthcoming.

Powell, Jane C., Amelia L. Craighill, Julian P. Parfitt and R. Kerry Turner (1996), 'A lifecycle assessment and economic valuation of recycling', *Journal of Environmental Planning and Management*, **39**(1), March, 97–112.

Repetto, Robert, Roger C. Dower, Robin Jenkins and Jacqueline Geoghegan (1992), *Green Fees: How a Tax Shift Can Work for the Environment and the Economy*, Washington, DC: The World Resources Institute.

Reschovsky, James D. and Sarah E. Stone (1994), 'Market incentives to encourage household waste recycling: paying for what you throw away', *Journal of Policy Analysis and Management*, **13**(1), Winter, 120–39.

Richardson, Robert A. and Joseph Havlicek, Jr. (1978), 'Economic analysis of the composition of household solid wastes', *Journal of Environmental Economics and Management*, **5**(1), March, 103–11.

Roberts, Roland K., Peggy V. Douglas and William M. Park (1991), 'Estimating external costs of municipal landfill siting through contingent valuation analysis: a case study', *Southern Journal of Agricultural Economics*, **23**(2), December, 155–65.

Rousso, Ada S. and Shvetank P. Shah (1994), 'Packaging taxes and recycling incentives: the German Green Dot programme', *National Tax Journal*, **47**(3), September, 689–701.

Saltzman, Cynthia, Vijaya G. Duggal and Mary L. Williams (1993), 'Income and the recycling effort: a maximization problem', *Energy Economics*, **15**(1), 33–8.

Savas, Emmanuel S. (1977), *The Organization and Efficiency of Solid Waste Collection*, Lexington, MA: Lexington Books.

Seguino, Stephanie, George Criner and Margarita Suarez (1995), 'Solid waste management options for Maine: the economics of pay-by-the-bag systems', *Maine Policy Review*, October, 49–58.

Silberberg, Eugene (1990), *The Structure of Economics: A Mathematical Analysis*, second edition, New York: McGraw-Hill.

Solid Waste Association of North America (1995), 'Integrated municipal solid waste management: six case studies of system costs and energy use: summary report', November.

Starreveld, P. Folkert and Ekko C. Van Ierland (1994), 'Recycling of plastics: a materials balance optimisation model', *Environmental and Resource Economics*, **4**, 251–64.

Stevens, Barbara J. (1978), 'Scale, market structure, and the cost of refuse collection', *The Review of Economics and Statistics*, **60**(3), August, 438–48.

Stone, Robert and Nicholas A. Ashford (1991), 'Package deal: the economic impacts

LIVERPOOL JOHN MOORES UNIVERSITY
LEARNING & INFORMATION SERVICES

of recycling standards for packaging in Massachusetts,' Working Paper, Massachusetts Institute of Technology.

Strathman, James G., Anthony M. Rufolo and Gerard C.S. Mildner (1995), 'The Demand for Solid Waste Disposal', *Land Economics*, **71**(1), February, 57–64.

Tawil, Natalie (1995), 'On the political economy of municipal curbside recycling programs: evidence from Massachusetts', Working Paper, Congressional Budget Office of the United States.

Tawil, Natalie (1999), 'Flow control and rent capture in solid waste management', *Journal of Environmental Economics and Management*, **37**(2), March, 183–201.

Tellus Institute (1991), 'Acting in the national interest: the transportation agenda,' Surface Transportation Policy Project, Washington, DC.

Tiller, Kelly J., Paul M. Jakus and William M. Park (1997), 'Household willingness to pay for dropoff recycling', *Journal of Agricultural and Resource Economics*, **22**(2), December, 310–20.

US Congress, Office of Technology Assessment (1989), 'Facing America's trash: what next for municipal solid waste', US Government Printing Office, Washington, DC, October.

Van der Kuil, Ir (1976), 'Recovery of materials by separate collection of domestic waste components', SVA, Amersfoort, Netherlands.

Walls, Margaret and Karen Palmer (1997), 'Upstream pollution, downstream waste disposal, and the design of comprehensive environmental policies', Discussion Paper 97–51–REV, Resources for the Future, Washington, DC, September.

Wertz, Kenneth L. (1976), 'Economic factors influencing households' production of refuse', *Journal of Environmental Economics and Management*, **2**, 263–72.

JOURNAL OF ENVIRONMENTAL ECONOMICS AND MANAGEMENT **29**, 78–91 (1995)

Garbage, Recycling, and Illicit Burning or Dumping

DON FULLERTON

Department of Economics, University of Texas at Austin, Austin, Texas 78712

AND

THOMAS C. KINNAMAN

Department of Economics, Bucknell University, Lewisburg, Pennsylvania 17837

Received July 15, 1993; revised February 18, 1994

With garbage and recycling as the only two disposal options, we confirm prior results that the optimal curbside fee for garbage collection equals the direct resource cost plus external environmental cost. When illicit burning or dumping is a third disposal option that cannot be taxed directly, the optimal curbside tax on garbage changes sign. The optimal fee structure is a deposit–refund system: a tax on all output plus a rebate on proper disposal through either recycling or garbage collection. The output tax helps achieve the first-best allocation even though it affects the choice between consumption and untaxed leisure. © 1995 Academic Press, Inc.

1. INTRODUCTION

Solid waste disposal has become more expensive recently due to rising land prices, strict environmental regulations, and host fees paid to localities to accept new landfills or incinerators. Tipping fees in the northeastern U.S. approach $125 per ton. Most towns still pay for garbage collection and disposal using general revenues, however, with no price per bag. Thus the resident views it as free.

As an alternative, more towns are beginning to sell special bags or stickers necessary for curbside collection of each bag or can of garbage (U.S. EPA [20]). These per-unit charges can help defray the cost of collection, and they help discourage waste. Two major recent studies describe the advantages of such charges. Project 88—Round II [14], sponsored by then Senators Timothy Wirth of Colorado and John Heinz of Pennsylvania, says that unit pricing "creates strong incentives for households to reduce the quantities of waste they generate, whether through changes in their purchasing patterns, reuse of products and containers, or composting of yard wastes" (pp. 49–50). The World Resources Institute (WRI, Repetto *et al*, [15]) further extols the virtues of "pay-by-the-bag." For densely populated areas, they estimate that each 32-gallon bag of garbage costs $1.12 in direct payments to waste haulers and landfill operators, and $1.83 including external costs to others near the landfill who may suffer from noise, odor, litter, and extra traffic. They go on to measure welfare gains from charging such a price.

In response to unit charges, however, households might not just recycle, compost, and adjust purchasing habits. They might also burn paper in fireplaces and carry trash to commercial dumpsters, back woods, and vacant lots. If New York City were to sell stickers for $1.83 each, and pick up only bags with stickers, we believe that revenue would be small and piles of unidentified garbage would be large. Welfare gains would be negative.

78

Should garbage be taxed to reflect its negative externality, or subsidized to avert illicit dumping? Maybe recycling should be subsidized. If not, could the same effect be achieved by a tax on virgin materials? What is the role for deposits on purchases with refunds on returns.

To address these questions, we build a simple theoretical general equilibrium model of household choice between consumption and leisure, and among three disposal options: garbage, recycling, and illicit burning or dumping. A single consumption good is produced using a single primary factor, recycled input, and virgin materials such as timber or minerals. We later consider disaggregate goods and services. The model also includes three externalities. First, municipal garbage collection and disposal may impose aesthetic and health costs on those who live near the landfill or incinerator. Second, improper burning and dumping may impose even higher costs on others. Third, the extraction of virgin materials involves clear-cutting or strip-mining that may adversely affect not only the landowner who sells timber or mineral rights, but others who enjoy wilderness and wildlife.

Others have addressed some of the above questions, usually with partial equilibrium models and only two disposal options. First, Sullivan [18] compares legal and illegal disposal. He finds both an optimal subsidy on legal disposal and an optimal degree of enforcement against illegal disposal. These are second-best policies since he does not allow for a tax on consumption (or, equivalently, a "deposit" upon purchase). Also, Dobbs [5] and Project 88—Round II [14] have discussed the problem of litter as a reason for deposits and refunds on particular commodities. Copeland [3] builds a general equilibrium model with international trade and waste from production, but no recycling or waste from consumption. Jenkins [6] and Sigman [16] consider waste and recycling, but not illegal dumping. Several other models of household decisionmaking deal with various important aspects of the solid waste problem, but also ignore illicit dumping (e.g., [4, 10, 15, 21]). Our study is unique in that (1) we address all of the above questions in (2) a single general equilibrium framework with (3) enough instruments to solve for first-best policies, and when (4) households can choose among all three disposal options: garbage, recycling, and illicit burning or dumping. Another advantage, we believe, is that our solution can be replicated easily on the back of an envelope.

To introduce our notation, and to characterize prior results, we start in Section 2 with a simple model in which garbage and recycling are the only two disposal choices. In this case the WRI study [15] is correct that the optimal garbage collection fee includes not only the direct resource cost ($1.12 per bag) but also the external cost (for a total of $1.83 per bag, in their study).

In Section 3, we add illicit dumping as a third disposal option. When all tax instruments are available, the first-best solution can be achieved by waste-end taxes on garbage *and* on illicit dumping. Not surprisingly, these two tax rates reflect only the corresponding externalities. Suppose, however, that a tax on illicit dumping is difficult or impossible to enforce. Does this mean that the first-best can no longer be supported? No. In general equilibrium, only relative prices matter—and therefore any tax can be set equal to zero as long as taxes on all other relevant activities are adjusted so as to induce first-best relative prices. Several points follow directly from this general equilibrium insight.

First, with the tax on illegal dumping set equal to zero, the proper relative price between legal and illegal disposal can be induced by subsidizing legal disposal (both garbage and recycling). That is, the optimal tax on garbage switches to a subsidy. If this subsidy for garbage is close to the direct resource cost ($1.12), then free collection of garbage is quite sensible.

Second, this subsidy for legal garbage disposal tends to subsidize consumption since it lowers the cost of waste disposal. Therefore, to restore the proper relative prices in general equilibrium, a tax on consumption is required. This result addresses a debate in the literature about whether optimal fees would be imposed "upstream" at the point of production, or "downstream" at the point of disposal.[1] In our model, if the downstream tax on illicit dumping cannot be enforced, the same first-best can be achieved by using an upstream tax instead. Consumption should be taxed at a rate that reflects not the good's disposal cost, but its possible externality from illicit burning or dumping. This tax is then returned as a subsidy on recycling and on proper disposal of garbage, leaving an implicit tax on burning or dumping. The result is a deposit–refund system, as in Bohm [2], but it applies to all consumption goods rather than just bottles or lead–acid batteries.

Third, many have suggested that recycling be encouraged by a tax on virgin materials (e.g., [9, 14, 16, and 19]). No such role arises in our model. Virgin materials are only taxed if their extraction has a negative externality (e.g., strip mining). Section 4 shows that if recycling *cannot* be subsidized for some reason, then all of the proper relative prices can still be achieved with a tax on virgin materials and on *all* other inputs except recycling.

Fourth, existing public finance literature generally finds that a consumption tax distorts the choice between taxed consumption and untaxed leisure. Here, we find that a consumption tax is part of a first-best policy, even though leisure is still untaxed. The reason is simply that consumption leads to disposal problems while leisure does not.

Section 5 considers disaggregate consumption goods, and Section 6 briefly discusses population density, multiple levels of government, and administrative cost.

2. JUST GARBAGE AND RECYCLING

Most models of household solid waste behavior ignore the possibility of illicit burning or dumping (e.g., [4, 6, 10, 15, 16, 21]). We therefore start with garbage and recycling as the only two disposal choices. The purpose of this section is not to provide any new results, but to set up our notation and to characterize prior results. Since none of the the discussion above involves distributional issues, we consider a single jurisdiction with n identical individuals or households. Each buys a single composite consumption good c, and each generates waste in two forms. We use g for garbage collection, and r for recycling and subsequent reuse in production. These alternatives are substitutes in the "technology" of household

---

[1] Wertz [21] finds that a (downstream) per-unit garbage fee raises the effective purchase price of goods with high disposal content. Menell [8] suggests retail disposal-content charges that reflect the subsequent disposal cost of each item. Porter [13] analyzes a deposit–refund system for bottles. Sigman [16] finds that a tax on virgin lead is equivalent to a deposit–refund system, when virgin lead and recycled lead are perfect substitutes in production. The pros and cons of alternative policies are nicely described in some of these papers, as well as in Miedema [9] and Project 88—Round II [14].

consumption,[2]

$$c = c(g, r), \tag{1}$$

where $c(\cdot, \cdot)$ is continuous and quasi-concave, and has positive first derivatives c_g and c_r. This relationship captures the degree to which the household is able to shift between disposal methods. With a given amount of consumption, the household may be able to reduce g and increase r by recycling newspapers, composting food waste, purchasing bottles in glass instead of plastic, collecting aluminum, and buying goods with less packaging. For simplicity, we specify each form of disposal as a single continuous variable. As a special case of (1), we will later discuss a "mass balance" example where $c = g + r$ (and $c_g = c_r = 1$).

Utility depends not only on household consumption, c, but also on home production, h, and the total amount of garbage, $G = ng$,

$$u = u[c(g, r), h, G], \tag{2}$$

where the first derivatives are $u_c > 0$, $u_h > 0$, and $u_G \leq 0$. For practical purposes, think of h as leisure use of time and resources. We use lower case letters to denote values per household and upper case letters for aggregates. Total garbage G may impose aesthetic and health costs, even if it is regulated in a "sanitary" landfill.[3]

On the production side of the model, output c may be produced using the constant returns to scale production function

$$c = f(k_c, r), \tag{3}$$

with input of resources k_c and recycled materials r from used consumption goods. Any reprocessing of r is folded into the production function. Also, just as we ignore transaction costs in the sale of c or k_c, we ignore the cost of collecting and trading r.

Provision of garbage collection services requires only one input, k_g, so constant returns to scale implies that production is linear. Home production uses resources k_h,

$$g = \gamma k_g, \quad h = k_h. \tag{4}$$

Finally, the model is closed by the resource constraint

$$k = k_c + k_g + k_h, \tag{5}$$

where k denotes a fixed total resource such as labor or capital. The results below do not require any distinction between labor and capital.

In this model, the social planner's problem is to maximize the utility of the representative household subject to the resource constraint, production constraints,

---

[2]Some readers may prefer to think of g and r as outputs of a function with input c, but Eq. (1) simply inverts that function. We think of g and r as amounts necessary to support c.

[3]In this static model of annual flows, G is total garbage per year. See V. L. Smith [17] for a dynamic treatment of waste flows into a landfill with a stock externality.

and $c(g, r) = f(k_c, r)$. The resource and production constraints can be substituted directly, to maximize

$$\mathscr{L} = u\big[c(\gamma k_g, r), k_h, n\gamma k_g\big] + \delta\big[f(k - k_g - k_h, r) - c(\gamma k_g, r)\big] \qquad (6)$$

with respect to k_g, r, and k_h. This optimization recognizes that every individual imposes costs on others through the use of garbage collection services.[4] The first-order conditions are

$$u_c c_g + u_G n = \delta(c_g + f_{kc}/\gamma) \qquad (7a)$$

$$u_c c_r = \delta(c_r - f_r) \qquad (7b)$$

$$u_h = \delta f_{kc}, \qquad (7c)$$

where f_{kc} is $\partial f/\partial k_c$, the marginal product of k used in the production of c. These equations will be employed shortly. They just indicate that the marginal utility made possible through additional g, r, or h must equal the marginal social cost.

For the case of private markets, individuals maximize utility in Eq. (2) subject to a budget constraint that may be affected by a tax or subsidy on each good,[5]

$$p_k k = (1 + t_c)c + (p_g + t_g)g + (p_r + t_r)r + p_k k_h, \qquad (8)$$

where p_k is the price earned on resources, the price of consumption equals one since c is numeraire, t_c is the tax per unit of consumption, p_g is the price paid for garbage collection, t_g is the tax per unit of garbage, p_r is the price paid by the consumer for recycling (which may be positive or negative), and t_r is the tax per unit of recycling. Note that consumers pays prices gross of tax, but producers receive prices net of tax. Here, however, households ignore the effect of their own activities on the total externality. Tax and subsidy rates can simply be set to zero for the case of private markets with no government interference.

Producers receive a price ($= 1$) for selling c, and they receive the price paid by consumers for recycling, p_r, which we said could be positive or negative. They maximize profits ($c + p_r r - p_k k_c$) under perfect competition with constant returns to scale. Thus $f_{kc} = p_k$ and $f_r = -p_r$. Producers of garbage collection services similarly maximize ($p_g g - p_k k_g$), so $p_g = p_k/\gamma$.

In this decentralized economy, the consumer chooses g, r, and h to maximize utility in (2) subject to the budget in (8). The resulting first-order conditions involve prices (p_k, p_r, and p_g), but we replace those with marginal products ($f_{kc}, -f_r, f_{kc}/\gamma$) to obtain

$$u_c c_g = \lambda\big[(1 + t_c)c_g + f_{kc}/\gamma + t_g\big] \qquad (9a)$$

$$u_c c_r = \lambda\big[(1 + t_c)c_r - f_r + t_r\big] \qquad (9b)$$

$$u_h = \lambda f_{kc}, \qquad (9c)$$

[4] We assume second-order conditions hold, solutions are internal, and a unique solution exists (see Baumol and Oates [1, pp. 37–38]).

[5] We ignore the government revenue requirement, assuming implicitly that lump-sum taxes are available to finance spending and to pay for necessary subsidies.

LIVERPOOL
JOHN MOORES UNIVERSITY
AVRIL ROBARTS LRC
TITHEBARN STREET
LIVERPOOL L2 2ER
TEL. 0151 231 4022

where λ is the marginal utility of income. These first-order conditions indicate that private marginal utility matches the cost to individuals of each activity. With tax rates of zero, it is easy to see that the outcome is not optimal. The right-hand sides of (7a) and (9a) would be similar, but only the left side of (7a) would account for the external cost of garbage, u_G.

With Pigouvian tax rates, however, private behavior in (9) can be induced to match the unique social optimum in (7). In this case, (7c) and (9c) indicate that $\delta = \lambda$. Since both problems maximize utility subject to a resource constraint, and both attain the same optimum, the social marginal utility equals the private marginal utility of the resource.

Next compare (7b) and (9b). By inspection, and using $\delta = \lambda$, these two equations will both hold when $t_c = t_r = 0$. In this model, no tax or subsidy is required for private behavior to yield this first-order condition of the social optimum.[6]

Finally, we compare (7a) and (9a). When $t_c = 0$, these equations both hold so long as $t_g = -nu_G/\lambda$. Since $u_G \leq 0$, this Pigouvian tax is ≥ 0. It increases with the size of the externality (u_G) and with the number of people adversely affected (n). To convert the tax into dollars, the marginal effect on utility, u_G, is divided by the marginal utility of income, λ.

Additional garbage collection is not a pure public good but uses scarce resources such as labor, capital, and landfill. Consumers should pay ($p_g + t_g$), equal to \$1.83 per bag in the WRI study [15], enough to cover both the resource cost and the negative externality from garbage.

3. VIRGIN MATERIALS AND ILLICIT BURNING OR DUMPING

This section makes two modifications to the model. First, for each individual, we allow a third disposal alternative,

$$c = c(g, r, b), \tag{1'}$$

where b stands for burning and other improper disposal, such as dumping by the side of the road. Again b is a single continuous variable, and $c_b > 0$. With given consumption, the household may reduce g and raise b by burning cardboard boxes in the fireplace, carrying trash to commercial dumpsters, or leaving it out in the woods. Total $B = nb$ may reduce the utility of others. In the "mass balance" example, $c = g + r + b$.

Second, we consider virgin materials, with per capita use v. Aggregate use $V = nv$ also may reduce the utility of others. Implicitly, this cost may represent the shadow price of over-using scarce minerals in a more complicated dynamic model.[7] More explicitly, in our model, total V may reduce the public enjoyment of natural areas through clear-cutting or strip-mining. Cutting timber may reduce biodiversity

---

[6]Actually, this condition allows for any tax on consumption t_c, as long as it is returned as a subsidy for both garbage and recycling such that the net tax is still zero. We use this property below.

[7]Neher [11, Chap. 13] shows conditions under which (1) economies systematically underprice environmental resources (p. 238), and (2) the static optimizing solution is the steady state solution of a corresponding dynamic problem (p. 243).

and increase global warming. The new utility function is

$$u = u[c(g,r,b),h,G,B,V], \tag{2'}$$

where $u_G \leq 0$, $u_B \leq 0$, and $u_V \leq 0$. In addition, we assume that $u_B \leq u_G$. In other words, garbage is bad enough in the landfill but even worse if thrown by the side of the road.[8]

Production of c is modified to use not only labor and capital resources, k, and recycling input, r, but also virgin materials, v,

$$c = f(k_c, r, v). \tag{3'}$$

These virgin materials are produced or extracted using a simple linear function,

$$v = \alpha k_v. \tag{4'}$$

Each of these goods can be provided for a market price, but improper burning and dumping cannot. Yet illegal burning does involve time, psychic costs, and perhaps risk of getting caught. We assume that burning uses private resources $k_b = \beta(b)$, with marginal costs that are positive ($\beta_b > 0$) and rising ($\beta_{bb} > 0$). We also assume that any direct tax or penalty on burning or dumping would be difficult or impossible to enforce.[9] Finally, the resource constraint becomes

$$k = k_c + k_g + k_h + k_v + k_b. \tag{5'}$$

The social planner maximizes consumer utility (2') in a Lagrangean like (6), subject to additional constraints (3') through (5'), with respect to k_g, r, k_h, b, and k_v.[10] First-order conditions (7a, b, c) are unchanged, and

$$u_c c_b + u_B n = \delta(c_b + f_{kc}\beta_b) \tag{7d}$$

$$u_V n = \delta(f_{kc}/\alpha - f_v). \tag{7e}$$

For the case of private markets, competitive firms set the marginal product f_v equal to their cost in terms of market price plus tax ($p_v + t_v$). Other firms produce v and maximize profits $[p_v(\alpha k_v) - p_k k_v]$, so $p_v = p_k/\alpha$.

---

[8] We are grateful to a referee for pointing out that it is not sufficient to assume the u_B schedule lies below the u_G schedule. Both schedules may be decreasing (with B or G). We assume that the marginal unit of B entails more externality than the marginal unit of G, even though the amount of burning B may be much less than the amount of regular garbage G.

[9] See Lee [7] for a full treatment of enforcement costs and taxpayer avoidance costs. A simple enforcement model might suggest arbitrarily high penalties, in order to save real police resources. Our model avoids this problem in two ways. First, an internal solution for the social optimum implies that a certain amount of burning may be less costly in social terms than more landfill or recycling. The optimal tax on b is finite. Second, in our model, no direct tax on b is required or even desirable. As long as the government can enforce taxes or pay subsidies on market transactions (of c, g, r, and v), we show that the first-best allocation is attainable.

[10] The Lagrangean is

$$\mathcal{L} = u[c(\gamma k_g, r, b), k_h, n\gamma k_g, nb, n\alpha k_v]$$
$$+ \delta[f(k - k_g - k_h - k_v - \beta(b), r, \alpha k_v) - c(\gamma k_g, r, b)].$$

The consumer's budget constraint in (8) must now include the cost of burning, $p_k \beta(b)$, which is not taxed for reasons cited above. First-order conditions (9a, b, c) are unchanged, and[11]

$$u_c c_b = \lambda[(1 + t_c)c_b + f_{kc}\beta_b] \qquad (9d)$$

$$f_{kc} = (f_v - t_v)\alpha. \qquad (9e)$$

Again we solve for the Pigouvian tax rates that induce private behavior in Eqs. (9) to match the social optimum in (7). Again (7c) and (9c) imply that $\delta = \lambda$. This time, however, (7d) and (9d) can be solved for a particular value of t_c that is not zero. Then (7b) and (9b) require that $t_r = -t_c c_r$. The full set of optimizing tax rates are

$$t_c^* = -nu_B/\lambda c_b \qquad (10a)$$

$$t_r^* = nu_B c_r/\lambda c_b \qquad (10b)$$

$$t_g^* = n[u_B c_g - u_G c_b]/\lambda c_b \qquad (10c)$$

$$t_v^* = -nu_V/\lambda. \qquad (10d)$$

If illicit burning or dumping has no external effect ($u_B = 0$), then this solution reduces to the previous solution, with $t_c = t_r = 0$ and $t_g = -nu_G/\lambda$. With $u_B < 0$, however, consumption must be taxed at $t_c^* > 0$ to attain the first-best conditions, even if leisure is still untaxed. This tax is returned on goods that are properly collected as garbage or recycling. The net effect is a tax on illicit burning, circumventing the problem that b could not be taxed directly.

Garbage receives the rebate of t_c^*, but it also receives a tax that depends on its own externality. In Section 2, above, the tax was positive. Here, the net tax t_g^* is likely to be negative. In the "mass-balance" case where $c_g = c_b = 1$, garbage receives a net subsidy because u_B is more negative than u_G. In general, the tax depends on the relative ease of burning versus garbage collection (c_b versus c_g). It may also depend on the consumer's willingness to break the law. If the optimal price $p_g + t_g^*$ is *near* zero, then the city or county can save administrative and billing costs by providing free garbage collection.

Finally, the tax on virgin materials is not part of any deposit–refund system. It is not used to encourage recycled input or to discourage the generation of garbage. Instead, the tax on virgin materials should only correct negative externalities from the use of virgin materials.

4. THE UPSTREAM VS DOWNSTREAM DEBATE

This model can be used to reconcile various policy recommendations, that is, to show the conditions under which different policies can each attain the first-best allocation of resources.

---

[11] The consumer maximizes utility (2′) subject to the new budget constraint by choosing g, r, h, and b, which yields four first-order conditions in prices. We replace those prices with marginal products as before, to get (9a) through (9d). The fifth condition (9e) results directly from producer behavior; the producer of v chooses input k_v to maximize profits $p_v(\alpha k_v) - p_k k_v$, which yields $p_v = p_k/\alpha = f_{kc}/\alpha$. Then the producer of c chooses inputs k_c, r, and v to maximize profits $f(k_c, r, v) + p_r r - p_k k_c - (p_v + t_v)v$, which yields $f_v = p_v + t_v$. Thus $p_v = f_v - t_v = f_{kc}/\alpha$, to get (9e).

TABLE I
Comparison of Various Tax Schemes to Achieve the First-Best

Case 1: illicit burning or dumping cannot be taxed	Case 2: all forms of household disposal can be taxed	Case 3: no recycling subsidy (requires tax on other inputs)	Case 4: disaggregate goods (illicit dumping cannot be taxed)
$t_c^* = -nu_B/\lambda c_b$	$t_c^* = 0$	$t_c^* = nu_B c_r/\lambda c_b f_r - nu_B/\lambda c_b$	$t_{ci}^* = -nu_{Bi}/\lambda c_{bi}$
$t_r^* = nu_B c_r/\lambda c_b$	$t_r^* = 0$	$t_r^* = 0$	$t_{ri}^* = nu_{Bi} c_{ri}/\lambda c_{bi}$
$t_g^* = n(u_B c_g - u_G c_b)/\lambda c_b$	$t_g^* = -nu_G/\lambda$	$t_g^* = n(u_B c_g - u_G c_b)/\lambda c_b$	$t_{gi}^* = n(u_{Bi} c_{gi} - u_{Gi} c_{bi})/\lambda c_{bi}$
$t_v^* = -nu_V/\lambda$	$t_v^* = -nu_V/\lambda$	$t_v^* = -nu_B c_r f_{kc}/\lambda c_b f_r \alpha - nu_V/\delta$	$t_v^* = -nu_V/\lambda$
	$t_b^* = -nu_B/\lambda$	$t_{kc}^* = -nu_B c_r f_{kc}/\lambda c_b f_r$	

Note. t_c^*, t_r^*, t_g^*, and t_v^* are, respectively, tax rates on consumption, recycling, garbage, and virgin materials. t_b^* is a tax on illicit burning or dumping (only in Case 2). t_{kc}^* is a tax on resources (labor or capital) used in production of the consumption good (only in Case 3). u_G, u_B, and u_V are the (negative) externalities from garbage collection, illicit burning, and virgin material extraction. c_g, c_r, and c_b are the (positive) derivatives of $c = c(g, r, b)$, the extra consumption enabled by more g, r, or b. λ is the private marginal utility of income, and δ is the social marginal utility of income. n is the number of individuals, and i is the index for disaggregate goods and services.

The first column of Table 1 repeats the deposit–refund system just described, and the second column shows an equivalent downstream tax on wastes. In this case we constrain t_c to zero, but we allow a tax on illicit burning or dumping at rate t_b. Equations (7b) and (9b) then require $t_r = 0$, while (7d) and (9d) require the enforcement of $t_b = -nu_B/\lambda$. `

Clearly the downstream tax system in column 2 can solve the problem in theory. It is the most direct policy, since the tax on each activity reflects its own externality. All tax rates are positive, but $u_B < u_G$ implies $t_b > t_g$. However, t_b would require enforcement of a tax or penalty upon actions that are easy to hide, such as burning trash in a fireplace or leaving it along a deserted road. Fortunately, the upstream tax t_c (in column 1) is easier to implement. It requires no litter penalties, and it still achieves the same first-best outcome in this model. We therefore return to the case where $t_b = 0$.

In addition, the CBO [19] echos others (e.g., [9, 14, 16]) in suggesting that a tax on virgin materials "could bring about an increase in the recycled content of some products and an overall decrease in the amount of waste disposal" [19, p. 41]. However, our equations (7e) and (9e) above show that $t_v = -nu_V/\lambda$ (as shown in columns 1 and 2 of the table). This simple Pigouvian tax only corrects for negative externalities from the extraction of virgin materials (e.g., strip mining). Some may believe that $u_V = 0$, in which case $t_v = 0$. The point is that t_v is *not* used to correct any problem related to garbage or recycling.

A reason for this nonresult is that recycling can be subsidized directly. In addition, production uses three inputs. A tax on v would encourage not only the use of r, but also the use of k_c. If recycling *cannot* be subsidized for some reason, and if k_c can be taxed at rate t_{kc}, then we can again appeal to multiple solutions. Since only relative prices matter, column 3 shows how the same first-best can be achieved using both an extra tax on virgin materials *and* a tax on k_c. In fact, the table shows that t_v and t_{kc} contain the same unambiguously positive term.[12] This term appears with the opposite sign in t_c. In other words, a subsidy for recycling in $f(k_c, r, v)$ is equivalent to a tax on v and k_c, which is then returned on output. The tax on g is unaffected.[13]

Although we show the equivalence of this result to the deposit–refund system, it is much more complicated. The tail wags the dog, since illicit dumping is corrected by multiple taxes on all inputs other than recycling, combined with a subsidy on all output.

5. DISAGGREGATE GOODS AND SERVICES

We can further modify the model to include different consumption goods c_i, where i is an index. These goods may have different technologies $c_i(g_i, r_i, b_i)$ and production functions $f_i(k_{ci}, r_i, v_i)$. Subscripts also are required for

---

[12] Slight differences appear in these terms. The tax on k_c uses $f_{kc} = \partial c/\partial k_c$ to convert to changes in c, whereas the tax on v uses $f_{kc}/\alpha = \partial c/\partial v$ to convert to changes in c.

[13] The derivation of Case 3 is a bit more difficult than the earlier cases, since λ is no longer equal to δ. We assume that p_k is the net return to individuals, so producers of c pay $p_k + t_{kc}$. Still the approach is to solve all equations (7) and (9) for t_c, t_g, t_v, and t_{kc}. Also, t_c can be manipulated to show a term $(c_r - f_r)$ which is unambiguously positive, from (7b), so t_c must be negative; the rebate of t_{kc} and t_v is within t_c, and this term exceeds the previous tax paid on c.

$u_G, u_B, \delta, t_c, t_g, t_r$, and the price of output (p). The results look exactly the same, except for the subscripts. In other words, the waste-end tax rates in column 2 must be modified to collect a specific tax rate on each good $t_{bi} = -nu_{Bi}/\lambda$, which reflects the social cost of burning or dumping that particular item. Alternatively, the deposit–refund system would collect $t_{ci} = -nu_{Bi}/\lambda c_{bi}$ on each purchase and rebate the corresponding amount upon proper disposal of that item (column 4 of Table I).

Differences arise because some goods are more toxic, more unsightly, or more easily burned. To get the details exactly right, the first-best policy would have to place a different tax rate on each item. With millions of goods and services, either of these first-best systems would be a nightmare to administer. Perhaps only some items could be targeted, or all items could be placed in just a few categories. Note, however, that this diversity among commodities is no reason to prefer waste-end taxes to the deposit–refund system: for any given commodity or category, the difficulty of enforcing a tax on illegal midnight dumping can still be avoided by taxing legal daytime purchases and subsidizing legal daytime disposal.

Consider three categories, for example. The purchase of "services" might be left untaxed, since this purchase requires no subsequent disposal.[14] A second category could receive a moderate rate, and a third, "hazardous" category would receive a higher rate. If goods with different-sized externalities were thrown into the same tax category, perhaps for reasons of administrative simplicity, then consumers would be encouraged to buy relatively too much of the goods that entailed relatively more costly disposal. Even if all goods were thrown in the same category, however, at least consumers would have some incentive to dispose of those goods properly. Results here can be taken simply to help explain existing policies that tax purchases and subsidize proper garbage collection.

6. LIMITATIONS, EXTENSIONS, AND DISCUSSION

Using broad brush strokes, this paper characterizes the optimal taxation of garbage, recycling, and general consumption. These broad strokes may miss some important details, however. One extension might consider how these optimizing fees are related to population density. We hypothesize that garbage fees would work best in suburban areas or small towns where the charges can be enforced. In densely populated urban areas, any price for garbage collection may be greeted by huge piles of unidentified garbage on the streets or vacant lots. In very rural areas, similarly, dumps may appear on back roads. Thus, these results may help explain differences in actual municipal pricing mechanisms.[15]

Another problem arises with different levels of government. States traditionally set sales tax rates, but municipal governments subsidize garbage collection. Perhaps some revenue should be transferred from one to the other. Goods may be purchased in one state, however, and then traded or carried across state lines before disposal. Various spillover effects might justify a national-level tax and

---

[14] On the other hand, the production of services such as legal and medical services generates plenty of paper and medical wastes. The model could be expanded to consider waste by-products from production.

[15] The U.S. EPA [10] lists sixteen towns that have unit fees for garbage collection, and we have extended that list for empirical work. All are small or moderate in size, with the exception of Seattle.

rebate system, but spillovers may still cross national boundaries. This issue deserves further scrutiny (as in Copeland [3]). Also, consideration of distributional issues might affect the optimal tax and refund system.

Finally, our model ignores some compliance costs and market imperfections. With regard to recycling, Nestor [12] points out that subsidies to households may generate supplies of recycled goods when the industrial capacity to make use of them does not exist. With regard to a per-unit garbage fee, the town would have to sell special bags or stickers. This administrative cost might further justify the subsidy inherent in free garbage collection.

None of these considerations alter our four main points, however. First, existing studies find that a negative externality from garbage can be corrected by a tax on garbage. When we add illicit dumping as a third disposal option, and assume that it cannot be taxed directly, then the tax on garbage may turn negative. Garbage collection may optimally subsidized to help prevent the worse environmental costs of improper disposal. Second, to restore all the correct relative prices, output would be taxed. The result is a deposit–refund system that is equivalent to the unenforceable waste-end tax. Third, existing literature suggests that a tax on virgin materials may help encourage recycling. In our basic model, a tax on virgin materials is not useful for that purpose. It only corrects directly for the ill effects of using virgin materials. Fourth, in existing public finance literature, a consumption tax distorts the choice between labor and leisure. This paper provides a first-best case for a consumption tax, however, even when leisure is untaxed. No tax on leisure is required, because leisure does not cause disposal problems.

APPENDIX: NOMENCLATURE

n	number of identical individuals in the single jurisdiction
c	a single composite commodity consumption good
$c(\ )$	consumption function (technology of consumption)
g	quantity of garbage collection
r	quantity of recycling
c_g	partial derivative of consumption with respect to garbage
c_r	partial derivative of consumption with respect to recycling
h	quantity of home production
G	total amount of garbage
$u(\ )$	utility function of the individual
u_c	marginal utility of consumption
u_h	marginal utility of home production
u_G	marginal utility of total garbage
$f(\ )$	production function
k_c	resources used in production of the consumption good
k_g	resources used in garbage collection
k_h	resources used in home production
γ	marginal product of resources in the collection of garbage
k	fixed total resources in the economy
$\mathscr{L}$	the Lagrange function
δ	social marginal utility of the resource (k)
f_{kc}	marginal product of the resource input (k_c)
f_r	marginal product of the recycled input
p_k	price earned on resources
t_c	tax per unit of consumption
p_g	price paid for garbage collection
t_g	tax per unit of garbage

p_r	price paid by the consumer for recycling
t_r	tax per unit of recycling
λ	private marginal utility of income
b	burning and other improper disposal
c_b	partial derivative of consumption with respect to burning
B	the total amount of burning in the economy
u_B	marginal utility of total burning
V	total amount of virgin material used in production
v	per capita virgin material used in production
u_V	marginal utility of total virgin material used in production
k_v	resources used in the extraction of virgin material
α	marginal product of resources in the extraction of virgin material
k_b	resources used in burning garbage
$\beta(\ )$	a function relating resources used in burning to the quantity of burning
β_b	the first derivative of $\beta(\ )$ with respect to burning
β_{bb}	the second derivative of $\beta(\ )$ with respect to burning
f_v	the marginal product of virgin material
p_v	price of virgin material
t_v	tax per unit of virgin material
t_b	tax per unit of burning
t_c^*	the optimal tax on consumption
t_r^*	the optimal tax on recycling
t_g^*	the optimal tax on garbage
t_v^*	the optimal tax on virgin material
t_{kc}	tax on the use of resources in the production of the consumption good
i	an index
c_i	consumption of good i
$c_i(\ )$	the consumption function for good i
g_i	garbage associated with good i
r_i	recycling associated with good i
b_i	burning associated with good i
$f_i(\ )$	the production function of good i
k_{ci}	the use of resources in the production of good i
r_i	the use of recyclables in the production of good i
v_i	the use of virgin materials in the production of good i
t_{bi}	tax on dumping for good i
u_{Bi}	the marginal utility from burning waste from good i
t_{ci}	tax on the consumption of good i
c_{bi}	the partial derivative of consumption with respect to burning

ACKNOWLEDGMENTS

This research began while both authors were at the University of Virginia. We are grateful for suggestions from Debbie Nestor, Ed Olsen, Jon Skinner, Margaret Walls, anonymous referees, and seminar participants at NBER, Carnegie Mellon, Georgia, Vanderbilt, and Virginia. We are also grateful for funding from NSF Grant SES91-22785, and from the Bankard Fund at the University of Virginia. This paper is part of NBER's research program in Public Economics. Any opinions expressed are those of the authors and not those of the National Science Foundation or the National Bureau of Economic Research.

REFERENCES

1. W. J. Baumol and W. E. Oates, "The Theory of Environmental Policy," 2nd ed., Cambridge Univ. Press, New York (1988).
2. P. Bohm, "Deposit–Refund Systems: Theory and Applications to Environmental, Conservation, and Consumer Policy," John Hopkins Univ. Press, Baltimore (1981).
3. B. R. Copeland, International trade in waste products in the presence of illegal disposal, *J. Environ. Econom. Management* **20**, March, 143–62 (1991).

4. T. M. Dinan, Economic efficiency effects of alternative policies for reducing waste disposal, *J. Environ. Econom. Management* **25**, 242–56 (1993).

5. I. M. Dobbs, Litter and waste management: Disposal taxes versus user charges, *Canad. J. Econom.* **24**, February, 221–7 (1991).

6. R. R. Jenkins, Municipal demand for solid waste disposal services: The impact of user fees, dissertation for the University of Maryland Department of Economics (1991).

7. D. R. Lee, The economics of enforcing pollution taxation, *J. Environ. Econom. Management* **11**, 147–60 (1984).

8. P. S. Menell, Beyond the throwaway society: An incentive approach to regulating municipal solid waste, *Ecology Law Quart.* **17**, 655–739 (1990).

9. A. K. Miedema, Fundamental economic comparisons of solid waste policy options, *Resour. Energy* **5**, 21–43 (1983).

10. G. E. Morris and D. M. Holthausen, The economics of household solid waste generation and disposal, *J. Environ. Econom. Management* **26**, 215–34 (1994).

11. P. A. Neher, "Natural Resources Economics: Conservation and Exploitation," Cambridge Univ. Press, New York (1990).

12. D. V. Nestor, Partial static equilibrium model of newsprint recycling, *Appl. Econom.* **24**, April, 411–7 (1992).

13. R. C. Porter, A social benefit–cost analysis of mandatory deposits on beverage containers, *J. Environ. Econom. Management* **5**, 351–75 (1978).

14. "Project 88—Round II, A Public Policy Study Sponsored by Senator T. E. Wirth and Senator J. Heinz, Directed by R. N. Stavins," Washington, DC (1991).

15. R. Repetto, R. C. Dower, R. Jenkins, and J. Geoghegan, "Green Fees: How a Tax Shift Can Work for the Environment and the Economy," World Resources Institute, Washington, DC (1992).

16. H. Sigman, A comparison of public policies for lead recycling, mimeo, UCLA Department of Economics (1991).

17. V. L. Smith, Dynamics of waste accumulation: Disposal versus recycling, *Quart. J. Econom.* **86**, November, 600–16 (1972).

18. A. M. Sullivan, Policy options for toxic disposal: Laissez-faire, subsidization, and enforcement, *J. Environ. Econom. Management* **14**, 58–71 (1987).

19. U.S. Congress, Congressional Budget Office, "Federal Options for Reducing Waste Disposal," U.S. Government Printing Office, Washington, DC (1991).

20. U.S. Environmental Protection Agency, "Charging Households for Waste Collection and Disposals: The Effects of Weight or Volume-Based Pricing on Solid Waste Management," EPA 530-SW-90-047, Washington, DC (1990).

21. K. L. Wertz, Economic factors influencing households' production of refuse, *J. Environ. Econom. Management* **2**, 263–72 (1976).

[3]

HOW A FEE PER-UNIT GARBAGE AFFECTS AGGREGATE RECYCLING IN A MODEL WITH HETEROGENEOUS HOUSEHOLDS

Thomas C. Kinnaman (Bucknell University)

and

Don Fullerton (University of Texas)*

INTRODUCTION

Nearly 2000 communities in the US have implemented user fees to finance garbage collection over the last five years. These user fees require households to pay for each bag of garbage presented at the curb for collection (Skumatz 1993). The revenue raised from these user fees has supplanted the use of general tax revenue to finance garbage collection and disposal costs. Benefits to the community include the social value of less garbage and more recycling. The costs include the social cost of additional litter and the value of resources used to administer the program. The magnitudes of both the benefits and costs depend on the waste removal choices of individual households within the community.

This chapter develops a model of household choice among waste removal options for various types of waste material. Each household in the model compares the cost of traditional curbside garbage collection, the cost of recycling, and the cost of littering for each type of waste material. We assume the marginal cost of traditional garbage collection is the same for all materials, and is zero in the absence of a user fee. The marginal cost of recycling is assumed to differ across materials. Households pay a positive price to recycle some materials,

* We are grateful for helpful suggestions from Lans Bovenberg, Hilary Sigman, and other Congress participants. We are also grateful for financial support from the National Science Foundation Grant SBR-9413334. This paper is part of NBER's research program in Public Economics. Any opinions expressed are those of the authors and do not necessarily represent those of the National Science Foundation or the National Bureau of Economic Research.

135

several others can be recycled for free if the community offers curbside collection, while still others can be recycled at a negative price if the material has market value. Finally, we assume the marginal cost of littering is zero; however, a fixed cost must be paid if the household chooses to engage in any littering.

A user fee for garbage collection is shown to affect the choice of each household over whether to discard, recycle, or litter each type of material. The user fee's effect on the disposal choices of the household is shown to depend on the household's degree of environmental awareness, on income, and on the availability of curbside recycling. In particular, our model explains (1) why some households participate in a curbside recycling program even in the absence of a user fee, (2) why other households still do not participate in recycling programs even in the presence of a user fee for garbage collection, and (3) why some households choose to litter when others do not.

The effect of a user fee on the disposal decisions of each household determines the communities aggregate changes of garbage, recycling, and litter quantities that would result from the implementation of a user-fee program. These aggregate changes comprise important costs and benefits to a community attributable to the implementation of a user-fee program. The model suggests that aggregate garbage will decrease with the value of the user fee. Aggregate litter increases with the user fee, but, perhaps surprisingly, aggregate recycling may decrease. The magnitude of each of these changes can vary across communities.

The consequence for empirical work, especially the use of a cross-section of communities with different user fees to estimate the demand for garbage collection, is that each local government's choice of user fee is not exogenous. The choice may, in fact, depend on the behavioral responses of households within the community. For example, a local government may be more apt to implement a user fee if the changes in garbage and recycling are expected to be large and the change in illegal dumping is expected to be small. Most empirical studies estimating the effect of a user fee on aggregate garbage quantities have treated the value of the user fee as exogenous.[1]

The next section of this chapter will introduce the model of household choice for methods of waste removal without the option to litter. The model is then expanded to include the littering option. A brief conclusion follows.

---

[1]   For example Repetto et al. (1992) and Jenkins (1991).

A MODEL OF HOUSEHOLD DISPOSAL CHOICE

Most models of household solid waste ignore the littering option.[2] In an important study for the World Resources Institute, Repetto et al (1992) claim that any potential increases in dumping can be alleviated by simple measures.[3] To characterize these existing studies, our initial model in this section ignores litter. Our analysis will suggest that a model without the littering option is inadequate to explain how local governments set user fees.

Individual Behavior

Assume that a community is comprised of several households. Each household may engage in consumption of different goods, each comprised of a single type of material, indexed by $j = 1,...,J$. Let c_j denote the consumption of good j by the household. Consumption generates waste material that must be disposed of. The quantity of waste material j (m_j) is assumed to be proportional to the consumption of good j:

(1) $$m_j = a_j c_j.$$

All waste material must be either collected as garbage (with amount g_j) or recycled (with amount r_j). We add litter to the model in the next section. Since all matter must be removed from the household in one form or another, we have:[4]

(2) $$m_j = g_j + r_j.$$

The household's total garbage and recycling quantities are $g = \Sigma_j g_j$ and $r = \Sigma_j r_j$, respectively.

---

[2]   For example, Jenkins (1991), Copeland (1991), Sigman (1991), Dinan (1993), Morris and Holthausen (1994), Wertz (1976).

[3]   They suggest locking dumpsters, vigorously publicizing and enforcing disposal rules in the initial months of the program, reporting households that put out no garbage, and requiring a one-bag minimum.

[4]   Households could conceivably compost garbage or reduce the quantity of their garbage by demanding less packaging at stores. Since these amounts are relatively small, however, we concentrate here on the major components of the waste stream: garbage and recycling. Later we introduce burning or dumping b_j.

Assume that the household's utility function is defined over its J consumption goods, and the total amount of garbage it contributes to the waste stream (g):

(3) $u = u(c_1, c_2, ..., c_J, g)$

Using a subscript to denote a first derivative, we assume that households receive positive marginal utility from consumption ($u_{c_j} > 0$), but they dislike their own contribution of garbage to the waste stream ($u_g < 0$). Households may differ with respect to their distaste for contributing garbage: a household with a large value of u_g (in absolute value) dislikes contributing garbage more than a household with a low value.

Each household is endowed with k units of time (or other resources) that can be supplied to a labor market to earn a wage p^k (which can also vary across households), or can be used to separate and store recyclable material. Let k^c denote the amount of household time supplied to the labor market, and let k^r denote the time devoted by the household to the separation of recyclable materials. Therefore, we have:

(4) $k = k^c + k^r$.

The amount of time devoted to separating and storing recyclable materials is assumed to be proportional to the amount of recycling conducted by the household:

(5) $k^r = \sigma r$.

We assume that σ is the same for all households and all materials (but the value of that time varies with the wage rate, p^k).[5]

With no city program to collect recyclable material, a household that wants to recycle must pay a recycling firm directly for the transfer of the material. Denote this payment by the household as p^r_j per unit of material of type j that is recycled. We assume that p^r_j is particular to the type of material being recycled and can take on a positive or negative value. For example, the cost to the household of paying a firm to recycle toxic waste could be very high, while the household may be able to *sell* precious metals to a recycling firm (p^r_j could be

---

[5]   We might expect the effort expended to separate and store recyclable material would differ over households and material types, but making this more realistic assumption only serves to cloud the model and adds little to the main conclusions.

negative). For used items sold on the second-hand market, we interpret p^r_j to include advertising costs.

Some materials may be collected from the curb as part of a curbside recycling program. The market price paid by households to recycle these materials is zero. A curbside recycling program represents an implicit subsidy to the household of s^r_j per unit of recycled material, which offsets p^r_j such that the overall cost $p^r_j - s^r_j = 0$. The value of s^r_j is zero for all materials not collected at the curb. The value of s^r_j will be negative for all collected materials that have positive market value. Therefore, s^r_j is a tax on households if the government mandates that households produce these materials at the curb.[6] Aluminum could be an example. A household that is not required to recycle a given material compares the cost of free curbside recycling pickup with the cost of sending used materials directly to secondary markets (bypassing curbside pickup). Thus our model is general enough to encompass second-hand sales.

The local government could also levy a user fee t^g per unit of garbage that is the same for every type of material. This fee is the household's only out-of-pocket marginal cost of curbside garbage disposal. The household may pay property taxes or a monthly fee, but, in the absence of a user fee for garbage collection, the price paid at the margin per bag of garbage is zero.

Household income ($p^k k - p^k k^r$) can be used to purchase consumption goods at market prices p^c_j, to recycle material j at unit cost p^r_j, and to pay any user fee that might be levied on garbage. Therefore, the budget constraint facing the household is:

(6) $$\Sigma_j p^c_j c_j + t^g g + \Sigma_j (p^r_j - s^r_j) r_j = p^k k - p^k (\sigma r)$$

where $s^r_j = p^r_j$ if the recyclable material j is collected for free, and s^r_j is zero for all other materials not collected for recycling.

Each household chooses consumption, and how to dispose of the resulting material, by maximizing utility (3) subject to (1), (2), and the budget constraint (6). The relevant first-order conditions from this maximization are:

(7a) $$dL/dg_j: \quad u_{c_j} \leq \lambda[p^c_j + a_j t^g] - a_j u_g \qquad \text{for all } j$$

(7b) $$dL/dr_j: \quad u_{c_j} \leq \lambda[p^c_j + a_j(p^r_j - s^r_j) + a_j \sigma p^k] \qquad \text{for all } j$$

---

[6] The model does not include such a law, so households are not expected to recycle valuable materials at the curb.

139

where λ is the marginal utility of income to household i. Define λ^* and u_g^* to be the values of λ and u_g at the solution to (7). The household's choice between waste removal options for each material is governed by:

(8a)	$m_j = g_j$	iff	$t^g - u_g^*/\lambda^* < (p_j^r - s_j^r) + \sigma p^k$
(8b)	$m_j = r_j$	iff	$t^g - u_g^*/\lambda^* > (p_j^r - s_j^r) + \sigma p^k$

The household compares the marginal cost of recycling material j ($p_j^r - s_j^r + \sigma p^k$) to the overall marginal "cost" of contributing garbage of material j -- which is the money payment (t_g) plus the value of marginal utility lost from contributing a unit of garbage ($-u_g^*/\lambda^*$). These conditions could imply a set of corner solutions. If the marginal cost of recycling a newspaper is less than the overall marginal cost of discarding it, then a household would be expected to recycle *all* of its newspaper, not just some portion of it.[7]

The household could choose an interior solution for a material j in which it discards some portion (g_j) and recycles some portion (r_j) of the material, if $t_g - u_g^*/\lambda^* = (p_j^r - s_j^r) + \sigma p^k$. This equality will hold only for very few materials at the knife's edge, where the cost of garbage collection exactly matches the marginal cost of recycling. However, the household will never choose interior solutions for two materials with different marginal costs. To see this, first remember that garbage and recycling are perfect substitutes in disposal ($m_j = g_j + r_j$) and that different materials provide equal disutility if discarded ($g = \Sigma_j g_j$). Now suppose the household *were* using both garbage and recycling for two kinds of waste materials with different marginal costs of recycling. This situation cannot be an optimal solution because the household could switch one unit of the higher-recycling-cost waste from recycling to garbage, and switch one unit of the lower-recycling-cost waste from garbage to recycling, while consuming the same amount of each material, generating the same total garbage and recycling, and saving the difference in marginal cost. Such switches would continue until the household is discarding all materials that meet condition (8a) and recycling all that meet (8b).[8]

---

[7]   This strong theoretical result is supported by casual observation. Households who recycle often devote space for virtually all quantities of certain materials, e.g. one bin for newspaper and another for aluminum cans.

[8]   The same maximization provides first-order conditions for consumption, not shown, in which the "effective" price of consuming good j depends on its purchase price, the relative waste generated ($m_j = a_j c_j$), and the cost of the chosen disposal method for that good. We thus capture the possibility that a garbage fee can discourage consumption of waste-intensive commodities.

With a few simplifying assumptions, we can use Figure 1 to illustrate the disposal choices of the household. First, assume that the income effect of an increase in the user fee is zero. In other words, the reduction of income attributable to an increase in the user fee does not change total consumption. Second, we assume that all types of materials can be ranked along the horizontal axis in a descending order according to the cost of recycling (p^r_j). For example, toxic waste would be ranked first and precious metals last. Third, we assume the household must dispose of one unit of each type of waste material on the spectrum. Given these assumptions, the overall schedule of recycling costs can be represented by P^r in Figure 1. Material types are ranked from highest cost to lowest cost from left to right. Discrete materials $(j = 1,...,J)$ would generate a step function, but we show a continuous P^r schedule for ease of exposition. This schedule does not have to be linear or even differentiable, it only has to be non-increasing.

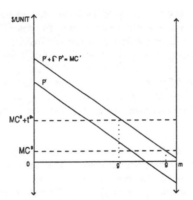

Figure 1 Household disposal choice

The first-order conditions indicate the marginal cost to the household of recycling is equal not only to the market transfer price (P^r), but to the value of resources devoted to separating and storing the material (σp^k) as well. The addition of this cost introduces another curve in Figure 1 higher than P^r but parallel, labeled MC^r. The MC^r curve indicates the overall marginal cost to the household of recycling each material type across the spectrum. The overall marginal cost of placing garbage at the curb in the absence of a user fee is the value of the marginal utility lost by household, $-u_g^*/\lambda^*$, which we assume is constant across materials. This cost is represented by the horizontal line labeled MC^g in Figure 1. The height of MC^g is unique to each household because each household has a different value of u_g^*/λ^*. These marginal cost schedules allow us to illustrate the amounts of garbage and recycling chosen by the household.

According to (8a) and (8b), the household can be expected to remove material j using the lowest cost alternative. This choice is illustrated by finding the lower envelope of marginal waste removal costs across all materials. In the absence of a user fee for garbage collection, the quantity of garbage is determined in Figure 1 by the horizontal distance between the origin and point g (where the cost to discard garbage is less than the cost to recycle). The quantity of recycling is indicated by the horizontal distance between point m and point g. The household transfers these materials directly to secondary markets in the absence of a curbside recycling program. Notice that all materials along the spectrum are either recycled or discarded as garbage. The amounts of garbage and recycling by each household will depend on where that household's unique MC^g curve intersects the MC^r curve. Households with a high opportunity cost of recycling (p^k) and those having a low disutility of throwing out garbage ($-u_g^*/\lambda^*$) will recycle less and throw out more in the garbage.

Figure 1 can also be used to indicate the amount of garbage and recycling produced by a household when a user fee for garbage collection is implemented. A user fee of $t^{g'}$ per bag increases the overall marginal cost to the household of contributing garbage to $MC^g + t^{g'}$. The user fee causes the amount of garbage presented by the household to decrease from g to g' and the amount of recycling to increase from (m-g) to (m-g'). The magnitudes of these changes depend on the slope of the MC^r curve through point g. The flatter MC^r is, the cheaper it is to recycle additional materials, and the greater the change in recycling.

The implementation of a curbside recycling program also affects the waste disposal choices of households. Assume that the local government has agreed to collect, transport, and recycle certain materials at no cost to the household (an implicit subsidy or tax of $s_j^r = p_j^r$). Therefore, the marginal cost of recycling materials that are collected from the curb is only the value of extra time (σp^k) devoted to separating and storing the material. In the absence of a user fee for garbage collection ($t^g = 0$), (8a) and (8b) suggest only households that have a strong dislike for contributing garbage ($-u_g^*/\lambda^* > \sigma p^k$) will participate in the curbside recycling program. All other households will not participate. Of course, all households might still recycle the more valuable materials directly to secondary markets if they receive a price such that the net cost MC^r is less than the cost of any alternative (either MC^g for garbage, or 0 for curbside recycling).

Figure 2 illustrates the disposal choices of households when a curbside recycling program has been implemented in the community. Again, let MC^r represent the schedule of marginal recycling costs and let MC^g represent the value of disutility from contributing garbage. Assume that all materials ranked to the right of point a are collected by the government at no cost to the household.[9] Households must still devote time to separate and store these materials (σp^k). Since this cost is assumed to be constant across all materials, the MC^r curve is flat over the range of materials that are collected for recycling by the government.

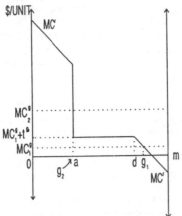

Figure 2 A curbside recycling program

The garbage cost function of two households in the same community, but with different preferences about contributing garbage, are labeled MC^g_1 and MC^g_2 in Figure 2. The household with MC^g_2 has strong distaste for contributing garbage ($MC^g_2 > \sigma p^k$) and will participate in the curbside recycling program in the absence of a user fee for garbage collection. The marginal cost of recycling the materials ranked between a and d is less than the overall marginal cost of throwing the material away. To see this, look again for the lower envelope of marginal costs in Figure 2. Household 2 discards all materials ranked to the left of g_2 (point a), recycles all materials ranked between g_2 and d at the curb, and sells all materials ranked to the right of d in secondary markets (where $p^r_j < 0$ so they get paid for those materials).

The household facing MC^g_1 has little distaste for contributing garbage ($MC^g_1 < \sigma p^k$) and will not recycle at the curb. This household discards all materials ranked to the left of g_1 (where MC^g_1 is less than MC_r) and sells material

---

9   The government is not willing to collect materials ranked to the left of point a, perhaps because it costs too much to recycle these materials. We assume that the government's decision over which materials to collect is exogenous to the model.

ranked to the right of g_1 directly to secondary markets. In order to encourage these households to recycle at the curb, the government must implement a user fee.

If $t^{g'} > \sigma p^k - MC^g_1$ is levied on each bag of garbage collected, the household with MC^g_2 will not change its disposal behavior. It will still recycle materials ranked between points a and d at the curb. However, the household represented by MC^g_1 is given the incentive to participate in the curbside recycling program. It discards all materials ranked to the left of point a, presents material ranked between a and d at the curb for recycling (since $MC^r_1 < MC^g_1 + t^{g'}$ for those materials), and sells all material ranked to the right of d in secondary markets. As indicated by equation (8b), t^g must be greater than $\sigma p^k - MC^g_1$ to induce these households to choose to recycle these materials ranked between a and d at the curb. Larger values of the user fee would be needed to encourage households with a lower distaste for contributing garbage to recycle at the curb.[10]

Aggregate Behavior

One point of the theory is to explain how a user fee for garbage collection affects the aggregate amounts of garbage and recycling produced by a community. These aggregate amounts are obtained by summing across the garbage and recycling quantities produced by each household in the community, for any possible value of a user fee. These aggregate quantities generated by two different communities for various values of a user fee are illustrated in Figure 3.

Assume, for comparison, that both communities have the same amount of aggregate material to discard and neither has implemented a curbside recycling program. The total amount of recycling in community 1 is measured by the horizontal distance between point M (the right vertical axis) and the curve labeled D^R_1. Aggregate garbage is the rest of M, and is measured by the horizontal distance between the left vertical axis and D^R_1. In the absence of a user fee for garbage collection, households in community 1 discard G_1 in a landfill and recycle $M-G_1$. A user fee of $t^{g'}$ will encourage this community to reduce its garbage to G_1' and increase its recycling to $(M-G_1')$. These changes arise because

---

[10]   A mandatory recycling law provides incentives similar to those of a user fee. For those materials that households are required to recycle, the expected cost of discarding increases as the expected fine for noncompliance increases or as the probability of getting caught increases. Households with very low values of MC^g would require a high penalty or greater enforcement to convince them to recycle.

households in the community choose to recycle more materials once a user fee is implemented (as in Figure 1).

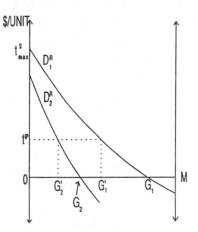

Figure 3 Aggregate behaviour

The D^R_2 function determines the aggregate quantity of garbage and recycling produced by community 2. This community recycles a greater quantity of material than the first community for all possible values of a user fee. For example, if a user fee with value $t^{g'}$ is levied, community 2 discards only G_2' and recycles $(M-G_2')$. Community 2 could be comprised of more households that have strong distaste for contributing garbage or have a low opportunity cost of time.

Empirical observation indicates that some local governments have chosen to implement user fees for garbage collection while most others have not. We assume that a local government will implement a user fee if the benefits of doing so outweigh the costs. Important benefits could be the reduction in garbage and increase in recycling that result from the user fee. Since households in this model engage in no dumping, the only cost is the value of resources used to administer the user-fee program.

As drawn in Figure 3, the change in garbage and recycling quantities resulting from the implementation of a user fee is greater for community one than for community two. The town of those with a strong distaste for contributing garbage (community two) does *not* necessarily experience a large *increase* in aggregate recycling due to a user fee. Households in community two already recycle in large quantities before the implementation of a user fee, leaving little

145

room for additional recycling. Therefore the benefits of implementing a user fee may be greater for community one than for community two. *Ceteris paribus*, we expect communities with flatter D^R schedules (like D^R_1) to be more likely to implement a user fee, since the benefits are greater.

Why is community one more conducive to the implementation of a user fee for garbage collection than is community two? Our model suggests that community one must be comprised of many households that increase their recycling amounts following the implementation of a user fee. These large increases would result if the MC^r schedule in Figure 1 is relatively flat near the horizontal axis, and if many households in the community do not participate in the curbside recycling program before the user fee. A flat MC^r schedule indicates that more materials can be recycled at a low additional cost to the household. In the presence of a curbside recycling program, for example, the marginal cost of recycling is *flat* across those materials collected at the curb. This serves to flatten the aggregate recycling schedule. Therefore, communities with curbside recycling may be more likely to implement a user fee.[11]

Suppose the value of the user fee does not affect administrative costs such as advertising the program, printing the stickers, and enforcing the law. Since the benefits of implementing the user-fee program increase with the value of the user fee, and the costs do not, this simple model without a litter option suggests that governments would be likely to levy a very high user fee.[12] For example, the government in community one could levy a user fee with a value of t^g_{max} and then collect no garbage. All materials would be recycled. The model suggests that all governments would either (1) not implement a user fee, if the administrative costs are greater than the benefit of having no garbage, or (2) charge at least t^g_{max} for each bag of garbage, if the benefits of no garbage exceed the administrative cost of the user-fee program.

Casual observations in the US reject this theoretical implication. Only 2000 communities across the US have implemented user fees for garbage collection. Most of these fees are moderate, like $0.80 per bag. One explanation for the failure of this model to explain government behavior could be that governments *are* concerned with the amount of illegal dumping that would arise following the implementation of a user fee. A more appropriate model would

---

[11]   Of a sample of 200 communities with user fees (sample collected by the authors), all have curbside recycling programs.

[12]   A user fee may change the relative price of a consumption good that is more waste intensive than others. Therefore, another cost or benefit of implementing a user fee is this effect on consumption.

146

include illegal dumping as a third removal option for households. We now proceed to develop such a model.

THE MODEL WITH A LITTERING OPTION

Several recent models of household solid waste behavior have considered the littering option. Kennedy and Laplante (1994) solve for the optimal user fee given the option to litter, but do not consider materials with different recycling costs. Fullerton and Kinnaman (forthcoming) argue that the possibility of illegal dumping implies that the optimal user fee for garbage collection could be zero. Sullivan (1987) and Dobbs (1991) also allow for litter in their models. We improve on these models by allowing heterogeneous households to choose among three removal methods for diverse types of goods.

Individual Behavior

Assume that households have the option to burn, dump, or litter garbage:

$$(9) \qquad m_j = g_j + r_j + b_j$$

where b_j is the amount of burning of material j done by the household. Also, assume that all households dislike the act of burning or littering garbage:

$$(10) \qquad u = u(c_1,...,c_J, g, b)$$

where $b = \Sigma_j b_j$, $u_b < 0$, and all other variables are defined as above.

No market or price exists for the littering or burning of garbage, but we assume that the household must pay a fixed cost f if it engages in such practice. This fixed cost could include, for example, the cost of finding a suitable dump site, the fixed portion of the cost of traveling to the dumpsite, the psychic cost of breaking a local ordinance, and the risk of a fine. In other words, dumping two bags is not twice as costly as dumping one bag, in terms of transport cost, the risk of getting caught, and feeling bad about this antisocial behavior. Later we address the possibility that fixed costs arise in recycling.

The new budget constraint facing the household is:

$$(11a) \qquad \Sigma p^c_j c_j + t^g g + \Sigma_j (p^r_j - s^r_j) r_j = p^k (k - \sigma r) \qquad \text{if } b = 0$$
$$(11b) \qquad \Sigma p^c_j c_j + t^g g + \Sigma_j (p^r_j - s^r_j) r_j + f = p^k (k - \sigma r) \qquad \text{if } b > 0.$$

147

The household maximizes utility (10) subject to (1), (9), and the budget constraint (11) by choosing the amounts of consumption, garbage, recycling, and litter. First-order conditions for disposal are:

(12a) $\qquad dL/dg_j:\ u_{cj} + a_j u_g \le \lambda[p^c_j + a_j t^g]$ $\qquad$ for all j

(12b) $\qquad dL/dr_j:\ u_{cj} \le \lambda[p^c_j + a_j(p^r_j - s^r_j) + a_j \sigma p^k]$ $\qquad$ for all j

(12c) $\qquad dL/db_j:\ u_{cj} + a_j u_b \le \lambda[p^c_j]$ $\qquad$ for all j

where λ is still the marginal utility of income to the household. Again, these results imply a set of corner solutions if the values of the right-hand sides of (13) are not equal to each other. If the household engages in no littering (b=0), then household behavior is described by (8a) and (8b). With some illegal dumping (b>0), choice on the margin over methods of removing the waste material of type j is determined by:

(13a) $\qquad m_j = g_j$ iff $\qquad t^g - u_g^*/\lambda^* < MIN[(p^r_j - s^r_j) + \sigma p^k, -u_b^*/\lambda^*]$

(13b) $\qquad m_j = r_j$ iff $\qquad p^r_j - s^r_j + \sigma p^k < MIN[t^g - u_g^*/\lambda^*, -u_b^*/\lambda^*]$

(13c) $\qquad m_j = b_j$ iff $\qquad -u_b^*/\lambda^* < MIN[t^g - u_g^*/\lambda^*, p^r_j - s^r_j + \sigma p^k]$

where λ^* and u_g^* are the values of λ and u_g evaluated at the maximum.

The household will again choose to remove material j using the lowest cost alternative (where the "cost" of contributing garbage includes effects on utility and the user fee). For most materials, households are again predicted to use only one method of removal.

With no curbside recycling program

Under what conditions will a household pay the fixed cost associated with littering garbage? In the absence of a curbside recycling program, the answer depends on the value of the user fee and the schedule of recycling costs. With a few simplifying assumptions, we can use Figure 4a to illustrate the conditions that create the incentive for a household to pay the fixed costs (f) and litter garbage. First, assume that the value of disutility associated with contributing garbage is equal to the value of disutility of burning or dumping garbage illegally ($u_g = u_b$). This assumption simplifies the graphical exposition while changing few of the conclusions of the model (see footnote 13 for an exception). Second, assume that the income effect of an increase in the user fee is zero. In other words, the reduction of income attributable to an increase in the user fee does not change total consumption. Furthermore, assume that we can once again order materials according to the marginal cost of recycling (MC^r), which includes the cost of household time spent separating and storing material and the market price for the transfer of the material. The marginal cost of functions associated with recycling (MC^r), and with contributing or illegally dumping garbage ($MC^g = MC^b$)

are illustrated in Figure 4a. The fixed costs associated with dumping introduces an average cost curve, which is also included in Figure 4a, and labeled AC^b.

According to (13a), (13b), and (13c), and as illustrated in Figure 4a, the household will discard all materials ranked to the left of g_o, will litter nothing, and will supply the remaining materials $(m-g_o)$ directly to secondary markets in the absence of a user fee for garbage collection. These results are again determined by looking for the lower envelope of disposal costs. Notice again that the removal of all materials is accounted for.

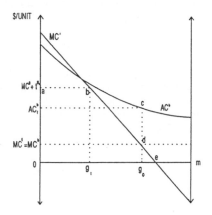

Figure 4a Household disposal choice with littering and no curbside recycling

A user fee for garbage collection will change the households disposal choices because it increases the marginal cost of contributing garbage to the curb. Small increases in the user fee (not shown in Figure 4a) will increase the amount of material that is recycled and will decrease the amount of material that is placed at the curb as garbage. These small increases do not provide the incentive to pay the fixed costs associated with illegally dumping garbage. However, a user fee of $t^{g'}$ increases the marginal cost of contributing garbage to $t^{g'} + MC^g$, and makes the household indifferent between paying the user fee for each unit of garbage and paying the fixed costs f to dump waste illegally. More specifically, a user fee of $t^{g'}$ makes the household indifferent between (1) putting into garbage all materials ranked to the left of g_t and supplying all other materials to secondary markets, and (2) dumping all materials ranked to the left of g_o and supplying the remaining materials to secondary markets. The threshold value of the user fee $(t^{g'})$ is found where the total cost of option (1), denoted by the trapezoidal area a,b,e,0 in Figure 4a (the cost of discarding g_t plus the cost of recycling), is equal to the total cost of option (2), which is AC^b_f,c,d,e,0 (the fixed cost of burning or dumping g_o plus recycling costs). The household would choose the second option for any user fee with value greater than t^g.

The information contained in Figure 4a can be captured in another manner using Figures 4b, 4c, and 4d. Figure 4b maps the demand curve for garbage as a function of the user fee. As stated above, the household decreases its quantity demanded for garbage collection (and increases recycling) as the price of garbage increases to t^g. Once the price of garbage exceeds this threshold value, the quantity demanded for garbage collection falls to zero. Figure 4c maps the cross-price relationship between the price of garbage and the quantity of recycling. Household recycling increases with larger values of the user fee over the interval between zero and t^g. At this point, recycling *decreases* as the household begins to litter garbage. Household recycling efforts are unresponsive to all values of the user fee that are greater than t^g. Figure 4d illustrates the effect of the user fee on the quantity of burning or dumping litter. No littering is conducted below the threshold value of the user fee, but the household litters g_o for all values of the user fee that are greater than t^g. Once the fixed costs of littering are paid, the marginal cost of littering items ranked from g_o leftward is less than the marginal cost of recycling them.

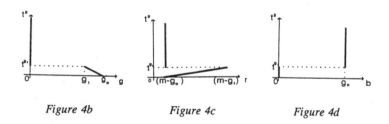

| Figure 4b | Figure 4c | Figure 4d |

Several points arise from this simple model. First, the household would never simultaneously engage in positive quantities of littering b and discarding garbage g. The household uses only garbage and recycling at low values of the user fee, and only uses dumping and recycling at high values. Second, the household will never recycle more than $(m-g_t)$ for any value of the user fee. Therefore, a very high user fee may *not* be optimal. In fact, free garbage collection may be optimal if (1) the administrative cost of operating a user fee program is high, and (2) t^g is relatively low.

Recall that $-u_g^*/\lambda^*$ is the marginal "cost" of contributing garbage. The values of g_o, g_t, and t^g in Figure 4a are determined, in part, by the value of $-u_g^*/\lambda^*$ and are, therefore, unique to each household. The values of g_o and g_t decrease as the value of $-u_g^*/\lambda^*$ increases. Households with a strong distaste for

150

contributing garbage will recycle more, discard less, and litter less than households with less of a distaste. The threshold value of the user fee ($t^{g'}$) increases as $-u_g^*/\lambda^*$ increases. Therefore, households that have a strong distaste for contributing garbage (and littering) wait for a higher value of the user fee before they are induced to litter their garbage. An increase in $-u_g^*/\lambda^*$ will also serve to shift the curves in Figure 4b and 4d to the left and shift the curve in Figure 4c to the right, while again, raising the threshold value of the user fee. A decrease in income produces similar effects on these variables.

With a free curbside recycling program

How will the implementation of a curbside recycling program influence household response to a user fee for garbage collection? A household will respond to a user fee in one of three ways, according to its value of $-u_g^*/\lambda^*$ relative to σp^k. A first category of households will never recycle at the curb, regardless of the value of the user fee. A second category of households will recycle at the curb for a certain range of the user fee, but will not recycle for values outside this range. A third category of households will still recycle at the curb even when it engages in littering. The households in higher numbered categories hold a greater distaste for contributing garbage ($-u_g^*/\lambda^*$) relative to the opportunity cost of recycling (σp^k).

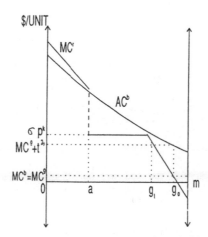

Figure 5a Category one households

The first category of households has the lowest distaste for contributing garbage; its choice among disposal methods is illustrated in Figure 5a. The overall marginal cost of presenting garbage, denoted by MC^g in Figure 5a, is very low relative to σp^k. These households either do not care too much about their garbage contributions or find the opportunity cost of recycling to be too high. Assume that the city is willing to collect materials ranked between point a and point m in Figure 5a at no monetary cost to the household. In the absence of a user fee, the household discards g_0 at no monetary cost and sends $(m-g_0)$ to secondary markets. This household will sell more material in secondary markets as the value of the user fee increases from zero, but will still not participate in a curbside recycling program. To try to induce these households to participate in the curbside recycling program, a user fee would have to be implemented with a value greater than $\sigma p^k - MC^g$. However, any value of the user fee that is greater than $t^{g'}$ would cause this household to pay the fixed costs and litter all materials ranked to the left of g_0 (as explained above). Since $\sigma p^k > t^{g'} + MC^g$, this household will never recycle at the curb. Most communities have households that fit in this category. No community has experienced 100% participation rates in its curbside recycling program, even those with substantial user fees.

Figures 5b, 5c, and 5d summarize the relationships between the value of the user fee and the quantities of garbage (g), recycling (r), and burning (b). A small user fee will induce this kind of household to sell more materials in secondary markets, but any user fee greater than $t^{g'}$ will induce this household to litter.

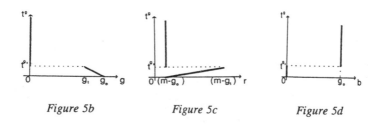

Figure 5b   Figure 5c   Figure 5d

The second category of households have a greater distaste for contributing garbage than the first category, however, the marginal cost of recycling material (σp^k) is still greater than the overall marginal "cost" of contributing garbage to the curb. This household will recycle at the curb, but only in response to very specific values of the user fee. The household will discard these materials if the user fee is too low or litter them if the user fee is too high.

152

Figure 6a illustrates the behavior of this category of households. In the absence of a user fee, this category will put into garbage all materials ranked to the left of g_o and will sell the remaining materials in secondary markets. As the value of the user fee increases from zero, the household will gradually discard less material and recycle more. It will recycle at the curb for values of the user fee slightly greater than σp^k. If a user fee of t^g is implemented, the household is indifferent between (1) discarding all materials ranked to the left of g_t and recycling the rest (including materials g_o-g_t collected at the curb), and (2) littering all materials ranked to the left of g_o and sending (m-g_o) to secondary markets. The total cost of method one is the area (f,a,h,c,e,0), while that of method two is (AC^b_f,b,d,e,0). The threshold value of the user fee (t^g) is found where these two areas are equal. The household chooses to litter g_o for all values of t^g greater than the threshold value.

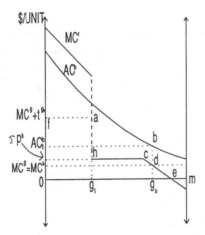

Figure 6a Category two households

These results are also summarized in Figures 6b, 6c, and 6d, where quantities of garbage, recycling, and litter are mapped over all positive values of the user fee. Figure 6b shows that, as the value of the user fee increases from zero, households in this category gradually reduce the quantity of garbage. As the user fee increases above σp^k-MC^g, the household sharply reduces its garbage and begins to recycle at the curb. Once the user fee rises above $t^g{}'$, the household stops discarding garbage, and, as Figure 6d illustrates, begins to litter. This response of recycling to a user fee is somewhat surprising. The household participates in curbside recycling for values of the user fee slightly greater than σp^k-MC^g, but it abandons its curbside recycling efforts once the user fee exceeds

153

t^{g}. At this high fee, the household has the incentive to pay the fixed cost f associated with dumping. Since the marginal cost of dumping materials (MC^{b}) is lower than the overall marginal "cost" of recycling them at the curb (σp^{k}), the household will litter these recyclable materials as well.

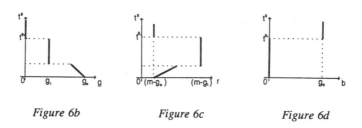

<table>
<tr><td>*Figure 6b*</td><td>*Figure 6c*</td><td>*Figure 6d*</td></tr>
</table>

Households in category three will recycle at the curb, even in the absence of a user fee. The marginal cost to recycle materials collected at the curb (σp^{k}) is less than the marginal "cost" of discarding garbage in the absence of a user fee MC^{g}. The logic can be seen in Figure 7a. The household discards all materials to the left of g_{o} and participates in curbside recycling in the absence of a user fee. Therefore, the implementation of a user fee for garbage collection will have no impact on this household's curbside recycling level. However, if the value of the user fee exceeds t^{g}, the household begins to litter all material ranked to the left of g_{o} (at marginal cost MC^{b}) and recycle the rest.[13]

Figures 7b, 7c, and 7d summarize these results. Notice in Figure 7c that the amount of recycling conducted by these households is fairly unresponsive to price. In fact, the only major change in waste removal methods attributed to a change in the user fee is a switch from discarding garbage (g) to burning or littering (b). This switch occurs for values of the user fee greater than t^{g}. This result suggests that garbage fees would have little success in increasing the recycling levels of households that have rather strong preferences for recycling.

---

[13]   A possible fourth category of households could involve $MC^{b} > \sigma p^{k} > MC^{g}$. These households would not recycle at the curb in the absence of a user fee. High user fees would still create the incentive for this household to litter, but it will still place those materials that are collected by the city out for recycling.

These households already participate in the curbside recycling program in the absence of a user fee, leaving little room to increase their recycling quantities following the implementation of the user fee.[14]

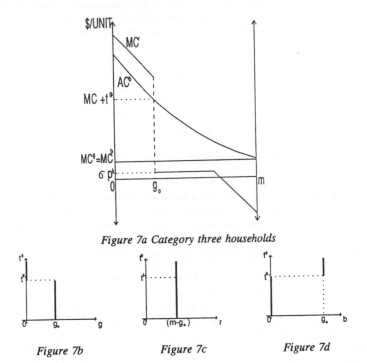

Figure 7a Category three households

Figure 7b   *Figure 7c*   *Figure 7d*

Aggregate Behavior

The community's demand schedule for garbage collection can be derived by adding the amounts of garbage thrown out by all households in the community, at each value of the user fee. Individual garbage quantities with curbside recycling are depicted in Figures 5b through 7b, where all types of households either reduce or leave unchanged their garbage quantities with increases in the value of

---

[14]   A possible fifth category of households will never litter garbage. The overall marginal "cost" of recycling even the most expensive items (the whole MC^r schedule) is less than the cost of burning or littering (the AC^b schedule).

the user fee. A higher user fee never increases the quantity of garbage. Therefore, aggregate garbage never increases with the user fee.

Similarly, Figures (5d) through (7d) illustrate that increasing values of the user fee either increase or leave unchanged amounts of litter for all households. Therefore, the aggregation of household litter must either increase or remain unchanged with higher values of the user fee. Aggregate litter will never decrease.

The same story cannot be told for aggregate recycling levels. One might expect that aggregate recycling would increase with higher values of the user fee, and this result certainly holds for some households over some ranges of the user fee. However, Figures (5c) through (7c) indicate that households can *reduce* recycling over *some* range of the user fee. Different households will decrease recycling by different amounts, and over different ranges of t^g. Therefore, the horizontal aggregation of recycling across all households could either rise or *fall* with increasing values of the user fee.

The logic is a bit different for each category of household, but increases in $t^{g'}$ will eventually induce all households to pay the fixed cost and begin to litter waste material. Once these fixed costs are paid, the household may find the marginal cost of dumping (MC^b) to be less than the marginal cost of recycling (MC^r). At this point, a higher value of $t^{g'}$ induces less recycling.

The relationships between the user fee and these aggregate amounts are illustrated in Figure 8 for two specific communities. The aggregate recycling function for community 1 (call it D^R_1) is drawn so that aggregate recycling (measured from the point M leftward) rises with the user fee. The litter function for community 1 (call it D^B_1) reflects the fact that some households, perhaps in category 1, litter garbage even at very low values of the user fee. As the user fee increases from zero, more households are predicted to pay the fixed cost associated with littering and contribute to aggregate litter.

If no user fee is charged for garbage, the community with recycling function D^R_1 and littering function D^B_1 litters an amount $B_1 = 0$, recycles $M\text{-}G_1$, and discards G_1. As long as the marginal cost of littering is positive and the marginal cost to discard garbage is zero, then all communities experience no litter in the absence of a user fee. Once a user fee of $t^{g'}$ is levied, the amount of litter increases to B_1', the amount of recycling increases to $M\text{-}G_1'$, and the amount of garbage decreases to $G_1'\text{-}B_1'$.

These functions for a second community are denoted by D^R_2 and D^B_2. With user fee $t^{g'}$, community two increases litter from B_2 to B_2', increases recycling from $M\text{-}G_2$ to $M\text{-}G_2'$ and reduces the level of garbage from $G_2\text{-}B_2$ to

156

G_2'-B_2'. Notice that the increase in litter is smaller than experienced by community one. As drawn, the change in recycling for community two is larger than for community one. Therefore, community two may realize greater benefits and lower costs from the implementation of a user fee.[15]

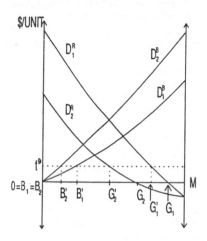

Figure 8 Aggregate behavior with littering

IMPLICATIONS AND CONCLUSION

This chapter has contributed to the literature on user fees for garbage collection in several ways. We introduced heterogeneity into a model of household choice over garbage removal methods. This model explained (1) why some households participate in curbside recycling programs in the absence of a user fee, (2) why other households do not recycle at the curb even in the presence of a user fee, and (3) why some households choose to litter garbage when others do not. We aggregated diverse households in each community to provide a prediction that a user fee will never increase garbage, and will never decrease illicit burning or dumping. At some point, however, the garbage fee becomes high enough to induce some people to pay the fixed cost of dumping and thus to switch away from recycling. As a consequence, the garbage fee might *decrease* aggregate recycling.

---

[15] The model does not suggest that the community with less littering will also experience a greater change in recycling (as drawn in Figure 9). This community could experience a smaller change in recycling.

The model is general enough to encompass fixed costs for recycling instead of for dumping. Individuals and recycling firms may incur search- and transport costs that do not vary with the amount recycled. If so, the same model could be employed to show that a rising garbage fee would generate monotonic decreases in garbage and monotonic increases in recycling. At some point, however, the garbage fee would become high enough to induce some people to pay the fixed cost of recycling and thus to switch away from dumping. As a consequence, the garbage fee might *decrease* aggregate dumping.

We found that the observed low or moderate garbage fees cannot be explained in a model where households cannot burn, dump, or litter. Therefore, we added this option to the model. We described three categories of households, and we aggregated individual behavior to find community demands. We found that individual behavior, and thus aggregate demands, depend upon (1) the community's distribution of household preferences for contributing garbage, (2) the fixed costs associated with dumping, (3) the price of recyclable materials, and (4) the presence of curbside recycling. Therefore, empirical work will require measures of those variables.

The theory also makes some specific predictions that can be tested empirically. In general, the own-price elasticity for garbage should be non-positive. The cross-price effect of the garbage fee on recycling quantities could be negative or positive at high values of the garbage fee (where it could induce people to pay the fixed cost of dumping and thus to switch out of recycling), but it should be non-negative at low values of the user fee.

We thought about how these aggregate outcomes affect the costs and benefits to a community from the implementation of a user-fee program. In particular, the heterogeneity of households implies that some communities will respond more than others. Thus a user fee is more likely to be adopted in communities with low administrative costs, large increases in recycling, and small increases in dumping. The important implication for empirical work is that the town's choice of user fee is not exogenous.

References

Copeland, B.R. (1991). "International Trade in Waste Products in the Presence of Illegal Disposal." *Journal of Environmental Economics and Management* 20, 143-162.

Dinan, T.M. (1993). "Economic Efficiency Effects of Alternative Policies for Reducing Waste Disposal." *Journal of Environmental Economics and Management* 25, 242-256.

Dobbs, I.M. (1991). "Litter and Waste Management: Disposal Taxes versus User Charges." *Canadian Journal of Economics* 24, 221-227.

Fullerton, D. and T.C. Kinnaman. (Forthcoming). "Garbage, Recycling, and Illicit Burning or Dumping." *Journal of Environmental Economics and Management*.

Jenkins, R. (1991). "Municipal Demand for Solid Waste Disposal Services: The Impact of User Fees." *Mimeo*. University of Maryland.

Kennedy, P.W., and B. Laplante. (1994). "Municipal Solid Waste Management: The Optimal Pricing of Garbage and Recyclables Collection." *Mimeo*. World Bank.

Morris, G.E., and D.M. Holthausen. (1994). "The Economics of Household Solid Waste Generation and Disposal." *Journal of Environmental Economics and Management* 26, 215-234.

Repetto, et al. (1992). *Green Fees: How a Tax Shift Can Work for the Environment and the Economy*. Washington DC: World Resources Institute.

Skumatz, L.A. (1993). "Variable Rates for Municipal Solid Waste: Implementation Experience, Economics, and Legislation." Policy Study 160. Reason Foundation.

Sigman, H. (1991). "A Comparison of Public Policies for Lead Recycling." *Mimeo*. Department of Economics UCLA.

Sullivan, A.M. (1987). "Policy Options for Toxic Disposal: Laissez-faire, Subsidization, and Enforcement." *Journal of Environmental Economics and Management* 14, 58-71.

Wertz, K.L. (1976). "Economic Factors Influencing Households' Production of Refuse." *Journal of Environmental Economics and Management* 2, 263-272.

[4]

Household Responses to Pricing Garbage by the Bag

By Don Fullerton and Thomas C. Kinnaman*

The average tipping fee paid by garbage collectors to landfills has tripled over a six-year period, largely due to rising land prices and new EPA regulations (Robert Steuteville and Nora Goldstein, 1993). Several communities and private firms have responded to these economic pressures by implementing volume-based pricing programs that require households to pay for each bag or can of garbage presented for collection. These towns employ unit pricing not only for additional revenue, but to reduce their direct costs and external costs from using landfills and incinerators. Households might recycle more, compost more, and demand less packaging at stores. Unfortunately, they might also burn garbage or dump it along deserted roads. The attractiveness of unit pricing depends crucially on the extent of each such method of garbage reduction.

The price per bag might also induce households to compact garbage into fewer bags. This practice, known as the "Seattle Stomp," was noticed first when Seattle started an early unit-pricing program. It is not helpful, since collectors compact the garbage anyway.

This paper employs individual household data to estimate the effect of such a program on the weight of garbage, the number of con-

tainers, the weight per can, and the amount of recycling. We also provide two indirect measures of illegal dumping. The data are based on a natural experiment that provides a unique opportunity to study human behavior in response to a change in price. On July 1, 1992, Charlottesville, Virginia, implemented a program to charge $0.80 per 32-gallon bag or can of residential garbage collected at the curb. Before and after the implementation of this program, we counted and weighed the bags or cans of garbage or recyclable materials of 75 households. In response to this new price, the average person living in these households reduced the weight of garbage by 14 percent, reduced the volume of garbage (number of containers) by 37 percent, and increased the weight of recycling by 16 percent. Our indirect measures suggest that additional illegal dumping may account for 28 percent to 43 percent of the reduction in garbage.

Based on these data, the change in weight of garbage is statistically significant, but small. The implied arc-price elasticity is only −0.076.[1] We also collect aggregate data on residential garbage (available only by weight) for 25 similar cities in Virginia over the same time period. Based on these aggregate data, the reduction in Charlottesville is less than one standard deviation beyond the mean reduction elsewhere. Using either set of data, we conclude that this pricing program has little effect on the weight of garbage. Using the household data, however, we find more substantial effects on volume, density, recycling, and illegal dumping.

* Fullerton: Department of Economics, University of Texas at Austin, Austin, TX 78712; Kinnaman: Department of Economics, Bucknell University, Lewisburg, PA 17837. This research began while both authors were at the University of Virginia. We are grateful for suggestions from Linda Babcock, John Engberg, Phil Heap, Debbie Nestor, Ed Olsen, Hilary Sigman, Jon Skinner, Dan Slesnick, Steve Stern, Lowell Taylor, Margaret Walls, anonymous referees, and seminar participants at the National Bureau of Economic Research, University of Virginia, Carnegie-Mellon University, University of Georgia, Vanderbilt University, University of Oregon, and University of Texas. We are also grateful for funding from National Science Foundation grant SES-91-22785, and from the Bankard Fund at the University of Virginia. This paper is part of NBER's research program in Public Economics. Any opinions expressed are those of the authors and not those of the National Science Foundation or the National Bureau of Economic Research.

[1] This response is not just to the change in price from zero to $0.80, but to the whole program. The demand-curve interpretation is useful, however, because any new price must be accompanied by a public-awareness campaign, a level of enforcement, and other program attributes. We use elasticities to compare with previous results, but the same $0.80 price could have different effects with a different program.

971

Other studies have estimated the demand for the collection of garbage, often using data for entire communities. Cross sections of cities are employed by J. M. McFarland et al. (1972), Kenneth L. Wertz (1976), Robin Jenkins (1991), and Robert Repetto et al. (1992). Aggregate time-series data from one city are used by Fritz Efaw and William N. Lanen (1979) and Lisa Skumatz and Cabell Breckinridge (1990).[2] Household surveys appear more recently. Seonghoon Hong et al. (1993) use a survey of 2,298 households in the area of Portland, Oregon, where 25 collection firms in 19 municipalities use a variety of block-pricing schedules (such as $12/month for one can per week and $24/month for two cans). Correcting for the endogeneity of price, they find small responses to changes in price or income. Finally, James D. Reschovsky and Sarah E. Stone (1994) survey 1,422 households around Ithaca, New York, facing a variety of unit-pricing and recycling rules. An important result is that curbside recycling pickup increases the probability of recycling more than does unit pricing of garbage.

We build upon these existing studies in several ways. First, by using individual households instead of just a cross section of cities, we avoid the problem that city tonnage data often include amounts from outside the jurisdiction and often mix residential garbage with commercial and industrial garbage.[3] Second, by collecting our own data, we avoid potential biases in surveys with self-reported amounts of garbage and recycling. Third, we measure the garbage itself, rather than the weekly number of cans contracted (some of which may be partially empty). Fourth, by taking direct measures of both weight and volume, we can measure the Seattle Stomp, that is, the change in weight per can. Fifth, our data include the

weight of recycling rather than just the frequency of recycling. Sixth, in our natural experiment, the change in price is truly exogenous to households. We thus avoid the problem in cross sections of cities that price is jointly determined with quantities (if cities self-select prices in a way that depends on resident characteristics).[4] Finally, our cross section of households contains more variation in demographic characteristics than does a cross section of communities, since the latter can only provide community-wide means.

Section I will describe the steps taken to gather the data from individual households in Charlottesville, including steps to control for seasonal or other variations. Results in Section II indicate that garbage weight is inelastic to price, but garbage volume does respond to this price per unit volume. We also estimate how these observed responses depend on demographic characteristics, and we provide two indirect measures of the increase in illegal dumping. Finally, in Section III, we consider policy issues. We discuss the pros and cons of collecting revenue from unit pricing, we calculate the effect of introducing a minimum of one bag per week, and we conduct a simple cost-benefit comparison. Welfare benefits from unit pricing range from $0.08 to $0.15 per $0.80 bag of garbage, but administrative costs are likely to exceed $0.19 per bag.

I. The Data

Charlottesville, Virginia, is a university town with a population of 40,341. Residential garbage collection has traditionally been provided by the city and financed by property taxes. To recycle, households had to haul materials to one of two drop-off centers that accepted newspaper, three colors of glass, and aluminum cans. Then, beginning in November of 1991, Charlottesville implemented a voluntary curbside recycling program. The city provided each household with a free plastic

---

[2] Also, Barbara Stevens (1977) and Peter Kemper and John M. Quigley (1976) use a cross section of cities to examine the effects of a change in the level of service for garbage collection. With a cross section of neighborhoods, Robert A. Richardson and Joseph Havlicek Jr. (1978) and William L. Rathje and Barry Thompson (1981) consider the effect of income on specific components of garbage.

[3] Jenkins (1991) and Douglas B. Cargo (1978) employ such data by estimating separate equations for commercial waste and mixed waste.

[4] Our individual households cannot self-select into unit pricing the same way, but Charlottesville could. Regressions below control for observable characteristics, but Charlottesville might have chosen unit pricing based on residents' characteristics that we cannot observe.

VOL. 86 NO. 4   FULLERTON AND KINNAMAN: PRICING GARBAGE BY THE BAG   973

recycling container in which to place any glass, tin, newspaper, aluminum, and certain plastics. The city also expanded the list of materials accepted at the drop-off locations.

In December 1991, the city council decided that a unit-pricing program would begin July 1, 1992. This program requires a sticker, costing $0.80, on each unit of garbage for collection, where a unit can be any container (bag or can) with a volume of approximately 32 gallons. A $0.40 sticker could be purchased for a 16-gallon bag, but garbage without a sticker would not be collected. Collection of recyclable materials would continue to be free and voluntary.

A. Our Procedures to Collect the Data

These events provide a natural experiment to study household response to price. Following the decision of the city council in December 1991, we began to assemble a sample of households. We first selected a set of streets spread throughout Charlottesville. This sample of streets represents all major neighborhoods and demographic groups. Then the city directory was used to select a random sample of households located on the selected streets.[5] A total of 400 households received a letter requesting their participation in our study. The letter indicated that their garbage and recycling would be weighed early in the morning over two four-week periods, and that participating households would be expected to complete a questionnaire. They were assured that their answers would be held confidential.[6]

A total of 97 households agreed to participate. Another 68 households responded that they would not participate, and several of these indicated they would be moving during the summer. Of the 97 positive responses, our final sample includes 75 with complete data.[7]

With only a 25-percent positive response rate, our sample could suffer from a self-selection bias. Perhaps only educated, environmentally-aware households would agree to have their garbage weighed. These households may already have been recycling as much as they could before unit pricing, with little opportunity for additional recycling. Conclusions based on such a sample might understate the reduction in garbage of an average household. The data do not allow us to conduct a formal test for selection bias. We cannot compare our sample's garbage per capita to the city's data on "residential" garbage per capita, because the latter includes garbage from small businesses that use bags, and includes population from apartments that use dumpsters. Nor can we usefully compare demographics of our sample to those of the city, because we intentionally excluded dormitories and all multi-family dwellings, which together make up 31 percent of housing in Charlottesville. Thus our sample has higher than average income and education, and it over-samples homeowners, married couples, and full-time workers. Our sample is not representative of the population as a whole, but it could provide useful information about other similar single-family neighborhoods that would be likely sites for similar unit-pricing programs.[8]

---

[5] We excluded streets located near the University of Virginia, to avoid sampling students who frequently leave town or change living locations. We also avoided apartments and town houses which often use dumpsters. With these exclusions, we then selected streets that appeared to be distributed uniformly across a map of Charlottesville. Density varies, so the sample is not representative of the population. This two-part selection process is designed to cluster households, in order to reduce the costs and complications involved with weighing household garbage each morning. Even though several households in the sample were located on the same street, they were most often located well apart from each other.

[6] The letter informed households that the Charlottesville City Council had been made aware of this study, and had agreed to all terms. Households were also informed

that they would receive $5 for completing the questionnaire. Each letter included a stamped postcard for their reply.

[7] Several households were removed from the sample because the original occupants had moved or because the building contained more than one family. Some other households refused to complete the questionnaire.

[8] We cannot test for selection bias, but we assess the potential sensitivity of our results to the problem induced by truncation of the sample (G. S. Maddala, 1983 pp. 165–70). We run an ordinary-least-squares (OLS) regression and compare it to a truncated regression that assumes our sample is truncated above our highest observed garbage per capita. The price coefficient changes only in the fourth significant digit.

Each household's garbage and recyclable materials were weighed each week over four weeks in May and early June before implementation of the unit-pricing program, and again over four weeks in September following its implementation. We skipped three weeks before the starting date to avoid anticipation effects, and we skipped two months afterwards to avoid vacations and to provide a short adjustment period. Garbage was not weighed during the week following Memorial Day, to avoid the extra garbage that can be generated over a holiday weekend. Care was taken throughout the term of the study not to weigh yard waste.[9] This involved some inspection of household garbage, which was not a difficult task.

Measurement error can arise from several sources in our data. First, rain can increase the weight of garbage and recycling, so we did not use observations from the two mornings that it rained.[10] Second, the recycling truck does not collect in certain parts of the city until well into the afternoon, so some households might wait to present their recycling. We could only measure amounts in the morning, but on one occasion we returned in the afternoon to households that did not recycle in the morning, and we saw no additional recycling. Third, the volume of garbage containers can vary, as households used different-sized cans, plastic bags, or cardboard boxes. Before implementation, we approximated each household's garbage by the number of 32-gallon containers it would have filled. Following implementation, we measured volume by counting the number of stickers. Thus our measure of volume is the same as the city's. We count the number of containers for which they were charged, rather than the precise volume of garbage per se.

We recorded each week separately, but household garbage and recycling amounts can vary substantially from one week to the next. To save on disposal costs, several households presented garbage only every other week. Therefore, we average the four weeks for each household before implementation, and we calculated a separate average for each household over the four weeks following implementation. We are left with two observations for each household. The first represents an average week's worth of garbage and recycling amounts at a price of zero, and the second provides the same at a price of $0.80.

Following measurement, each household was sent a questionnaire with a self-addressed stamped envelope to report their demographic statistics such as household size, ages, race, income category, marital status, education, and other information that might influence the generation of garbage or recycling. They were also given the opportunity to express their opinions on several subjects relating to the unit-pricing program. Some of their responses are reported in Table 1. Support for the sticker program runs fairly high, with 78 percent of households favoring it over an increase in property taxes,[11] and 73 percent favoring it over mandatory recycling. Yet households found it more inconvenient to purchase and place stickers on their garbage than to recycle. Households had been recycling for more than one year by that time, and may have become accustomed to it, whereas the sticker program was relatively new to them. See Stuart Oskamp et al. (1991) or Seattle Solid Waste Utility (1991) for more elaborate survey studies.

B. Control for Seasonal and Other Effects

The change in garbage from May to September might not all be due to the change in price. How can we control for changes attributable to seasonal or other factors? Ideally, we would like to compare these months in Charlottesville to the same months in another similar town that did not introduce unit pricing, and then take "differences in differences." Unfortunately, we did not have resources to collect similar data for

---

[9] Residents are not supposed to mix yard waste with regular garbage. Instead, Charlottesville conducts special collection of yard waste several times each year. Some households still included yard waste with regular garbage, however, and we took care to exclude it.

[10] We did note whether each household presented any garbage for collection. If so, we designated the following week's garbage as one week's worth. If not, the following week's garbage was assumed to represent two week's worth (or the number of weeks since the last presentation).

[11] Among owner-occupied households, 79 percent prefer unit pricing to an increase in property taxes.

VOL. 86 NO. 4   *FULLERTON AND KINNAMAN: PRICING GARBAGE BY THE BAG*   975

TABLE 1—RESPONSES TO SELECTED QUESTIONS IN OUR SURVEY

Questions	Response	Percentage
Assuming that the city must face higher costs for the collection and disposal of your garbage, would you rather have your property taxes increase or participate in a sticker program such as the one Charlottesville currently has implemented to pay for the higher costs?	Sticker Property tax	77.7 22.3
Other cities across the United States have passed laws requiring households to recycle certain material each week or they must pay a fine. Would you rather have such a law instead of the sticker program?	Yes No	27.8 72.8
How inconvenient is it for you to purchase and place stickers on your garbage?	Not Very Somewhat Very Extremely	46.7 36.4 11.7 5.2
How inconvenient is it for you to place your newspaper, plastic, aluminum and tin in the green recycling container?	Not very Somewhat Very Extremely	75.3 14.3 5.2 5.2
Do you think the city of Charlottesville should collect a larger variety of recyclable material from households each week?	Yes No	86.9 13.1
Have you observed a greater incidence of litter in Charlottesville since the sticker program began in July?	Yes, a lot Yes, a little No	15.6 24.7 59.7
Have you experienced any problems with people stealing garbage stickers?	Yes No	3.9 96.1

individual households at the same time in a different city. Instead, we take several approaches. First, we searched the literature for information on seasonal effects. Only Richardson and Havlicek (1974) measure monthly household waste components to determine the size and sources of seasonal variation. The first row of Table 2 indicates that their average weekly weight of garbage fell by 4.8 percent from May to September. That information is only from one city, and only from 1970–1971. Second, we therefore collected aggregate garbage data for Charlottesville (excluding the University of Virginia) in May and September of seven years *other* than 1992. The second row shows that garbage weight fell by an average of 3.8 percent between those months (for 1986–1991 and 1993–1994).[12] That informa-

tion does not control for events specific to 1992. Third, we therefore collected our own aggregate data for May and September of 1992 by calling solid waste officials of 25 other cities in Virginia. This sample represents virtually every city in Virginia that is similar in size to Charlottesville and not near a beach. It can be used to control for effects of changes in the Virginia economy, changes in the price of newsprint, or changes in any other variables likely to affect garbage in Charlottesville between May and September of 1992. As shown in the third row, garbage fell in those other cities by 3.5 percent.

The three estimates of seasonal effects are close to one another, but their standard errors are high. Aggregate garbage per capita is poorly measured because cities combine the different categories of residents, small businesses, and apartments. The variance is large,

---

[12] The aggregate garbage weight in Charlottesville fell by 6.0 percent from May to September of 1992, which is not significantly different from the 3.8 percent average change in other years, but these aggregates include small

businesses that use garbage bags instead of dumpsters. The 14-percent reduction in our sample includes only single-family households.

976 THE AMERICAN ECONOMIC REVIEW SEPTEMBER 1996

TABLE 2—AVERAGE WEEKLY MEASURES PER CAPITA

	May	September	Difference (standard error)	Percent change	Arc-elasticity
Elsewhere (garbage in pounds):					
Richardson and Havlicek, 1970–1971	11.39	10.84	−0.55[a]	−4.8	
Charlottesville, 1986–1991, 1993–1994[b]	11.78	11.33	−0.45 (0.32)	−3.8	
25 Cities in Virginia, 1992[c]	9.68	9.34	−0.34 (0.34)	−3.5	
For our 75 households:					
Weight of garbage (pounds)	10.90	9.37	−1.54** (0.69)	−14.1	−0.076
Volume of garbage (cans)	0.73	0.46	−0.27*** (0.04)	−36.8	−0.226
Density (pounds per can)	15.04	21.49	6.44*** (1.02)	42.8	0.176
Recycling (pounds)	3.69	4.27	0.58* (0.31)	15.6	0.073

[a] Standard error not available.
[b] Includes small businesses that use garbage bags instead of dumpsters.
[c] Some cities' garbage figures include small businesses, and some apartments, whereas population is taken from the census and thus includes the whole city.
* Statistically different from zero at the 10-percent level.
** Statistically different from zero at the 5-percent level.
*** Statistically different from zero at the 1-percent level.

so the observed change in Charlottesville is not statistically different from changes in those other cities.

This estimated aggregate seasonal effect is small, but most importantly, Richardson and Havlicek (1974) find that it is primarily attributable to yard waste, as well as to vacations, holidays, and changes in household composition. Therefore another approach to correct for seasonal effects is given by our data collection procedures. As noted above, we carefully avoided yard waste, we excluded households that moved or went on vacation, we excluded households whose composition changed, and we selected measurement dates to avoid holidays. In addition, we checked whether other events could have affected household waste. We found no changes in state or local recycling laws, no changes in packaging restrictions, and no changes in dumping laws during this period.[13]

[13] On this issue, we benefited from discussions with Nancy Williams, the local government recycling-program analyst of the Virginia Department of Environmental Quality. A remaining source of seasonal variation might be changes in consumption habits between those months.

We feel that these steps constitute the best correction for seasonal and other effects. First, the aggregate statistics are poorly measured. Second, aggregate statistics relate only to weight of garbage, whereas our steps in the collection of household data also correct for seasonal effects on volume and recycling. Third, our data already exclude yard waste and thus should not be corrected again by other cities' seasonal variations that are primarily due to yard waste. Therefore our primary results are based on no further correction. For completeness, we provide estimates based on the 3.5-percent correction for other cities in Virginia, but we show it makes very little difference.

II. Results

This section estimates how the change in garbage depends on price and demographic variables. Our previous working paper (Fullerton and Kinnaman, 1994) estimates how the level of garbage and the probability of recycling depend on demographic variables.

A. Direct Measures

The second panel of Table 2 reports the average across our 75 households of per capita garbage weight, garbage volume, garbage density, and recycling weight. The average person in our sample reduced the weight of garbage from 10.90 to 9.37 pounds per week, a 14-percent decrease. This change is statistically different from zero at the 5-percent level.[14] Using this difference, the arc-price elasticity of demand is −0.076 for the collection of garbage, measured in pounds, at mean levels of price and weight. This estimate is a bit closer to zero than in previous studies.[15]

If these figures are adjusted for the 3.5-percent reduction from May to September of 1992 in other cities, then the change is still significant at the 10-percent level. The adjusted arc-elasticity is −0.058, which is similar to (but even smaller than) the unadjusted elasticity.

The average individual reduced the volume of garbage from 0.73 to 0.46 containers per week, a 37-percent decrease, which is statistically different from zero at the 1-percent level. The arc-price elasticity of demand, measured in volume, is −0.226 at mean levels of price and volume. Thus volume fell in greater proportion than weight. Density increased by 43 percent, from 15.04 to 21.49 pounds per container. After all, this "volume-based" pricing program charges not by weight but by the number of bags. Unfortunately, social costs depend on volume after compacting at the landfill, which is better proxied by weight at the curb than by volume at the curb.

Finally, the weight of recycling increased from 3.69 to 4.27 pounds per week, a 16-

percent increase. The implied cross-price elasticity is 0.073 at mean levels.[16]

B. Garbage Reduction and Household Characteristics

Overall change in weight is small, but this change is averaged over diverse households. We now investigate briefly whether these responses depend on household income or demographic characteristics. These estimates would help some other town that is considering unit pricing. Specifically, the change in each of the four measures is regressed on household income and demographic variables listed in Table 3. For this fixed-effects model,[17] the ordinary-least-squares estimator is efficient. Table 4 reports results from four separate regressions.

Our survey provides much information about each household, but several variables have no effect in any of these four regressions. We wish to conserve degrees of freedom, with only 75 observations, so we omit variables for homeownership, employment, age, and household size. Coefficients on these variables always have large standard errors. Their exclusion has virtually no effect on the coefficient estimates of remaining variables, but reduces their standard errors. Even with the fewer variables, the null hypothesis that all slope coefficients are zero cannot be rejected for three of the four regressions. It is barely rejected at the 5-percent level for the garbage-weight regression.

In the garbage-weight equation, shown in the first column, the (negative) baseline

---

[14] This test presumes a normal distribution. Using a less-restrictive nonparametric Fisher-sign test, the change in weight of garbage is *not* significant. The reason is that only 38 of the 75 households reduced the weight. However, significant numbers decreased volume, and increased both density and recycling.

[15] No other study employs a cross section of households around the start of unit pricing. Using aggregate data, others have estimated the price elasticity to be −0.12 (Jenkins, 1991), −0.15 (Wertz, 1976), −0.26 and −0.22 (Glenn E. Morris and Denise Byrd, 1990, in two communities), and −0.14 (Skumatz and Breckinridge, 1990).

[16] Using two observations from each city, the U.S. Environmental Protection Agency (1990) estimates this cross-price elasticity for Perkasie, PA (0.49), Illion, NY (0.48), and Seattle, WA (0.06 in 1985–1986 and 0.10 in 1986–1987).

[17] As described in Fullerton and Kinnaman (1994), the garbage level can be expressed as a linear function of price P, exogenous variables X, and interactions PX. Taking first differences, where ΔX is zero, the change in garbage becomes a function of ΔP (a constant 0.8) and $\Delta P \cdot X$. Thus the estimated constant reflects the "baseline" price effect (if all $X = 0$), the coefficients on X reflect interaction terms, and the average price effect can be evaluated at the mean values of X.

TABLE 3—DESCRIPTION OF VARIABLES USED IN REGRESSIONS

Independent variables	Mean (standard deviation)	Description
NEWS	0.47 (0.42)	Number of newspapers delivered daily per person
INFANT	0.03 (0.10)	Fraction of those in the household less than age three
COLLEGE	0.75 (0.44)	1–At least one person with some college in the household 0–No individual with some college
INC	4.63 (2.66)	The household annual income level: 1–Less than $20,000 3–From $20,000 to $40,000 6–From $40,000 to $80,000 9–Greater than $80,000
LINC	0.41 (0.86)	Natural log of per capita income
MARRY	0.65 (0.51)	1–An adult married couple lives in the household 0–No married couple
WHITE	0.95 (0.28)	1–A white household 0–A nonwhite household

price effect given by the constant term is dampened for households that subscribe to more daily newspapers, for those with infants, and for married couples. Interestingly, the reduction in garbage is greater for households with more income. Column (2) shows the effect on the number of bags. These coefficients are similar in sign to those in the garbage-weight equation.

Who stomped on their garbage in response to unit pricing? Column (3) of Table 4 shows how demographic characteristics affect the change in garbage density. Stomping is a bit higher for married couples and lower for those with more income. The stomping problem could be addressed by charging households according to the weight of their garbage, but such a system would require scales on collection trucks and more elaborate billing.[18]

C. Illegal Dumping Behavior

The biggest concern to policy makers considering unit pricing in their communities is

the possibility of increases in illegal forms of garbage disposal. We could not provide direct measures of such behavior, and we could not trust answers to direct survey questions about it either. Instead, we asked each household to indicate whether they 1) did not attempt to reduce garbage, or 2) recycled more, 3) composted more, 4) demanded less packaging at stores, or 5) used "other" means to reduce garbage. Since the first four options would seem to cover all legal alternatives, we think the "other" option is a strong indicator of illegal disposal such as burning, littering, or using commercial dumpsters.[19] Eight of our 75 households (10.7 percent) indicated "other."

We offer two indirect methods of estimating the amount of illegal dumping that took place in Charlottesville during the period of our experiment.[20] For our first measure, we use two

---

[18] The city of Seattle has been considering a weight-based system for later in this decade. A pilot project (Seattle Solid Waste Utility, 1991) revealed that operation and administrative costs would not be prohibitive, but scales were not sensitive enough to meet federal standards for weights and measures.

[19] The other category might include in-sink garbage disposal, but changes in this behavior must be small. It might include changes in the level or composition of consumption. Fullerton and Kinnaman (1994) estimate the probability of using each method, but the sample size is too small for definitive results.

[20] Daniel R. Blume (1991) interviews officials from 14 unit-pricing communities. Four reported significant dumping problems, 4 reported minor problems, and 6 reported no problems. He was unable to explain what causes these differences, even considering the price of garbage collection.

TABLE 4—OLS ESTIMATES OF COEFFICIENTS

Independent variables	Dependent variable is the change in:			
	Weight (1)	Volume (2)	Density (3)	Recycle (4)
Constant	−4.83	−0.52	2.21	1.23
	(−1.76)	(−3.40)	(0.51)	(0.96)
NEWS	4.49	0.17	−0.66	2.36
	(2.04)	(1.37)	(−0.18)	(2.28)
INFANT	13.14	0.75	11.75	5.01
	(1.57)	(1.59)	(0.92)	(1.27)
COLLEGE	1.57	0.13	−0.68	0.02
	(0.75)	(1.11)	(−0.19)	(0.02)
LINC	−3.15	−0.11	−3.31	−0.07
	(−2.71)	(−1.75)	(−1.61)	(−0.12)
MARRY	3.44	0.17	4.54	0.33
	(2.04)	(1.76)	(1.63)	(0.42)
WHITE	−0.48	0.06	4.42	−2.38
	(−0.16)	(0.37)	(0.96)	(−1.69)
R^2:	0.165	0.117	0.143	0.121
$F(6,68)^a$:	2.243	1.505	1.698	1.558

Note: All variables are defined in Table 3. Descriptive statistics at the bottom of the table show the goodness of fit. *t* statistics are given in parentheses.

ᵃ The number of observations is 75 for columns (1), (2), and (4). The number is 68 for column (3), because density is undefined for the seven households who put out zero garbage for the entire four-week measurement period following implementation. Therefore the F statistic in column (3) is $F(6,61)$.

criteria. We suspect illegal dumping only if a) the household indicated that "other" means were used to reduce garbage, *and* b) the amount of garbage presented for collection fell to zero for the *entire* four-week measurement period following implementation of unit pricing. These households were not on vacation, and they were still presenting recyclable materials.

Based on these two criteria, we find that 4 of our 75 households (5.33 percent) disposed of garbage illegally.[21] To estimate the amount, we take their garbage before unit pricing, minus the increase in their recycling, minus an estimate of additional composting.[22] We find that these households dumped an average of 13.38 pounds per person per week. Furthermore, this estimate constitutes 28 percent of the total reduction in garbage at the curb. For comparison, additional recycling constitutes 38 percent of the total reduction in garbage. Thus households may have increased dumping by almost as much as they increased recycling. The remaining 34 percent of the total reduction in garbage could be explained by additional composting, less packaging demanded at stores, additional recycling at drop-off locations, or even additional illegal dumping.

For our second measure, we use only the second criterion. Altogether, 7 of the 75 households (9.33 percent) presented zero

[21] These results should be viewed with caution. First, the sample size is small. Second, our sample includes a disproportionate number of high-income, well-educated, single-family households. Third, households who dump could have selected themselves out of our sample either by refusing to participate in the study or by refusing to return the questionnaire.

[22] Some households indicated more composting as well as "other" methods. We regress the change in garbage on the same demographic variables and a dummy variable for composting. The coefficient on this dummy is an estimate of per capita change in garbage due to composting.

garbage for the entire four-week period following the price hike (and were not away on vacation). After we account for their additional recycling, and an estimate of additional composting, the missing garbage of these seven households represents 43.0 percent of the total reduction in garbage at the curb.

Social costs can vary over methods of illegal disposal. If a person takes the weekly garbage to a commercial dumpster of an employer, and has permission, the social costs could be quite low. However, if this individual throws garbage along a rural route or burns it in the back yard, then social cost could be quite large. Unfortunately, we have no means to identify what kind of "other" methods were used by households in our study.

Recent stories in newspapers tell of increased dumping.[23] The recycling coordinator of the University of Virginia is aware of "many, many" private reports of individuals dumping in UVA dumpsters. The Albemarle school system has also observed quantities of unidentified garbage in their dumpsters. One person who was warned to stop dumping his garbage in a commercial dumpster was subsequently convicted for continuing the practice. Major department stores around Charlottesville have placed locks on their dumpsters to prevent residents from dumping their garbage. Over 40 percent of households in our sample stated that they had observed more littering since the implementation of the sticker program (see Table 1). Of those observing "a lot" of littering, 75.0 percent lived in densely-populated areas of the city near downtown.

III. Policy Issues

A community may be interested in the amount of revenue it could earn with a unit-pricing program. These revenues could be used to finance recycling-collection programs and to pay tipping fees. Based on our post-change average of 1.0822 cans per household

---

[23] The Charlottesville *Daily Progress*, Tuesday October 26, 1993, "Illegal Dumping Has County, Landowners Sifting for Answers," tells of increased dumping at more than 30 illegal dumpsites.

per week, at a price of $0.80, the revenue would be $0.86 per single-family household per week.

A. Pros and Cons

Several arguments favor unit charges as a source of revenue. First, they can help reduce the city's garbage and thus its expenditures on disposal. Second, garbage collection is not a "public good." Each bag incurs additional cost (is rival), and collection can be limited to bags with paid stickers (is excludable). Third, the "benefit principle" suggests that charges are "fair," since each household pays only according to its use of this service. Fourth, we find that the demand for garbage collection is inelastic. Established optimal-tax theories suggest that total deadweight loss can be reduced by taxing goods with inelastic demand.

Other arguments can be made against this type of taxation. First, administrative and enforcement costs may be higher than for other sources of revenue. Second, the social cost of noncompliance can be large. Illegal dumping could require costly cleanups of backwoods dump sites. Third, our results suggest the tax on garbage is regressive. With unit pricing, the volume of garbage is 0.55 containers per person for the lowest-income group and 0.46 containers per person for the highest-income group. Fourth, communities that use property taxes to pay for garbage collection enable their residents to take deductions against their federal income tax. Depending on the number who itemize, and their marginal tax rates, this deduction can pass to the federal government a third of the cost of this local public service. A community that switches to unit pricing thus loses a substantial federal subsidy on this portion of revenue.

B. A One-Bag Minimum

Some other communities with unit pricing have tried to reduce illegal dumping by using property taxes or monthly fees to collect funds to pay for one bag each week for each household. They then require stickers only for additional bags. The advantage is that households who would otherwise dump their gar-

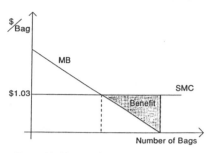

FIGURE 1A. MARGINAL BENEFIT (MB) AND SOCIAL
MARGINAL COST (SMC) OF GARBAGE COLLECTION
AND DISPOSAL

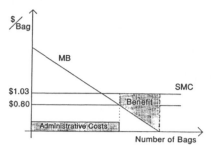

FIGURE 1B. BENEFIT AND COST OF UNIT-PRICING
IN CHARLOTTESVILLE

bage might present at least one bag for collection each week. The disadvantage is that nobody has any incentive to reduce garbage below one bag per week.

We can calculate the effects of such a policy in Charlottesville if we assume a) that households dumping all of their garbage would now dump only the excess over one bag, b) that their regular garbage would increase by the amount not dumped, and c) that others presenting up to one bag of garbage per week (33 percent of our sample) are then unaffected by unit pricing. With these assumptions, illegal dumping falls from 0.42 to 0.07 pounds per person per week—an 83-percent reduction. The average person would reduce garbage weight by 1.04 instead of 1.54 pounds per week, reduce volume by 0.21 instead of 0.27 cans per week, and increase recycling by 0.50 instead of 0.58 pounds per week. The one-bag minimum would reduce dumping substantially, but it would also reduce some of the desirable changes in garbage and recycling.

C. A Simple Cost-Benefit Comparison

What are the social benefits of a unit-pricing program? Repetto et al. (1992) use a diagram like our Figure 1A, where the demand for garbage collection is the marginal benefit (MB). They also find that the social marginal cost (SMC) for a town like Charlottesville is $1.03 per bag. Thus a price of zero generates too much garbage, and a price of $1.03 creates a

welfare benefit shown by the shaded triangle in Figure 1A. This calculation ignores illegal dumping.

We follow Repetto et al. (1992) by assuming that the social marginal cost of garbage collection and disposal is $1.03 per bag. Charlottesville charges only $0.80 per bag of garbage, so their benefit is represented by the shaded trapezoid in Figure 1B. The estimated dollar amounts are shown in the first column of Table 5. With no increase in illegal dumping, this gain is $3.59 per person per year.[24] With illegal dumping, to be conservative, we ignore the cost of cleaning up backwoods dump sites and instead suppose illegal dumpers just use commercial dumpsters. In this case the "true" reduction in garbage at the landfill would be less than the reduction in garbage observed at the curb. The "true" demand curve in Figure 1B is steeper, so the welfare gain trapezoid is smaller, only $2.67 or $2.17 per person per year.

These benefit estimates are converted into an amount per bag, in the second column of Table 5, to indicate "threshold" costs per bag that would yield zero net gain. With no illegal

---

[24] We ignore the benefits of additional recycling and composting. Market prices are near zero for most types of recyclable materials, but see William J. Baumol (1977) for potential costs and benefits. Also, SMC in Figure 1B must refer to "constant density" bags of garbage, so we calculate the change from old volume to "constant density" new volume (given by the new weight divided by the old density).

TABLE 5—A SIMPLE COST-BENEFIT COMPARISON

Assumption	Benefits (per person per year)	Threshold administrative, enforcement and compliance costs (per bag)	Estimated administrative costs to government (per bag)[c]
No minimum:			
No dumping	3.59	0.149	0.193
DUMP1[a]	2.67	0.111	0.193
DUMP2[b]	2.17	0.090	0.193
One bag minimum:			
No dumping	2.54	0.105	0.193
DUMP1[a]	2.38	0.099	0.193
DUMP2[b]	1.95	0.081	0.193

Note: All figures are in dollars.
    [a] Includes the missing garbage of households who used "other" methods to reduce garbage *and* set out no garbage for collection following the implementation of unit pricing.
    [b] Includes the missing garbage of households who may or may not have used "other" methods, but who set out no garbage for collection following implementation.
    [c] Excludes enforcement costs to government and compliance costs to households.

dumping, estimated benefits would be completely offset by administrative and enforcement costs that were $0.149 per bag. With dumping, thresholds are lower.

What are the costs of imposing a price which is per bag of garbage? The municipality must pay to print the stickers, pay commissions to area merchants to sell the stickers, pay employees to distribute the stickers and administer the program, pay to enforce dumping laws, pay to clean up illegal dump sites, and pay to promote the program. In addition, the household must travel to outlets that sell the stickers, spend time and effort to compact more garbage into each container, and spend time and effort to dump their garbage. Private businesses may have to lock dumpsters and pay to remove garbage that has been dumped on their property.

We cannot begin to estimate all such costs, but we do have some information on just the first three. Charlottesville twice purchased stickers from the printer at a cost of at least $0.13 per sticker. In addition, the city pays a 5-percent commission on sales by merchants, $0.04 per sticker. Third, the city pays one part-time clerical person (20 hours per week) to administer the program, and another part-time person to deliver the stickers to the 35 vendors and to follow the garbage trucks to

report violations.[25] At just $6/hour, this labor cost would be $12,000/year, or $0.023 per sticker actually sold. The sum of just these three costs is $0.193 per sticker, well above any threshold in Table 5. Consideration of illegal dumping not only makes the benefits smaller in Table 5, but would also make the social costs higher.

IV. Conclusion

This paper has used original data gathered from individual households to estimate responses to the implementation of a price per bag of garbage. We find that households reduced the number of bags, but not necessarily the actual weight of their garbage. Thus households stomped on their garbage to reduce their costs. They also increased the weight of recycling, and they might have increased illegal dumping.

The reduction in weight of garbage at the curb is 14 percent. If we account for the

---

[25] We are grateful for this help from city officials Chase Anderson and Mike Timberlake. Competition among bids by printers and competition among vendors would suggest that these payments represent social costs, but any pure profits would be a transfer rather than a cost.

VOL. 86 NO. 4   FULLERTON AND KINNAMAN: PRICING GARBAGE BY THE BAG   983

amount of illegal dumping, using our lower estimate, then the true reduction in garbage is only 10 percent. Recycling increased by 16 percent. Many in Charlottesville were already participating in the voluntary recycling program before unit pricing began. Thus the incremental benefit of unit pricing is small. In our simple comparison, this social benefit does not cover the administrative cost.

REFERENCES

Baumol, William J. "On Recycling as a Moot Environmental Issue." *Journal of Environmental Economics and Management,* January 1977, *4*(1), pp. 83–87.

Blume, Daniel R. "Under What Conditions Should Cities Adopt Volume-Based Pricing for Residential Solid Waste Collection?" Manuscript, Office of Management and Budget, Office of Information and Regulatory Affairs, Natural Resources Branch, May 1991.

Cargo, Douglas B. *Solid wastes: Factors influencing generations rates.* Chicago: University of Chicago, 1978.

Efaw, Fritz and Lanen, William N. *Impact of user charges on management of household solid waste.* Princeton, NJ: Mathtech, Inc., August 1979.

Fullerton, Don and Kinnaman, Thomas C. "Household Demand for Garbage and Recycling Collection with the Start of a Price per Bag." National Bureau of Economic Research (Cambridge, MA) Working Paper No. 4670, 1994.

Hong, Seonghoon; Adams, Richard M. and Love, H. Alan. "An Economic Analysis of Household Recycling of Solid Wastes: The Case of Portland, Oregon." *Journal of Environmental Economics and Management,* September 1993, *25*(2), pp. 136–46.

Jenkins, Robin. "Municipal Demand for Solid Waste Disposal Services: The Impact of User Fees." Manuscript, University of Maryland, 1991.

Kemper, Peter and Quigley, John M. *The economics of refuse collection.* Cambridge, MA: Ballinger Publishing, 1976.

Maddala, G. S. *Limited-dependent and qualitative variables in econometrics.* New York: Cambridge University Press, 1983.

McFarland, J. M. et al. *Comprehensive studies of solid waste management.* Berkeley: University of California, May 1972.

Morris, Glenn E. and Byrd, Denise. "The Effects of Weight or Volume-Based Pricing on Solid Waste Management." Unpublished report, U.S. EPA, January 1990.

Oskamp, Stuart; Harrington, Maura J.; Edwards, Todd C.; Sherwood, Deborah L.; Okuda, Shawn M. and Swanson, Deborah C. "Factors Influencing Household Recycling Behavior." *Environment and Behavior,* July 1991, *23*(4), pp. 494–519.

Rathje, William L. and Thompson, Barry. *The Milwaukee garbage project: A report for the solid waste council of the paper industry.* Tucson: University of Arizona, March 1981.

Repetto, Robert; Dower, Roger C.; Jenkins, Robin and Geoghegan, Jacqueline. *Green fees: How a tax shift can work for the environment and the economy.* Washington, DC: World Resource Institute, 1992.

Reschovsky, James D. and Stone, Sarah E. "Market Incentives to Encourage Household Waste Recycling: Paying for What You Throw Away." *Journal of Policy Analysis and Management,* Winter 1994, *13*(1), pp. 120–39.

Richardson, Robert A. and Havlicek, Joseph, Jr. "An Analysis of Seasonal Household Waste Generation." *Southern Journal of Agricultural Economics,* December 1974, *6*(2), pp. 143–55.

———. "Economic Analysis of the Composition of Household Solid Wastes." *Journal of Environmental Economics and Management,* March 1978, *5*(1), pp. 103–11.

Seattle Solid Waste Utility. *Garbage by the pound: Pilot project summary.* Draft report completed for the U.S. Environmental Protection Agency, Seattle, 1991.

Skumatz, Lisa and Breckinridge, Cabell. *Handbook for solid waste officials,* Vol. 2. Washington DC: EPA 530-SW-90-084B, June 1990.

Steuteville, Robert and Goldstein, Nora. "State of Garbage in America, 1993 Nationwide Survey." *Biocycle,* May 1993, *34*(5), pp. 42–50.

Stevens, Barbara. "Pricing Schemes for Refuse Collection Services: The Impact on Refuse Generation." Research Paper No. 154, Columbia University Graduate School of Business, 1977.

U.S. Environmental Protection Agency. "Charging Households for Waste Collection and Disposals." Washington, DC: EPA 530-SW-90-047, September 1990.

Wertz, Kenneth L. "Economic Factors Influencing Households' Production of Refuse." *Journal of Environmental Economics and Management,* May 1976, 2(3), pp. 263–72.

[5]

JOURNAL OF ENVIRONMENTAL ECONOMICS AND MANAGEMENT **36**, 131–148 (1998)
ARTICLE NO. EE981044

Policies for Green Design[1]

Don Fullerton

Department of Economics, University of Texas at Austin, Austin, Texas 78712

and

Wenbo Wu

*H. John Heinz III School of Public Policy and Management, Carnegie Mellon University,
Pittsburgh, Pennsylvania 15213*

Received June 18, 1997; revised June 1998

A simple general equilibrium model is used to analyze disposal-content fees, subsidies for recyclable designs, unit-pricing of household disposal, deposit-refund systems, and manufacturer "take-back" requirements. Firms use primary and recycled inputs to produce output that has two "attributes": packaging per unit output, and recyclability. If households pay the social cost of disposal, then they send the right signals to producers to reduce packaging and to design products that can more easily be recycled. If garbage is collected for free, then socially optimum attributes can still be achieved by a tax on producers' use of packaging and subsidy to recyclable designs. © 1998 Academic Press

Key Words: green design; source reduction; household waste; disposal content; deposit refund; green dot; packaging tax; recycling subsidy.

A consumer durable may be composed of a hundred different parts, each designed by a different team that selects the best type of plastic or other material for its own purpose. Assembly may use different sized bolts, or one-way fasteners. The firm does not care about disassembly because the buyer does not care; the unit can most often be discarded for free. If somebody had to worry about the social cost of disposal, however, a better solution might use a design with fewer types of plastic, and one sized bolt, for easier subsequent disassembly and recycling.

The U.S. Office of Technology Assessment [33] defines green design as a "process in which environmental attributes are treated as design objectives." The purpose is to reduce pollution at its source, that is, to "avoid the generation of waste in the first place" [33, p. 7]. It also finds that "better product design offers new opportunities to address environmental problems, but that current governmental regulations and market practices are not sufficient to fully exploit these opportunities" [33, p. 3].

[1] We are grateful for financial assistance from the National Science Foundation's Grant SBR-9413334 and EPA Grant R824740-01-0, and for helpful suggestions from Bob Haveman, Arik Levinson, Wally Oates, Hilary Sigman, Lowell Taylor, Margaret Walls, anonymous referees, and various seminar participants. This paper is part of NBER's research program in Public Economics. Any opinions expressed are those of the authors and not those of the National Science Foundation, the EPA, or the National Bureau of Economic Research.

131

A variety of reforms have been proposed to deal with these perceived problems, both at state and federal levels. Packaging could be subjected to standards, taxes, deposit-refund systems, or recycling requirements. Other proposals would tax toxic substances, require a minimum percentage of recycled content in certain products such as newspapers, require manufacturers to "take back" certain products such as batteries, provide tax credits for machinery used in recycling, require local governments to collect household recycling at the curb, and require households to pay a price per unit of garbage. Table I lists 34 such policy interventions, from a table in OTA [33, p. 17].

Existing studies have analyzed economic and environmental effects of selected policies, usually in partial equilibrium models, but comparison across policies is made difficult by differences in the design of those studies.[2] In this paper, we extend prior contributions by constructing a single general equilibrium model that can be used to compare virtually all of the 34 policies listed in Table I. A single framework is important, because these policies may not be consistent with each other. For example, the U.S. General Accounting Office [36] points out that a major effort to collect curbside recycling would not work in places where the recyclable materials are already diverted by a beverage container deposit-refund system.

This model has several important attributes. First, it encompasses the entire life-cycle of each product from design to production, packaging, sale, use, and disposal. Table I shows how proposed policies target different stages of this life-cycle, and our model shows how the stages are connected. Policies to affect product design will also affect product disposal, and vice versa. Another policy directed at consumers may similarly affect market prices and firm behavior.[3] Our model can be used to find the equivalence between different policies directed at producers, consumers, and waste managers.

Second, the model can also be used to analyze the distinction in Table I between regulatory instruments and economic instruments. Since we assume perfect certainty, we can show how a behavioral mandate raises production costs and thus product prices in a way that may be equivalent to a price incentive.[4]

Third, the model includes a negative externality from total waste generation, and it specifies exactly when a particular market failure precludes exchange at an equilibrium price. This attribute is important, because many of the proposals in Table I really address different problems altogether. The goal is not recycling *per*

---

[2] Policy options are discussed in Miedema [16], *Project 88—Round II* [23], and the U.S. Congressional Budget Office [32]. A complete review of analytical studies is not possible here, but several are noteworthy. In a model of the toxic disposal market, Sullivan [31] finds the optimal subsidy on legal disposal and degree of enforcement against illegal disposal. Bohm [3] and Dobbs [8] avoid the problem of enforcement by finding the optimal tax on the product (deposit) and subsidy to proper disposal (refund). Sigman [27] compares policies for lead recycling, while Palmer and Walls [20] assess efficiency implications of an output tax, recycling subsidy, and recycled-content standard. Such policies are implemented numerically in Palmer, Sigman, and Walls [21] for several different materials to find specific effects on source reduction, recycling, and waste.

[3] Thus disposal charges can reduce initial demand for the product. The U.S. Environmental Protection Agency (EPA, [34]) places this kind of "source reduction" at the top of its "solid waste management hierarchy," ahead of recycling or waste-to-energy. Palmer, Sigman, and Walls [21] point out that the optimal allocation of resources probably involves an optimal *mix* of these alternatives.

[4] Weitzman [38] shows how the equivalence between quantity restrictions and price incentives depends on uncertainty, and Stavins [29] shows how it depends on transaction costs.

POLICIES FOR GREEN DESIGN   133

TABLE I

Policy Options that Could Affect Materials Flows

Life-cycle stage	Regulatory instruments	Economic instruments
Raw material extraction and processing	1. Regulate mining, oil, and gas nonhazardous solid wastes under the Resource Conservation and Recovery Act (RCRA). 2. Establish depletion quotas on extraction and import of virgin materials.	1. Eliminate special tax treatment for extraction of virgin materials, and subsidies for agriculture. 2. Tax the production of virgin materials.
Manufacturing	1. Tighten regulations under Clean Air Act, Clean Water Act, and RCRA. 2. Regulate nonhazardous industrial waste under RCRA. 3. Mandate disclosure of toxic materials use. 4. Raise corporate average Fuel Economy Standards for automobiles. 5. Mandate recycled content in products. 6. Mandate manufacturer take-back and recycling of products. 7. Regulate product composition, e.g., volatile organic compounds or heavy metal. 8. Establish requirements for product reuse, recyclability, or biodegradability. 9. Ban or phase out hazardous chemicals. 10. Mandate toxic use reduction.	1. Tax industrial emissions, effluents, and hazardous wastes. 2. Establish tradable emissions permits. 3. Tax the carbon content of fuels. 4. Establish tradable recycling credits. 5. Tax the use of virgin toxic materials. 6. Create tax credits for use of recycled materials. 7. Establish a grant fund for clean technology research.
Purchase, use, and disposal	1. Mandate consumer separation of materials for recyling.	1. Establish weight/volume-based waste disposal fees. 2. Tax hazardous or hard-to-dispose products. 3. Establish deposit-refund system for packaging, hazardous products. 4. Establish a fee/rebate system based on product energy efficiency. 5. Tax gasoline.
Waste Management	1. Tighten regulation of waste management facilities under RCRA. 2. Ban disposal of hazardous products in landfills and incinerators. 3. Mandate recycling diversion rates for various materials. 4. Exempt recylers of hazardous wastes from RCRA Subtitle C. 5. Establish a moratorium on construction of new landfills and incinerators.	1. Tax emissions or effluents from waste management facilities. 2. Establish surcharges on wastes delivered to landfills or incinerators.

SOURCE: Office of Technology Assessment [33, p. 17].

se, or even "reduction of waste," because some wastes might be too low while others are too high. If all prices for all products and all forms of disposal reflected full social costs, then markets would send the "right" signals about how to consume and how to dispose of each waste. Thus the "problem" in each case can be defined by identifying exactly where markets fail. Then a policy can be designed to correct that market failure.

In our model, firms produce output using primary resources (labor or capital) and recycled materials. They also choose an amount of packaging, and a level of "recyclability," intended to reflect the resources needed to implement a design that would allow the subsequent recycler to take apart the item more easily, separate the different types of plastic, and recycle a higher percentage of it.[5] Households in this model supply primary resources (labor or capital), retain some resources for home production or leisure, and generate amounts of garbage and recycling that depend upon the firm's choice of packaging and the firm's choice of recyclability. All markets clear, in this closed economy, so the amount of recycling generated by households must match the amount of recycling that gets reused in production. Also, the amount of garbage generated by households must match the supply of disposal services by a collection firm.

At this point, the model allows for various possible market failures. In Case A, private collection firms charge a price per unit of disposal that reflects the private cost of disposal but not negative externalities. A landfill imposes aesthetic or health costs on neighbors, an incinerator generates air pollution and hazardous residue, and collection trucks create noise, odor, and litter. In Case B, the collection of a price or tax per bag of garbage is not possible at all, either because it would cause difficulties of administration, costs of compliance, or an overabundance of illegal dumping on the back roads or vacant lots.[6] Indeed, most local governments collect garbage for free.[7] This zero price can avoid illegal dumping and administrative cost, but it leaves households with insufficient incentive to reduce waste by demanding that firms design and produce goods with less packaging and greater recyclability. In this case, government policy can be used to present firms directly with the right incentives to reduce packaging and to increase recyclability. Thus, different policy packages can be used to induce the same socially optimum outcome. Cases C and D involve a failure in the recycling market, and Case E considers a manufacturer "take-back" requirement. In Case F, where a subsidy to the firm's choice of "recyclability" is not feasible, we show that again the same optimum can be achieved with a tax on packaging and subsidy to the consumer's choice of recycling. The choice among these alternative but equivalent policy packages can depend on their relative administrative feasibilities.

---

[5] The idea of design for recyclability appears in Henstock [12], and modifications to packaging are suggested in Stilwell *et al.* [30]. Further discussion appears in Denison and Ruston [6]. As described below, we model the choice among existing designs with different degrees of recyclability, not the uncertain process of research to develop new designs.

[6] Jenkins [14] and Repetto *et al.* [25] indicate that illegal dumping can be addressed by other policies, and they calculate the welfare gain from charging a curbside fee equal to the marginal social cost of disposal. When illegal dumping is a problem, however, Fullerton and Kinnaman [10] show that the optimal curbside fee may be close to zero. In a case study of an actual curbside fee program, Fullerton and Kinnaman [11] provide evidence on the amount of dumping, and show that administrative cost may outweigh any gain in efficiency from charging a price equal to the social cost of disposal.

[7] Sixteen towns with unit pricing are studied in EPA [35]. Recent empirical work on unit pricing includes Jenkins [14], Hong, Adams, and Love [13], Reschovsky and Stone [24], and Miranda *et al.* [17]. The great majority of towns still charge no price per bag of garbage.

We analyze enough of the policies listed in Table I to clarify how the model would be used to analyze any of them. For each market failure, we show how alternative policies can correct it. In a later section, we extend the model to consider heterogeneous goods with different degrees of packaging, recyclability, and toxicity. The model could also be extended to consider trade between jurisdictions with different disposal costs, or households with different incomes.

I. A SIMPLE GENERAL EQUILIBRIUM MODEL

The model in this paper is designed to convey basic intuition about materials flows in general equilibrium from the producer to the household and possibly back to the producer before disposal or reuse in production. Initially, therefore, we build a simple static model with one type of household and one commodity.[8]

A. Model Assumptions

Our simple economy has n identical individuals or households that buy a single composite commodity q. This product possesses two "attributes": a degree of recyclability ρ and a packaging rate θ. We can interpret ρ as the fraction of the weight of the product that can be recycled at the end of its useful life, and θ as the weight of the box and other protection that accompanies each unit of the product. In order to focus on the recycling of the product itself, we assume that the packaging cannot be recycled.

Households dispose of solid waste either in the form of garbage collection g or in the form of recycling r. The generation of g is given by the household's technology:

$$g = g(q, \rho, \theta), \tag{1}$$

where $g(.,.,.)$ is continuous and quasi-concave, with first derivatives $g_q > 0$, $g_\rho < 0$, and $g_\theta > 0$. That is, garbage collection g increases with the quantity of consumption q, all else equal. Garbage would decrease if the product had more recyclability ρ, or increase if it had more packaging θ. The generation of recycling is given by:[9]

$$r = r(q, \rho), \tag{2}$$

where $r(.,.)$ is continuous and quasi-concave, with first derivatives $r_q > 0$, $r_\rho > 0$. All else equal, recycling increases with the quantity q and increases with recyclability ρ.

---

[8] Smith [28] presents a dynamic model where disposal creates a stock externality. Our model here is similar to one in Fullerton and Kinnaman [10], but we add the two attributes as well as other contributions listed above. The model has only one period, but more "recyclability" could be interpreted as more "durability": a product that lasts longer will generate less disposal per period. To put it another way, longer continued use is like recycling and reusing the product.

[9] The amount of packaging θ could easily enter the recycling generation function, since people reuse boxes for storing or shipping other items and brown paper bags for wrapping postal packages. This added realism would come at the expense of some added clutter, however, and it would not change the basic insights below. We focus on how disposal costs affect recycling of the product, and the amount of packaging, without mixing the two concepts together.

Household utility then depends on the amount of this good, q, purchased in the market, and on the amount of another good, h, produced and consumed at home. In order to capture the possibility of a negative externality from others' garbage, we assume that each household's utility also depends on $G = ng$, the total amount of garbage generated in the economy. Utility then is

$$u = u(q, h, G), \qquad (3)$$

with first derivatives $u_q > 0$, $u_h > 0$, $u_G \leq 0$. Later, with heterogeneous commodities, we can include different externalities from hazardous and nonhazardous wastes. In this formulation, households do not care about recyclabllity or packaging *per se*. Instead, those attributes affect waste generation (through Eqs. (1) and (2)) and thus disposal costs. In other words, ρ and θ do not affect households directly through the utility function but indirectly through the resource constraint.[10]

Competitive firms produce output q under conditions of constant returns to scale, using inputs of resources k_q and recycled materials r. In equilibrium, the firm's use of r must match the household's generation of it. In its production decision, the firm also chooses the product's recyclability ρ and packaging rate θ. We could think of production with three outputs (q, ρ, θ) as a function of two inputs (k_q, r). Instead, we just move the two attributes over to the other side of the equation. Thus the production function is[11]

$$q = f(k_q, r, \rho, \theta), \qquad (4)$$

where some first derivatives are $f_k > 0$, $f_r > 0$, $f_\rho < 0$. As usual, output increases with greater use of either input k_q or r. In order to make the output more recyclable, however, the firm needs to use up some inputs. Given a total use of k_q and r, therefore, more ρ implies less output q. With regard to θ, we consider the cost of producing and distributing the product safely to the consumer. At low levels of packaging, the firm might need to replace broken units or pay for damages resulting from impurities. Thus more packaging can free inputs for use in producing output ($f_\theta > 0$). At higher levels of θ, on the other hand, more packaging can use up resources unnecessarily ($f_\theta < 0$). Thus we assume that production cost is minimized at a point θ^* where $f_\theta = 0$, as shown in Fig. 1.

In the garbage collection industry, firms use resources k_g as the only input, with constant returns to scale, so the production function is linear:

$$g = \gamma k_g. \qquad (5)$$

---

[10] In general, packaging may serve as a form of advertising and promotion, as well as protection and transportation. Packaging θ could enter the demand for q, or directly into utility. Also, recycling itself could provide utility, as in Mrozek [19]. Instead we focus on incentives. These suggestions would introduce extra terms into results below but would not alter our basic insights.

[11] Three comments about this formulation. First, production does not directly generate any solid wastes, air pollution, or liquid effluents. Those topics are thoroughly treated elsewhere, as in Baumol and Oates [2]. The concern here is with post-consumption waste and disposal. In some ways, however, θ can be viewed as direct waste, skipping the rest of the product life-cycle through the consumer. Second, Fullerton and Kinnaman [10] consider extraction of virgin materials and associated externalities, but these are omitted here to avoid clutter. A straightforward extension of this model could integrate the extraction phase of the product life-cycle. Third, although we omit transactions costs *per se*, we do not omit the recyclers' costs of collection, sorting, cleaning, and other processing. These activities are incorporated in the production function f which specifies the transformation of r into q.

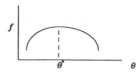

FIG. 1.   The effect on net output (f) from packaging (θ).

The good h is produced from home use of time and resource, k_h:

$$h = k_h, \tag{6}$$

which can be interpreted as leisure. Finally, the model is closed by the resource constraint:[12]

$$k = k_q + k_g + k_h, \tag{7}$$

where k denotes a fixed total resource such as capital, labor, or land. No distinction between labor and capital is necessary to obtain our results below about optimal policies toward households or firms regarding garbage, recycling, packaging, or recyclability.

B. Outcome in the Social Planning Model

The social planner's goal is to maximize utility of a representative household Eq. (3), subject to the resource constraint Eq. (7), production functions Eq. (4–6), and waste generation technologies Eq. (1–2). We maximize the appropriate Lagrangian and use first-order conditions to show:[13]

$$\frac{u_q}{u_h} = \frac{1}{f_k} + \left(\frac{1}{\gamma} - \frac{nu_G}{u_h}\right)g_q + \left(-\frac{f_r}{f_k}\right)r_q, \tag{8a}$$

$$-\frac{f_\rho}{f_k} + \left(\frac{1}{\gamma} - \frac{nu_G}{u_h}\right)g_\rho + \left(-\frac{f_r}{f_k}\right)r_\rho = 0, \tag{8b}$$

$$-\frac{f_\theta}{f_k} + \left(\frac{1}{\gamma} - \frac{nu_G}{u_h}\right)g_\theta = 0. \tag{8c}$$

All of these expressions employ the marginal social cost per unit of garbage, which we call MSC_g, defined to include both the direct resource cost ($1/\gamma$) and the external cost ($-nu_G/u_h$). This external cost includes the negative externality ($u_G < 0$) on all n households. We will use these equations below, but the first just says that the marginal utility from another unit of q would equal the marginal

---

[12] Also, we could have said that household recycling activities require some time and resources for handling and storage, as in Wertz [37], Morris and Holthausen [18], or Choe and Fraser [4]. Then k_r could enter the resource constraint Eq. (7) and the recycling function Eq. (2). Again, however, this variation does not alter the basic insights below. In any case, these costs are similar in nature to costs of transactions in any market: time to get to the store to buy q, or time needed to dispose of g.

[13] We assume convexity, with no corner solutions, for a unique global optimum.

social cost of producing *and* disposing of it. The second condition says that recyclability ρ should increase until its marginal resource cost offsets the savings in disposal costs. Similarly, Eq. (8c) says that society cannot gain from alterations in packaging θ. Note that f_θ must be positive, along the upward sloping portion of the curve in Fig. 1. That is, optimal packaging is below the point that minimizes production cost, to account for disposal cost.

This model captures a full general equilibrium, since prices and quantities are determined using demand and supply simultaneously for several different "goods" including recyclability ρ, and packaging θ, as well as garbage collection g, recycling r, and output q. An extension below considers many outputs q_i where $i = 1, \ldots, m$. It is a "first-best" model, however, because it does not incorporate any other distorting taxes on labor supply or capital. To achieve this social optimum in the decentralized economy described next, the government can use lump sum taxes to raise any revenue needed to pay for subsidies to garbage collection or recycling.[14] Similarly, any revenue from a tax on packaging or on garbage disposal is returned to consumers in lump sum form. This assumption considerably simplifies the analysis, because we do not need to keep track of those lump sum taxes or transfers: any exogenous change to income of the consumer will affect the quantities demanded, and the *values* of the marginal utilities (such as u_q or u_h), but do not affect the appearance of the first-order conditions. Each of these equations simply states that the marginal benefits of having more of the good equals the marginal cost, and such an equation still holds with any lump sum tax or transfer.

While we do not include distorting taxes, we do include a simple treatment of other possible market failures due to illegal dumping, transactions costs, enforcement problems, or the administrative cost of trying to collect a tax on a tax-base that is difficult to measure. For simplicity, we consider only two extremes: the sum of these costs in a particular market is either zero or prohibitive. Thus, we do not specify a particular form for these costs. In one case we assume "perfect markets" in the sense that the firm can charge a price and the government can charge a tax per unit of garbage collection, with no administrative cost. In other cases the collection of that price or tax is impossible, and we do not need to specify whether it is because of transactions costs, fear of illegal dumping, or administrative costs. We then find alternative policies that can restore the first-best allocation (Eqs. (8)). Note that when the market "fails" in this sense, and the price or tax per unit of garbage is not collected, then illegal dumping and administrative costs are again zero.

C. Outcome in the Decentralized Model

Now we turn to the case of private markets, where government can provide various tax incentives to households or firms. In particular, the household budget is affected by a tax or subsidy on each good:

$$(k - k_h) + (p_r - t_r)r = (p_q + t_q)q + (p_g + t_g)g. \tag{9}$$

[14] Many "second-best" general equilibrium models assume that lump sum taxes are not available, and that government must use distorting taxes to meet an explicit revenue requirement. A review of this large literature appears in Auerbach [1].

The household owns k of resources and sells $(k - k_h)$ to the market at a price of one (since k is numeraire). The household earns p_r for each unit of recycling, which might be taxed at rate t_r per unit. Any tax rate may be positive or negative. With this income, the household can buy the consumption good at price p_q with per-unit tax rate t_q. For each unit of garbage, the household might have to pay price p_g and tax t_g.

Firms' decisions are also affected by taxes. Producers of q maximize profits:

$$\pi = p_q q - p_r r - k_q - q \rho t_\rho - q \theta t_\theta, \tag{10}$$

where t_θ is the tax per unit of packaging, on a measure such as weight, and t_ρ is the tax per unit of recyclability. This tax may be difficult to implement, as discussed more below, but could apply to the percentage of the weight of the item that satisfies prespecified criteria for recyclability.[15] To investigate permit requirements or other quantity restrictions, such as a recycled content standard, Eq. (10) would be maximized subject to a constraint on r per unit production of q.

Individual firms are price-takers, but in the aggregate they face "demand" schedules for ρ and θ that are reflected in the price p_q that consumers are willing to pay. If consumers have to pay for garbage disposal, then they will be willing to pay more for a product with greater recyclability $(\partial p_q / \partial \rho \geq 0)$ or for a product with less packaging $(\partial p_q / \partial \theta \leq 0)$. We undertake the appropriate maximization and use first-order conditions to show

$$p_q = \frac{1}{f_k} + \rho t_\rho + \theta t_\theta, \tag{11}$$

$$p_r = \frac{f_r}{f_k}, \tag{12}$$

$$\frac{\partial p_q}{\partial \rho} \cdot q = q t_\rho - \frac{f_\rho}{f_k}, \tag{13}$$

$$\frac{\partial p_q}{\partial \theta} \cdot q = q t_\theta - \frac{f_\theta}{f_k}. \tag{14}$$

With competition, the sales price just covers resource cost plus taxes per unit of output. Firms use more r until its marginal product is offset by its cost to the firm.

In the garbage collection industry, competitive firms maximize profits $(p_g g - p_k k_g)$, where $g = \gamma k_g$ and $p_k = 1$, so $p_g = 1/\gamma$. This price just covers cost.

In this decentralized economy, the household maximizes utility in Eq. (3) subject to budget constraint Eq. (9) by choosing h, q, and attributes ρ and θ (which together determine g and r). These choices are available because competing firms offer different designs (even though the equilibrium with identical households will

---

[15] For example, the electronic news service *Greenwire* (May 3, 1995) reports that "cars built before the 1995 model year are about 75% recyclable; the remaining 25% is sent to landfills. New cars such as the Ford Contour and the Chrysler Cirrus are 80% recyclable, and the goal is to make all vehicles built by the year 2000 85% recyclable."

involve a single outcome for attributes ρ and θ).[16] Individual consumers are price-takers, but in the aggregate they face "supply" schedules for ρ and θ that are reflected in the price p_q for which firms are willing to sell. If firms devote more resources to "green design," then they will have to charge more for a product with greater recyclability or for a product with better packaging. Also, the household's optimization ignores the impact of its own g on the utility of others through the increment to total G.

Maximization of the appropriate Lagrangian yields first-order conditions in terms of the prices and tax rates faced by households, but we use Eqs. (11)–(14) above to replace each price with the corresponding cost of production:

$$\frac{u_q}{u_h} = \frac{1}{f_k} + \rho t_\rho + \theta t_\theta + t_q + \left(\frac{1}{\gamma} + t_g\right)g_q + \left(-\frac{f_r}{f_k} + t_r\right)r_q, \qquad (15a)$$

$$qt_\rho - \frac{f_\rho}{f_k} + \left(\frac{1}{\gamma} + t_g\right)g_\rho + \left(-\frac{f_r}{f_k} + t_r\right)r_\rho = 0, \qquad (15b)$$

$$qt_\theta - \frac{f_\theta}{f_k} + \left(\frac{1}{\gamma} + t_g\right)g_\theta = 0. \qquad (15c)$$

These expressions reflect a general equilibrium where all firms are on their supply curves and all households are on their demand curves for each commodity and attribute. The first condition says that marginal utility is set equal to the "full effective price" of consumption. For each unit of q the consumer must pay the firm's cost in terms of resources and taxes, plus the private cost of disposal.

Expressions (15) are written in a form comparable to the social optimum conditions in Eqs. (8). To check on efficiency of private markets with no government interference, suppose that tax rates in Eqs. (15) were all set to zero. In this case, it is easy to see that the private market does not yield the social optimum, because the externality u_G appears in the social conditions Eqs. (8) but not in the market conditions Eqs. (15). In addition, private firms might not be able to charge a price for garbage collection at all, if transactions costs are high or households can avoid the charges by dumping in commercial dumpsters or vacant lots. If local governments must provide collection for free, then households face neither the direct cost $(1/\gamma)$ nor the external cost $(-nu_G/u_h)$.

II. MARKET FAILURES AND CORRECTIONS

In this section, we consider several possible market failures. In each case, we solve for the tax rates of Pigou [22] that induce private behavior in Eqs. (15) to match the social optimum in Eqs. (8). Assuming this optimum is unique, it might be achieved using several different combinations of taxes and subsidies.

Case A: Negative Externality with Unit-Pricing of Garbage

In the simplest case, suppose that competitive waste disposal firms just break even, so, $p_g = 1/\gamma$, and that consumers pay $(p_g + t_g)$ per unit of garbage col-

---

[16] An important assumption is full information. Direct regulations might be proposed by those who would not rely on consumers to know product characteristics and to signal their preferences.

lected. Then Eq. (15c) can be made to match Eq. (8c) if $t_g = -nu_G/u_h$ and $t_\theta = 0$. Next, Eq. (15b) matches Eq. (8b) if $t - \rho$ and t_r are zero. Finally, Eq. (15a) matches Eq. (8a) if $t_q = 0$ as well. In other words, if consumers have to pay the full marginal social cost of disposal MSC_g, then they will induce firms to design products with the right combinations of ρ and θ. In this case the government does not do anything about household recycling, or consumption, or about the producer's choice of inputs. The tax on garbage corrects for the only externality.

Case B: Free Garbage Collection

   Because of illegal dumping, or tax collection costs, many communities do not or cannot charge for garbage collection. We therefore consider the case where $p_g + t_g = 0$. Free garbage collection means that collection firms are receiving a per-unit subsidy equal to the price. In this case the consumer does not care about disposal cost and is *not* willing to pay any extra for greater recyclability or for green design of packaging. Manufacturers do not receive those market signals from consumers, but they can still be given the right signals by appropriate taxes and subsidies. Eq. (15c) will match Eq. (8c) if the tax rate on packaging is $t_\theta = (1/\gamma - nu_G/u_h)g_\theta/q$. This tax is $MSC_g \cdot g_\theta/q$, the marginal disposal cost per unit of output from a change in θ. This tax is positive, to induce firms to reduce packaging which contributes to direct resource costs and external costs of disposal. Then Eq. (15b) will match Eq. (8b) if $t_r = 0$ and $t_\rho = (1/\gamma - nu_G/u_h)g_\rho/q = MSC_q \cdot g_\rho/q$. This tax rate is negative and reflects the cost *savings* from a change in ρ that reduces disposal costs per unit of output.

   Finally, Eq. (15a) matches Eq. (8a) if

$$t_q = \left(\frac{1}{\gamma} - \frac{nu_G}{u_h} \right) \left(g_q - \frac{\rho g_\rho + \theta g_\theta}{q} \right),$$

which equals $MSC_g \cdot g_q - \rho t_\rho - \theta t_\theta$. The first term looks a lot like the proposal for "disposal-content charges"[17] since it collects the cost of disposal of the extra g from an extra q. The other terms correct for the effects of other instruments on the price of output. The subsidy t_π is intended to increase ρ, but it also would reduce the cost of production, reduce output price, and increase the quantity demanded. Thus the output tax takes back that implicit subsidy per unit of output. Similarly, in the final term, the output tax gives back the effect of the packaging tax on the output price. The result is a system that just discourages packaging, and not output generally. The sign of the overall tax rate depends on the relative size of the recyclability and packaging parameters.

   This case where consumers pay nothing for disposal provides a coherent rationale for a tax on packaging and a subsidy to designs that improve recyclability.[18] It does not include a subsidy to recycling, since recycling has no externality (but see

---

[17] See, for example, Menell [15]. In this case, the output tax is combined with a subsidy to recyclability, an example of what Fullerton [9] calls a "two-part instrument."

[18] These policies directed at the firm are enough to reach the social optimum in this model, because the firm chooses packaging and recyclability. If household garbage and recycling also depended on effort at the household level, as in Choe and Fraser [4], then an additional instrument would have to be directed at the behavior of those households.

Case F below). This "upstream" policy package involves three different instruments (t_θ, t_p, t_q) that each contain a number of terms, so it entails substantial
information requirements, but it may still be the most feasible policy if illegal
dumping or collection costs prevent the use of the simpler "downstream" policy
with a single fee per unit trash (t_g).

Case C: No Payment for Recycling

To deal with possible market failures separately, we return to the case with no
failure in the market for garbage collection (so $p_g = 1/\gamma$ and $t_g = -nu_G/u_h$) and
instead consider a failure in the market for recycling collection. The price p_r paid
by the firm for its input of recycling may be close to zero, and the cost of counting
out the pennies per pound of glass or plastic recycling may outweigh the value of
the material. We do not model these transactions costs explicitly, but suppose they
preclude the formation of a private market for recycling. Households would then
place this recyclable material into the garbage for the landfill, unless the municipality collects curbside recycling for free. Effectively, the municipal subsidy matches
the price, so households face $(p_r - t_r) = 0$. A remaining problem is that households do not get paid for recycling, so they do not demand enough recyclability.

This problem can be corrected by a subsidy $t_p = -f_r r_p/f_k q = -p_r r_p/q$, which
reflects the marginal social value of the extra recycling generated by the change
in ρ. The optimal tax rate on packaging in this case is $t_\theta = 0$, since packaging is
effectively discouraged by the optimal charge for garbage. We still need to impose
consumption tax $t_q = (f_r/f_k)(\rho r_p/q - r_q)$, which equals $-\rho t_p - p_r r_q$. The first
term collects a tax per unit of output to correct for the fact that t_p is supposed to
subsidize recyclability and not output generally. The second term is the opposite
sign, to reflect the marginal social value of the recycling generated by the extra q.

Case D: No Payment for Recycling **and** Free Garbage Collection

The purpose of separate Cases B and C is to prepare for this case where
households face no price either for garbage collection or for recycling ($p_g + t_g = 0$
and $p_r - t_r = 0$). Municipal subsidies enable free curbside collection of garbage
and recycling, so the household is totally freed from worrying about solid waste
disposal. Even though the model now includes multiple constraints and market
failures, it also includes multiple policy instruments. Government can still correct
these market failures. The optimal tax rate on recyclability is

$$t_p = \left(\frac{1}{\gamma} - \frac{nu_G}{u_h}\right)\frac{g_\rho}{q} + \left(-\frac{f_r r_p}{f_k q}\right),$$

which is exactly the sum of the subsidies from the two cases above. The rationale
for policies to encourage "green design" is doubly strong in this case. The tax on
packaging is still $t_\theta = (1/\gamma - nu_G/u_h)g_\theta/q$, from Case B, because it was zero in
Case C. The tax per unit of output is also the sum of the tax rates from Cases B
and C, and can be written as $t_q = MSC_g \cdot g_q - p_r r_q - \rho t_p - \theta t_\theta$. The first two
terms reflect the costs and benefits of the extra disposal and recycling generated by
an extra unit of output. The other two terms correct the output price for the
subsidy on recyclability and the tax on packaging.

Case E: Manufacturer Take-Back Requirement

Table I also includes a proposal to "mandate manufacturer take-back and recycling of products." The idea is that firms would have the right incentives to reduce packaging and to design for recyclability if they had to dispose of all their own packaging and products. Firms might *choose* to use fewer different types of plastic, and to use fewer one-way fasteners, if they had to take apart and recycle their own product. This idea has been at least partially implemented in Germany's Green Dot program.[19]

This proposal can be illustrated with modifications to our model. First, the household does not pay for garbage disposal and recycling, so its budget constraint changes to

$$k - k_h = (p_q + t_q)q. \tag{16}$$

The take-back requirement shifts responsibility for garbage disposal and recycling to the firm, so the profit function becomes

$$\pi = p_q q - k_q - (p_g + t_g)g - t_r r - q\rho t_\rho - q\theta t_\theta. \tag{17}$$

We could set all of these tax rates to zero for the case with *just* the take-back requirement, to see if private markets match the social optimum. If not, we can then find what additional tax instrument might be necessary.

Into this profit function, we substitute the firm's production function for q and the solid waste generation technologies $g = g(q, \rho, \theta)$ and $r = r(q, \rho)$. We also need to add the constraint that this r generated by households is the same as the r that enters the production function. The firm maximizes profits subject to this constraint, and it determines the amount of garbage and recycling it will receive by its choice of q, ρ, and θ. Since the firm gets to use the resulting r back in production, we find that it faces a shadow price (the Lagrangian on the constraint) equal to what the market price would have been ($p_r = f_r/f_k$, in Eq. (12)). Since the firm is also setting all variables that determine g, it will face all the correct market signals if it has to pay the social marginal cost of garbage disposal. In other words, we find that optimality requires the firm to pay $p_g = 1/\gamma$ and $t_g = -nu_G/u_h$. All other tax rates are zero.

With the take-back requirement, plus $t_g = -nu_G/u_h$, the firm has all the right incentives. This solution does not require any extra tax on packaging, disposal-content charges, recycled-content standards, or subsidies for "green design" that would encourage recyclability. These results are intuitive, given the nature of the model, but an important corollary result is that the "take-back requirement" by itself is not enough. Even a firm that pays the market price for garbage disposal does not account for all social costs if u_G is not zero.

---

[19] Transaction costs could become important. In Germany, manufacturers do not take back the packaging themselves but subscribe to the "Duales System Deutschland" (DSD). The firm puts a green dot on their packages and contracts with a recycling company that collects all packages with green dots. See Rousso and Shah [26].

144   FULLERTON AND WU

Case F: A Deposit-Refund System

Only relative prices affect behavior in this general equilibrium model, so a tax on one activity may be equivalent to a combination of taxes and subsidies on other activities. The choice between these policies can depend on which combination is more easily administered and enforced. The fee per unit of household disposal in Case A would require the difficult enforcement of antidumping laws. That problem is avoided in Case B, with the same optimal outcome, by setting the disposal fee to zero and instead using a tax on the firm's packaging, subsidy to recyclability, and tax on output.

Our final case is similar to Case B, where the disposal fee is zero ($p_g + t_g = 0$), and instruments are directed at firms instead of households. But suppose the subsidy is not feasible for "recyclability." That concept may be difficult to quantify. With $t_\rho = 0$, the same outcome can again be obtained, with the use of a subsidy to recycling. The optimal tax on packaging from Case B is unchanged at $t_\theta = (1/\gamma - nu_G/u_h)g_\theta/q$, which equals $MSC_g \cdot g_\theta/q$, the marginal disposal cost per unit of output from a change in θ. Then the subsidy to recycling is $t_r = (1/\gamma - nu_G/u_h)g_\rho/r_\rho$, which equals $MSC_g \cdot g_\rho/r_\rho$. Finally,

$$t_q = \left(\frac{1}{\gamma} - \frac{nu_G}{u_h} \right) \left(g_q - \frac{g_\rho r_q}{r_\rho} - \frac{\theta g_\theta}{q} \right),$$

which equals $MSC_g \cdot g_q - r_q t_r - \theta t_\theta$. The first term is positive to account for the disposal cost of output, and the second term is positive to correct output price for the subsidy to recycling. This term is the "deposit" of a deposit-refund system: this tax on output is given back if the item is recycled. Only the third term of this output tax is negative, to correct for the tax on packaging.

As usual, the "refund" is intended to encourage recycling and thereby avoid the socially costly disposal of waste. In this model, however, the rate of subsidy depends on g_ρ and r_ρ, so it encourages design for recyclability. Profit-seeking firms change their design because of the demand for recyclability by consumers who want to get the subsidy for recycled items.

III. HETEROGENEOUS COMMODITIES AND OTHER EXTENSIONS

This section will consider several extensions to the basic model. First, suppose the utility function in Eq. (3) is modified to include a vector of commodities q_i, where $i = 1, \ldots, m$. Each good then requires its own attributes ρ_i and θ_i, its own garbage generation function in Eq. (1), its own recycling generation function in Eq. (2), and its own production function in Eq. (4). In the simplest case, each output is produced using a recycled amount of the same good ("closed-loop" recycling). Total garbage is the sum from all consumption goods, and each industry may face its own set of tax rates.

This extension involves keeping track of more goods, but results are remarkably similar to those above. As long as only total garbage G enters utility, the first-best outcome can still be obtained by a single fee per unit of garbage (Case A). If illegal dumping or collection costs prohibit the use of a price or tax per bag of garbage, then the first-best allocation can still be achieved (Case B), but only by meeting substantial information requirements since the solution then requires many policy instruments. The optimal tax on packaging still looks like $t_\theta = (1/\gamma - nu_G/u_h)g_\theta/q$, except subscripts are added to q and g_θ. All other tax rates in Section II are modified by adding similar subscripts. Thus, in Case B, each industry would need a unique tax on packaging, subsidy to recyclability, and tax on output. This complicated result points to an advantage of the "take-back" rule (Case E), since each industry then deals only with its own packaging and with recycling its own product.

A second extension would replace closed-loop recycling and allow a good to be recycled as an input to production of a different good.[20] In Dinan's [7] model, a tax on one industry's use of virgin materials encourages that industry to use recycled input, but it does not encourage other industries to use this output as recycled input. Similarly, in our model, the subsidy to recycling (in Case F) would have to be provided to all possible users of a recycled good. In contrast, the subsidy to recyclability (in Cases B, C, and D) would only have to be provided to the original producer. A question, however, is whether one kind of "recyclability" would make the good equally reusable in all other industries.

In a third extension, suppose the m goods have different toxicity. Batteries in household garbage are more damaging than vegetable matter. In this case, the utility function must be modified to include a vector of negative externalities (and not just one externality from total garbage). This complication means that the first-best cannot be achieved by a single fee per bag of garbage: a different fee must apply to each component of the household's waste. These different disposal fees could be impossible to administer, providing some reason to use policies directed at firms. The optimum in this model can still be achieved with an appropriate differential tax (that is, deposit) on each output and subsidy (refund) to anyone who recycles it, or a subsidy to recyclable designs, as long as the extra recyclability helps all others who reuse that good.

In a fourth extension, not undertaken here, the model could be modified to consider heterogeneous jurisdictions. States might differ in terms of natural endowments, and they might trade in various outputs, recycled goods, and types of waste.[21] A jurisdiction with abundant land suitable for waste disposal would charge a lower disposal fee (Case A), and import waste, even accounting for all the social costs of disposal at that location. The optimal disposal fees would differ by location, however, so this solution could *not* be replicated by a system of taxes and subsidies on producing firms as in Case B.

Fifth, the model could allow for altruism by households who recycle even without compensation, simply because they feel good about helping the environment. This modification would presumably reduce the optimal level of policy intervention, but it could make the optimal policies more complicated.

Finally, the model could be extended to allow for a number of other possibilities. Markets could be added to consider tradable permits, and other quantity constraints could be used to represent command and control regulations such as recycled-content standards. A model with more significant modifications such as

---

[20] *Greenwire* (March 25, 1996) reports that Ford uses recycled drink containers in its door padding, grille reinforcements, and luggage-rack side rails. The top cover of some of Chrysler's instrument panels are made from recycled compact disks, water bottles, and computer parts.

[21] See, for example, Copeland [5].

other distorting taxes could be used to solve for a second-best revenue-raising system of taxes and subsidies. Or, the model could be modified to account for heterogeneous households at different levels of income, in order to analyze distributional effects of environmental policies.

IV. CONCLUSION

The advantage of this general equilibrium model is that it encompasses the entire life-cycle of each product from the design phase to production, consumption, and disposal. It also captures each price paid along the way, so a tax at one stage of production or sale has an equivalent counterpart at another stage of consumption or disposal. We show conditions where the efficient solution can be obtained either by a "downstream" tax on waste disposal or by an equivalent "upstream" tax on production processes that give rise to the subsequent waste.

If market signals can be corrected by the appropriate disposal charges (Case A), then consumers will induce firms to use less packaging and to design products for easier subsequent recycling. If market signals cannot be corrected in this way, however, then welfare can be improved by policies directed at the firm. The solution might involve a subsidy to recycling (Case F), or if that is not possible, a subsidy to recyclability (Cases B, C, and D). In the extended model, with disaggregate commodities of differing toxicity, separate output taxes and recycling subsidies can deal with hazardous and nonhazardous generation of waste. With other modifications, the model can be used to compare virtually all of the 34 policy options listed in Table I.

The reason for comparing all of these options is that some may be implemented more easily than others. The difficult enforcement of penalties on improper waste disposal is not necessary, if the equivalent outcome can be obtained by a tax (deposit) on all output in combination with a subsidy (rebate) on all proper waste disposal. Indeed, the objections of municipalities to unit pricing of curbside garbage collection may be motivated not by a lack of appreciation for the scarcity of space in landfills, but instead just by these problems of implementation. Any charges for household waste might have to deal with 100 million taxpaying units, while equivalent instruments could apply to substantially fewer firms. If the downstream tax on waste disposal cannot be administered effectively, this paper shows how to derive the equivalent upstream tax on packaging and subsidy to recyclability.

REFERENCES

1. A. J. Auerbach, The theory of excess burden and optimal taxation, *in* "Handbook of Public Economics," (Alan J. Auerbach and M. Feldstein, Eds.), Vol. 1, Elsevier, Amsterdam (1985).
2. W. J. Baumol and Wallace E. Oates, "The Theory of Environmental Policy," 2nd ed., Cambridge University Press, New York (1988).
3. P. Bohm, "Deposit-Refund Systems: Theory and Applications to Environmental, Conservation, and Consumer Policy," Johns Hopkins University Press, Baltimore, MD (1981).
4. C. Choe and I. Fraser, "An Economic Analysis of Household Waste Management," Department of Economics, La Trobe University, Bundoora, Victoria, Australia (1998).
5. B. R. Copeland, International trade in waste products in the presence of illegal disposal, *J. Environ. Econom. Management* **20**, 143–162 (1991).

6. R. A. Denison and J. Ruston, "Recycling and Incineration: Evaluating the Choices," Island Press, Washington, DC (1990).

7. T. M. Dinan, Economic efficiency effects of alternate policies for reducing waste disposal, *J. Environ. Econom. Management* **25**, 242–256 (1993).

8. I. M. Dobbs, Litter and waste management: Disposal taxes versus user charges, *Canad. J. Econom.* **24**, 221–227 (1991).

9. D. Fullerton, Environmental levies and distortionary taxation: Comment, *Amer. Econom. Rev.* **87**, 245–251 (1997).

10. D. Fullerton and T. C. Kinnaman, Garbage, recycling, and illicit burning or dumping, *J. Environ. Econom. Management* **29**, 78–91 (1995).

11. D. Fullerton and T. C. Kinnaman, Household responses to pricing garbage by the bag, *Amer. Econom. Rev.* **86**, 971–984 (1996).

12. M. E. Henstock, "Design for Recyclability," The Institute of Metals, London (1988).

13. S. Hong, R. M. Adams, and H. A. Love, An economic analysis of household recycling of solid wastes: The case of Portland, Oregon, *J. Environ. Econom. Management* **25**, 136–146 (1993).

14. R. R. Jenkins, "The Economics of Solid Waste Reduction," Edward Elgar, Brookfield, VT (1993).

15. P. S. Menell, Beyond the throwaway society: An incentive approach to regulating municipal solid waste, *Ecology Law Quart.* **17**, 655–739 (1990).

16. A. K. Miedema, Fundamental economic comparisons of solid waste policy options, *Resour. Energy* **5**, 21–43 (1983).

17. M. L. Miranda, J. W. Everett, D. Blume, and B. A. Roy, Jr., Market-based incentives and residential municipal solid waste, *J. Policy Anal. Management* **13**, 681–698 (1994).

18. G. E. Morris and D. M. Holthausen, The economics of household solid waste generation and disposal, *J. Environ. Econom. Management* **26**, 215–234 (1994).

19. J. R. Mrozek, "Beverage Container Recycling: Incentives versus Attitudes as Explanations of Behavior," working paper, Georgia Institute of Technology, Atlanta (1995).

20. K. Palmer and M. Walls, Optimal policies for solid waste disposal: Taxes, subsidies, and standards, *J. Public Econom.* **65**, 193–205 (1997).

21. K. Palmer, H. Sigman, and M. Walls, The cost of reducing municipal solid waste, *J. Environ. Econom. Management* **33**, 128–150 (1997).

22. A. C. Pigou, "The Economics of Welfare," 4th ed., Macmillan, London (1932).

23. Project 88—Round II," A Public Policy Study Sponsored by Senator Timothy E. Wirth and Senator John Heinz, Directed by Robert N. Stavins, Washington, DC (1991).

24. J. D. Reschovsky and S. E. Stone, Market incentives to encourage household waste recycling: Paying for what you throw away, *J. Policy Anal. Management* **13**, 120–139 (1994).

25. R. Repetto, R. C. Dower, R. Jenkins, and J. Geoghegan, "Green Fees: How a Tax Shift Can Work for the Environment and the Economy," World Resources Institute, Washington, DC (1992).

26. A. S. Rousso, and S. P. Shah, Packaging taxes and recycling incentives: The German green dot program, *National Tax J.* **47**, 689–701 (1994).

27. H. Sigman, A comparison of public policies for lead recycling, *RAND J. Econom.* **26**, 452–478 (1995).

28. V. L. Smith, Dynamics of waste accumulation: Disposal versus recycling, *Quart. J. Econom.* **86**, 600–616 (1972).

29. R. N. Stavins, Transaction costs and tradeable permits, *J. Environ. Econom. Management* **29**, 133–148 (1995).

30. E. J. Stilwell, R. C. Canty, P. W. Kopf, and A. M. Montrone, "Packaging for the Environment: A Partnership for Progress," A. D. Little, Inc., New York (1991).

31. A. M. Sullivan, Policy options for toxic disposal: Laissez-faire, subsidization, and enforcement, *J. Environ. Econom. Management* **14**, 58–71 (1987).

32. U.S. Congress, Congressional Budget Office, "Federal Options for Reducing Waste Disposal," U.S. Government Printing Office, 1991 0-304-900 QL 3, Washington, DC (1991).

33. U.S. Congress, Office of Technology Assessment, "Green Products by Design: Choices for a Cleaner Environment," U.S. Government Printing Office, OTA-E-541, Washington, DC (1992).

34. U.S. Environmental Protection Agency, "The Solid Waste Dilemma: An Agenda for Action," EPA Technical Report EPA/530-SW-89-019, Washington, DC (1989).

35. U.S. Environmental Protection Agency, "Charging Households for Waste Collection and Disposals: The Effects of Weight or Volume-Based Pricing on Solid Waste Management, EPA 530-SW-90-047, Washington, DC (1990).

36. U.S. General Accounting Office, "Solid Waste: Tradeoffs Involved in Beverage Container Deposit Legislation," GAO/RCED-91-25, Washington, DC (1990).

37. K. L. Wertz, Economic factors influencing households' production of refuse, *J. Environ. Econom. Management* **2**, 263–272 (1976).

38. M. L. Weitzman, Prices vs. quantities, *Rev. Econom. Stud.* **41**, 477–491 (1974).

[6]

Journal of Urban Economics **48**, 419–442 (2000)

doi:10.1006/juec.2000.2174, available online at http://www.idealibrary.com on **IDE🅰L**®

Garbage and Recycling with Endogenous Local Policy*

Thomas C. Kinnaman

Department of Economics, Bucknell University, Lewisburg, Pennsylvania 17837
E-mail: kinnaman@bucknell.edu

and

Don Fullerton

Department of Economics, University of Texas at Austin, Austin, Texas 78712
E-mail: dfullert@eco.utexas.edu

Received April 6, 1999; revised January 25, 2000

This paper estimates the impact of garbage fees and curbside recycling programs on garbage and recycling amounts. Without correction for endogenous policy, a price per bag of garbage has a negative effect on garbage and a positive cross-price effect on recycling. Correction for endogenous local policy increases the effect of the user fee on garbage and the effect of curbside recycling collection on recycling. Introducing a fee of $1 per bag is estimated to reduce garbage by 412 pounds per person per year (44%), but to increase recycling by only 30 pounds per person per year. © 2000 Academic Press

Most communities in the United States pay for municipal solid waste services using general revenues or monthly fees that do not vary per unit of garbage collected at the curb. Thus households think that more garbage is free. This public provision might be warranted if the service were nonrival, but the marginal cost of collecting and disposing of another unit of garbage is decidedly nonzero. The community must pay for additional labor, truck space, and tipping fees at regional landfills or incinerators.

*We are grateful for suggestions from Jan Brueckner, Gaby Inchauste, Robin Jenkins, Arik Levinson, Debbie Nestor, Ed Olsen, Michael Podolsky, Jon Skinner, Steve Stern, Joe Terza, and anonymous referees. We are also grateful for funding from NSF Grants SES-91-22785 and SBR-94-13334, and from the Bankard Fund at the University of Virginia. This paper is part of NBER's research program in Public Economics. Any opinions expressed are those of the authors and not those of the National Science Foundation or the National Bureau of Economic Research.

419

0094-1190/00 $35.00
Copyright © 2000 by Academic Press
All rights of reproduction in any form reserved.

Similarly, free public provision might be warranted if the service were nonexcludable, but providers can indeed extract a price per unit of garbage collected. An increasing number of communities have begun to sell special stickers or tags that must be attached to any bag of garbage at the curb—or else it will not be collected.

This local policy innovation can have several beneficial effects. The price per bag of garbage can help reduce household generation of garbage that must be put in a landfill, help raise revenue, alleviate budget problems, and allow property tax reductions. It provides incentives for recycling, composting, and even for source reduction—demanding less packaging at stores. Unfortunately, these policies also have costs. The new programs must be advertised, promoted, administered, and enforced. And the price per bag of garbage might induce households to litter or burn their garbage, or dump it in vacant lots.

Many communities have also adopted curbside recycling programs to help deal with their solid waste problems. A curbside recycling program can be expensive to operate, but reduces disposal costs at the landfill and could produce revenue if collected materials are sold.

Both of these local solid waste management policies are still relatively new and more could be known about their effectiveness at reducing garbage and increasing recycling. Communities considering the adoption of curbside recycling and a user fee (price per bag of garbage) could benefit from economic estimates of the incidence of these policies. The U.S. EPA [23] describes case studies of 17 communities with pricing programs, and Jenkins [7, 8] uses a panel of 14 communities to initiate a growing econometric literature that estimates the demand for garbage collection as a function of the price per bag, the presence of a free curbside recycling program, and household demographic characteristics.

Our paper makes three main contributions to this literature. First, we collect original data from a significantly larger cross-section of communities. No existing econometric study uses data with more than 12 communities with a user fee.[1] We started with a list of 32 communities with user fee programs from the U.S EPA [23], and through extensive probing and

---

[1] Jenkins [7, 8] and Repetto *et al.* [17] estimate fixed effects using a monthly panel of 14 communities, 9 with a user fee, for a total of 636 observations. Podolsky and Spiegel [16] use a cross-section of 180 cities, 12 with a user fee. Miranda *et al.* [12] show data from 21 communities before and after implementation of a user fee but do not use econometrics to control for changes in other variables. Other kinds of data have been used as well. Aggregate time series from one city are employed by Efaw and Lanen [3] and Skumatz and Breckinridge [20]. Household surveys with self-reported garbage and recycling behavior appear in Hong, Adams, and Love [5] and Reschovsky and Stone [18]. Fullerton and Kinnaman [4] take direct measures of garbage and recycling weight and volume for 75 households before and after the implementation of a user fee program.

word-of-mouth communications, we expanded this list to include 114 communities with a user fee. We called each of these communities on the phone to find the appropriate solid waste official and to ask about the pricing program, the recycling program, actual tonnages of residential garbage and recycling (for 1991), and whether they knew of any other communities that charge a price per unit of garbage at the curb.[2] We combine this original data with similar information for 845 communities without a user fee but with and without curbside recycling. This second set of data is provided by the International City Managers Association (ICMA [6]). We use U.S. Census data for demographic characteristics of all these communities and data published by *Biocycle* magazine's annual survey for regional tipping fees and any state mandates expected to affect garbage and recycling (Steuteville and Goldstein [21]).[3]

Second, while other studies estimate the demand for garbage collection or for recycling collection, we estimate both as comparable functions of the price of garbage, the presence of a curbside recycling program, and other relevant variables. Thus we can estimate the cross-price effect of garbage price on recycling quantity.[4] In addition, the comparable estimation of both garbage and recycling demands allows us to infer changes in source reduction or other possibly illegal methods of disposal: as discussed below, the user fee decreases the weight of garbage by more than it increases recycling.

Third, and perhaps most important, we allow for the possibility of endogenous policy choices. As pointed out by Besley and Case [1, p. 1], "If state policy making is purposeful action, responsive to economic and political conditions within the state, then it may be necessary to identify and control for the forces that lead policies to change if one wishes to obtain unbiased estimates of a policy's incidence." No existing study of

---

[2] After collecting much of this information, we discovered that some towns had provided us an estimate of their aggregate garbage (our dependent variable) that was obtained by multiplying their local population times the EPA estimate of the U.S. average garbage per person! We did not include these communities in our sample. We also excluded towns that were unable to provide data on residential waste separately from commercial waste.

[3] See an earlier unpublished version of this paper (Kinnaman and Fullerton [10]) for a detailed written description of the data gathering process. Enough years of a panel could be used to estimate a fixed-effects model, but that effort will have to wait.

[4] Several papers mentioned above estimate the demand for garbage collection, but not recycling amounts. Using a survey of 2298 households, Hong, Adams, and Love [5] are able to estimate the frequency that households recycle. Using a different survey of 1422 households, Reschovsky and Stone [18] estimate the probability that a household will recycle, for each material. Tawil [22] estimates the probability of adopting curbside recycling. Only Browne [2] estimates the amount of household recycling as a function of a user fee for garbage collection, and other variables, using 34 communities (16 with a user fee). None of these studies estimates both garbage and recycling quantities.

garbage demand includes a correction for the endogeneity of local government decisions about the price per bag of garbage collected and whether to implement curbside recycling.[5]

The bias in the estimate of a policy's incidence from treating the policy variable as exogenous could go in either direction. Both the positive effect on recycling and the negative effect on garbage could be *overstated* if the estimation processes omit an unobservable variable such as the environmental awareness of the community. The omitted variable might (i) increase the probability that a community implements "green" policies such as a user fee and curbside recycling program, (ii) increase the observed quantity of recycling by these "environmentally aware" citizens, and (iii) consequently reduce the observed quantity of garbage. On the other hand, the effects of such policies could be *understated* if the likelihood of implementing these local policies is a positive function of the quantity of garbage collected in the community. Such a relationship could exist if the benefits of implementing these policies (including the expected reduction in garbage) are larger for towns with relatively large quantities of garbage collected. In general, previous estimates of the effect of price or curbside recycling could be biased in either direction if they leave in the error term these unobserved characteristics that are correlated with the price or curbside recycling variables.

To control for the possibility of endogenous policy choices, we model the local government's decisions about curbside recycling, whether to charge a price and what price to charge. These local policy choices are estimated as functions of observable exogenous variables such as the region-wide tipping fee, the population density, several state policy variables, and demographic characteristics. We then use the predicted values for these policy variables to correct for possible endogeneity in the garbage and recycling demand equations using two-stage least squares (2SLS).

Relative to the results obtained from treating these policies as exogenous, we find that this correction increases the estimated impact of a user fee on garbage quantities, and it increases the effect of curbside recycling on the quantity of recycling. That is, previous studies may have underestimated the effects of these programs on garbage and recycling totals. Thus, our results confirm the second scenario described in the paragraph above.

---

[5] Most studies assume the price is exogenous. Hong, Adams, and Love [5] correct for the endogeneity that arises from the fact that the household's quantity choices determine its location on a fixed price schedule, but they do not deal with the setting of the price schedule. Browne [2] considers endogeneity of the town's chosen price, and rejects it. Tawil [22] corrects for the self-selection of towns into curbside recycling programs, to estimate the probability of adopting such programs. None of these papers corrects for this kind of self-selection or endogeneity in the estimation of garbage or recycling quantities.

LIVERPOOL
JOHN MOORES UNIVERSITY
AVRIL ROBARTS LRC
TITHEBARN STREET
LIVERPOOL L2 2ER
TEL. 0151 231 4022

Accounting for endogeneity in local policy choices, we find that raising the fee from 0 to $1 per bag reduces collected garbage from 942 to 530 pounds per capita (by 44%). Of the 412-pound decrease, we estimate that approximately 30 pounds goes into local recycling. At present we are unable to trace the remaining 382 pounds. Clearly, the wisdom of garbage collection fees depends critically on the ultimate whereabouts of these 382 pounds of missing garbage; it is an important topic for future research.

I. A MODEL OF HOUSEHOLD DEMAND FOR GARBAGE AND RECYCLING

Our full model involves a sequence of decisions by different agents. In order to explain the model, we start with the household's waste disposal choices, and then work our way back to the local government's policy choices.

Assume that a community with a single local government is composed of N households. Each household buys a single composite consumption good c, and each generates waste in three forms. All waste must appear as regular garbage collection (with amount g), recycling (with amount r), or illicit burning and dumping (with amount b). Household preferences among these three disposal methods may depend on a set of demographic characteristics, α. Thus each household maximizes utility:[6]

$$u = u[c, g, r, b; \alpha] \qquad (1)$$

subject to

$$m = c + p_g g + p_r r + p_b b \qquad (2)$$

where m is income, the consumption good c is numeraire, and p_j denotes the price of disposal option j for $j = g, r, b$. This maximization process yields demand functions for each method of waste removal:

$$g = g(p_g, p_r, p_b, m, \alpha) \qquad (3a)$$

$$r = r(p_g, p_r, p_b, m, \alpha) \qquad (3b)$$

$$b = b(p_g, p_r, p_b, m, \alpha). \qquad (3c)$$

The price of garbage collection facing the household (p_g) may include the value of a user fee charged by the community (P), plus time and effort

---

[6] As pointed out by a referee, utility could be a function only of consumption c, where c is produced at home using purchased inputs, household time, and disposal (g, r, and b). Then that home-production function for c can be substituted into utility to obtain Eq. (1). Our formulation is somewhat more general, however, in that it allows for the possibility that altruistic households do care directly about their own g, r, and b.

to store garbage and to put it out to the curb.[7] We have no data on the time and effort components, but we assume they are functions of household income and demographic characteristics (m, α). Other variables might also affect the household cost of disposing of garbage. First, several states prohibit yardwaste from entering landfills. We define the indicator variable $I^{YW} = 1$ if the community bans yardwaste from the garbage, and 0 otherwise. We expect such a ban to increase the cost of disposing of yardwaste. Second, many states require local mandates for household curbside recycling ($I^{MAN} = 1$, and 0 otherwise).[8] This law increases the cost of disposing of garbage at the curb by the expected fine for not recycling. These considerations explain the first of our three price equations:

$$p_g = p_g(P, m, \alpha, I^{YW}, I^{MAN}) \qquad (4a)$$

$$p_r = p_r(I^R, m, \alpha, I^{DR}, I^{MAN}) \qquad (4b)$$

$$p_b = p_b(m, \alpha, D, D^2) \qquad (4c)$$

where all variables are carefully defined in Table 1.

In Eq. (4b), the household's price of recycling (p_r) includes the cost of separating, storing, transporting, and possibly paying a firm to accept the recycled material (this last component could be negative). Time costs can be functions of household income and demographic characteristics (m, α). The presence of a curbside recycling program diminishes these costs significantly, since transportation and payments to firms are handled by the community. Let $I^R = 1$ if the community has free curbside recycling collection, and 0 otherwise. Several states have a deposit-refund program for certain types of drink containers. We define $I^{DR} = 1$ for communities in such states, and 0 otherwise. A refund for bottles returned to the store might increase the cost of putting those bottles into curbside collection.

The household's price for burning or dumping (p_b) is not a market price, but it includes implicitly the time required to find a suitable dump site, the costs of traveling to the dump site, and the possible fine for breaking a local litter ordinance.[9] We tried to collect information on litter

---

[7] Throughout this paper we use lower case letters to denote household variables and upper case letters to denote community variables.

[8] In most cases, this decision is imposed by the state and is therefore exogenous to the community. We treat all state policy variables defined in the paper as exogenous in order to focus on local choices about whether to implement a curbside recycling program and a pricing program.

[9] Some of these costs may be fixed or marginal. Implicitly, therefore, we allow for the possibility that a higher price for garbage could induce the household to incur the fixed cost of dumping, and thus to reduce both its garbage and its recycling (Kinnaman and Fullerton [9]).

TABLE 1

Definitions of Variables

Endogenous variables:

G	Pounds per person per year of collected residential garbage
R	Pounds per person per year of collected recyclable material
I^R	1 if city-wide, free curbside recycling collection (0 otherwise)
$P1$	Price of first 32-gallon bag or can, divided by local price index
$P2$	Price of second 32-gallon bag or can, divided by local price index

Exogenous variables in household demand (X_i in Eq. (6)):

m = INCOME	Per capita income in 1000's of dollars, divided by local price index
RETIRE	The percentage of all persons that are 65 years and older
FAM SIZE	Average number of persons per household
EDUC	Percentage of those 25 years or older with bachelor's degree or higher
OWNER	The percentage of households that own their own home
D = DENSITY	The number of 1000's of persons per square mile
I^{YW}	1 if a state law prohibits yardwaste from landfills (0 otherwise)
I^{DR}	1 if the state has a deposit/refund system for bottles (0 otherwise)
I^{MAN}	1 if the state mandates that households recycle (0 otherwise)

Exogenous variables in probability of recycling (Z_i^R in Eq. (7)) include X_i plus:

P_T	The region-wide tipping fee, divided by the local price index
I^{SH}	1 if state helps incentives to buy recycled materials (0 otherwise)
I^{SB}	1 if state agencies must buy recycled materials (0 otherwise)
Q = QUOTA	State mandated minimum for the recycling rate, $R/(R + G)$
$QTIME$	Number of years until quota takes effect
I^{SL}	1 if state law "requires" the city to collect recycling (0 otherwise)

Exogenous variables in the optimal price (Z_i^P in Eq. (9)) include the Z_i^R plus:

I^{PT}	1 if state law limits the town's property taxes (0 otherwise)
I^{MUN}	1 if collection is handled by municipal employees (0 otherwise)

laws and fines in each community, but enforcement varies widely. Adequate data on penalties are not available. Instead, we hypothesize that easier opportunities for illegal dumping are provided in areas where population density is very high or very low: urban areas with commercial dumpsters and rural areas with remote spots for dumping. Communities with middle densities (suburbs and residential communities) provide fewer opportunities to dump. Suburban areas could also provide greater social pressure not to dump. We therefore enter density (D) in a nonlinear fashion, using both population density and its square in the regressions. Hence (4c) above.

Upon substitution of (4a–c) into 3(a–c), we get demands for garbage (G), recycling (R), and burning or dumping (B) as functions of observed variables defined above:

$$G = G(I^R, P, m, \alpha, D, D^2, I^{YW}, I^{DR}, I^{MAN}) \tag{5a}$$

426   KINNAMAN AND FULLERTON

$$R = R(I^R, P, m, \alpha, D, D^2, I^{YW}, I^{DR}, I^{MAN})$$ (5b)

$$B = B(I^R, P, m, \alpha, D, D^2, I^{YW}, I^{DR}, I^{MAN}).$$ (5c)

We do not observe each community's quantity of burning or dumping (B) and, therefore, do not estimate (5c). Though the system of equations in (5) is simultaneously determined, the bias from estimating one equation at a time is zero since the set of independent variables is the same in all equations. The reason for discussing B, however, is two-fold. First, the instruments for the *price* of burning and dumping can affect the quantities of observed garbage and recycling in (5a) and (5b). Second, the availability of this third option (B) to households implies that the two observed options (G and R) are not *necessarily* substitutes.

A linear econometric specification of these equations is:[10]

$$Y_i = \beta_0 + I_i^R\beta_1 + P_i\beta_2 + X_i\beta_3 + \mu_i$$ (6)

where Y_i denotes either the per capita weight of garbage (G) or recycling (R) for community i (where $i = 1, \ldots, M$), I_i^R is the indicator variable for the presence of a curbside recycling program, P_i denotes the (observed) price of garbage collection, X_i is a vector of exogenous variables in (5) defined in Table 1, and μ_i is an error term. The vector X_i includes variables such as income, demographic characteristics, population density, its square, and state laws (m, α, D, D^2, I^{YW}, I^{DR}, and I^{MAN}).

Summary statistics appear in Table 2. We gathered information on two types of user fee pricing systems. The first is a "subscription" system, in which residents pay a monthly fee for a specified number of cans each week. The second is a "bag or tag" program, where residents must purchase special program bags or stickers to place on each of their own garbage containers. Because different communities state prices for different bag or can sizes, we convert all observations to a price per 32-gallon container.

Although we gather data from 959 towns, 50 had implemented "subscription" pricing programs. For reasons explained below, we eliminate these communities from most of our regressions–which reduces our sample size to 909. (For comparison, we also estimate the model with the full sample including "subscription" programs.) All remaining 909 communi-

---

[10] One might naturally include an interaction term to account for the idea that curbside recycling ($I^R = 1$) could increase the effect of the price (P). Without curbside recycling, households have few options to reduce their garbage and might react to a fee by dumping illegally. Probably for this very reason, no city in our sample has a positive price without curbside recycling. That is, every town with $I^R = 0$ also has $P = 0$. The interaction term is exactly colinear with P and cannot be included separately in (6). Thus the coefficient on P should always be interpreted as the effect of price *given* curbside recycling collection.

TABLE 2

Summary Statistics

	Mean	SD	Min.	Max.	No.
Endogenous Variables					
G (in pounds per person per year)	911.68	392.17	88.75	2115.	756[a]
R (in pounds per person per year)	47.84	103.41	0	1155.	658[b]
I^R (curbside recycling is in place)	0.44	0.50	0	1	909
$P1$ (price of first bag of garbage)	0.08	0.31	0.00	2.76	909
$P2$ (price of second bag of garbage)	0.07	0.28	0.00	2.18	909
Household demand (X_i in Eq. (6)):					
INCOME (per capita, in $000)	12.69	5.31	4.46	51.2	909
RETIRE (% $\geq$ 65 years of age)	14.12	6.07	2.10	56.0	909
FAM SIZE (number per household)	2.57	0.29	1.80	4.13	909
EDUC (% with bachelor's)	23.60	13.51	2.76	82.8	909
OWNER (% homeowners)	64.12	13.30	17.6	98.3	909
DENSITY (1000's per square mile)	2.59	2.10	0.03	21.0	909
I^{YW} (ban on yardwaste in garbage)	0.39	0.49	0	1	909
I^{DR} (state has deposit-refund)	0.17	0.37	0	1	909
I^{MAN} (mandatory recycling)	0.48	0.50	0	1	909
Curbside recycling (Z_i^R in Eq. (7)):					
P_T (regional tipping fee)	26.07	20.70	2.41	107.7	909
I^{SH} (state help to recycling)	0.55	0.50	0	1	909
I^{SB} (state buys recycled materials)	0.72	0.45	0	1	909
Q (quota for min % recycled)	0.12	0.17	0	0.5	909
QTIME (years before quota)	1.74	3.07	−1	9	909
I^{SL} (state law on city recycling)	0.11	0.31	0	1	909
Optimal price (Z_i^P in Eq. (9)):					
I^{PT} (property tax limitation)	0.38	0.49	0	1	909
I^{MUN} (municipal collection)	0.52	0.50	0	1	909

[a] Number of towns with garbage quantity data available.
[b] Number of towns with recycling quantity data available.

ties are used in first-stage regressions, but only 756 report data on garbage quantity (for garbage regressions) and 658 report data on the quantity of recyclable materials (for recycling regressions). Garbage averages 911.68 pounds per person per year. Recycling averages only 47.84 pounds per person per year, but the third row of Table 2 shows that only 44% of the communities have curbside collection.

In some towns, residents pay one price ($P1$) for their first bag of garbage each week and another price ($P2$) for the second bag. Households may *have* to use at least one bag each week, so we use $P2$ as the marginal price for additional garbage in most of our regressions. We compare these results to those using $P1$, below, and find that the results are fairly robust to alternative specifications of price. The price variable ($P2$) ranges from zero to $2.18 per 32-gallon bag, and it averages $.07 per 32-gallon bag.

Table 2 also shows that our communities display considerable variation in income and demographic characteristics. Using the U.S. Census, per capita income varies from $4,461 per person to $51,170 per person. The retired population varies from 2 to 56%, family size varies from 1.8 to 4.1, the fraction with college degrees varies from 3 to 83%, and the fraction that own homes varies from 18 to 98%. The overall average fraction for homeowners in our sample is 64%, closely matching the overall average for the United States. Population density varies from 32 per square mile to 21,040 per square mile. Finally, 39% of our communities ban yardwaste from their garbage, 17% are located in states with deposit-refund systems, and 48% require households to recycle.

Previous studies have estimated (6) directly by ordinary least squares (OLS) or generalized least squares (GLS). Estimates of β_1 and β_2 are used to interpret the effects of free curbside recycling and of the user fee. These OLS estimates are biased, however, if I_i^R and P_i are endogenous. The next section describes instruments for these variables.

II. A MODEL AND ESTIMATION OF LOCAL GOVERNMENT BEHAVIOR

Each local government has several policy instruments available to control the quantities of garbage, recycling, and illegal dumping. The two primary policies of concern are free curbside recycling and a user fee for garbage.

A. The Choice to Implement a Curbside Recycling Program

1. *A Probit Model.* Each local government is assumed to compare the costs and benefits of implementing a curbside recycling program. The first benefit to the community is the reduction in garbage collected (ΔG) times the tipping fee that must be paid to the regional landfill (P_T). As shown in Table 2, the average tipping fee faced by our communities is $26 per ton and varies from $2.41 to just over $107. The reduction in garbage collected depends on the vector X_i of variables in the household's demand for garbage collection in equation (6) above. A second benefit to the community is the price that it receives (P_R) for the collected recycling times any increase in recycling (ΔR). This latter amount also depends on household income and characteristics in X_i of Eq. (6).[11] For the price P_R, we use two proxies described below.

The cost to the community of curbside recycling includes the total cost of labor and capital to collect the recycled materials from the household

---

[11] In the reduced form below, the probability of curbside recycling depends directly on household characteristics X_i, so the policymaker's decision can equivalently be said to depend directly on local voter preferences rather than on a formal cost-benefit test.

(TC_R). We have no data on the labor or capital costs of collection, but proxy it with the population density of the community. Recycling trucks in communities with high densities do not have to drive as far between houses. The benefits and costs of curbside recycling might also be affected by a number of state laws described below. These considerations give us the following equation for I_i^{R*}, a latent variable defined as the net benefits to the community from providing curbside recycling collection:

$$I_i^{R*} = Z_i^R \gamma + \varepsilon_i \tag{7}$$

where $\varepsilon \sim N(0,1)$, and γ is a vector of parameters to be estimated. The vector Z_i^R includes all of the variables that help determine household choices (the X_i), and it includes other exogenous variables defined in Table 1 (and discussed below).

We do not observe the net benefits from having curbside recycling. Instead, we only observe whether a community has implemented such a program. We assume:

$$I^R = 1 \qquad \text{iff } I^{R*} > 0 \tag{8a}$$

$$I^R = 0 \qquad \text{otherwise.} \tag{8b}$$

We use the Probit model to estimate the γ, and then we use these coefficients to generate a predicted probability that each town will choose to implement curbside recycling. This predicted variable is used to replace the actual (endogenous) variable I^R in Eq. (6) to estimate household demands.

2. *Results of recycling Probit.*   Results from the Probit model defined in Eqs. (7) and (8) are presented in Table 3. The third column of Table 3 presents the marginal effect of a change in any independent variable on the probability that a government implements free curbside recycling. The probability of this program is estimated to decrease by about 20% for an additional person per household and to increase by 0.77% for a 1-point increase in the percentage of citizens with bachelor degrees. Perhaps college-educated residents have greater preference for a clean environment and thus encourage their local government to implement curbside recycling. An increase of 1000 persons per square mile is estimated to increase the likelihood of this recycling program by 3.9%.

We estimate that communities in states with deposit-refund programs are 18% less likely to implement curbside recycling collection. Households in these states can take recyclable materials directly to stores for a refund. A community in one of these states would therefore realize fewer benefits from implementing curbside recycling.

430   KINNAMAN AND FULLERTON

TABLE 3

Probit Estimation of the Probability of Curbside Recycling
(Dependent Variable: I^R (= 1 iff Curbside Recycling))

Variable	Coefficient	Standard error	Marginal effects
CONSTANT	−1.3436	(0.8956)	
INCOME	−0.0195	(0.0190)	−0.0062
RETIRE	−0.0014	(0.0139)	−0.0044
FAM SIZE	−0.6218*	(0.3426)	−0.1995
EDUCATION	0.0241***	(0.0073)	0.0077
OWNER	0.0092	(0.0071)	0.0030
DENSITY	0.1199*	(0.0665)	0.0385
DENSITY SQUARED	−0.0064	(0.0049)	−0.0020
I^{YW} (yardwaste ban)	0.3854	(0.3346)	0.1236
I^{DR} (deposit refund)	−0.5501**	(0.2718)	−0.1765
P_T (tipping fee)	0.0242***	(0.0046)	0.0078
I^{SH} (state helps)	0.4026	(0.3210)	0.1292
I^{SB} (state buys)	0.2115	(0.2105)	0.0679
Q (quota)	−0.0072	(0.9924)	−0.0023
QTIME	0.0357	(0.0740)	0.0115
$Q \times TIME$	0.0730	(0.2092)	0.0234
I^{SL} (state law)	−0.2041	(0.2306)	−0.0655
Sample size		909	
ZM statistic		0.570	
Likelihood ratio index		0.363	
−2[L(0) − L(b)]		452.6639***	

Note. *, **, and *** indicate significance at the 0.10, 0.05, and 0.01 level, respectively. The ZM statistic and Likelihood ratio index measure goodness of fit. The last row jointly tests whether all coefficients are equal to zero.

The model also suggests that the probability of implementing a curbside recycling program increases with the regional tipping fee (P_T). Faced with additional costs for disposing of garbage in landfills, these communities can use curbside recycling to decrease collections of garbage. Indeed, much of the previous literature attributes the recent popularity of curbside recycling programs to higher tipping fees. Our data support these claims. After controlling for other relevant variables, we find that the likelihood of implementing a curbside recycling program increases by 7.8% with every $10 increase in the regional tipping fee.

We do not have direct observations of the price received for recycling (P_R), but we have a couple of proxies. First, we have an indicator variable I^{SH} = 1 if the state helps stimulate demand by providing economic incentives to firms that purchase recycled materials (and 0 otherwise). Second, we have another indicator variable I^{SB} = 1 if the state buys recycled materials for its own operation (and 0 otherwise). Though the estimated effects are positive, the coefficients are not statistically different from zero.

Several states have implemented quotas that require communities to recycle more. For example, every community in the state of California must recycle 50% of its waste by the year 2000. The effect of such a quota (Q) may depend on the time until it must be achieved ($QTIME$). For completeness, we include Q, $QTIME$, and their interaction in the regression, but we find none of these to be significant.

Some states like New Jersey have passed laws requiring all communities to implement curbside recycling ($I^{SL} = 1$, and 0 otherwise). This law does not guarantee that communities actually implement the required program, but it may increase the probability. The final choice still remains with the community, and only 57% of communities in these states had implemented curbside recycling in the year of our data. Controlling for other variables in the model, results in Table 3 indicate that this mandate has *no* effect on a community's decision to implement a curbside recycling program.

Though results in Table 3 are useful and interesting in their own right, the major purpose of estimating this Probit model is to generate a prediction to substitute for the endogenous dummy variable I^R in the estimation of Eq. (6) above. Before estimating those demand equations, however, we still need to calculate an instrument for the price per unit garbage.

B. The Choice to Implement a User Fee

1. *A Tobit Model.* In order to decide whether to charge a price per bag, community officials first calculate the optimal price to charge. This optimal fee, P^*, is determined by a tradeoff between benefits and costs at the margin. A higher fee might generate more revenue (if demand is inelastic), reduce the amount of garbage that has to be sent to the landfill, and increase the amount of curbside recycling that can be sold by the community. Unfortunately, it may also increase the quantity of illegal dumping. The locations of the marginal cost and benefit curves and thus P^* will vary across communities. Each town implements the program only if its optimal price is positive.[12]

Thus we expect the chosen price per bag of garbage to depend upon marginal conditions that are proxied by many of the variables that entered

---

[12] Marginal curves may not include the fixed costs necessary to print and distribute the stickers or bags, to promote the program, and to enforce litter laws. Thus an alternative specification might say that the town finds P^* and then implements the program only if the net social gain is positive. A problem with this alternative is that net social benefits are not monotonic in price, since a higher price might increase dumping. Thus the decision to implement would not be based on any threshold involving P^*.

into the curbside recycling equation above, including the region's tipping fee (P_T), the price received for recycled materials (P_R, or its proxies I^{SH} and I^{SB}), and the household's determination of G and R (which depend upon income and household characteristics in X_i). We add two additional variables to this list. First, the revenue from a higher user fee might help alleviate the problem of dealing with a state limitation on local property taxes. We define a dummy variable $I^{PT} = 1$ if the community is located in a state with a property tax limitation (and 0 otherwise). Second, the marginal cost of the program may depend on whether garbage collection is conducted by the municipality or by a private regulated firm. Private firms may be more efficient. We define a dummy variable $I^{MUN} = 1$ if the community employs municipal resources for collection and 0 for those that franchise or contract the collection service to a single private firm.[13] These considerations together suggest that the optimal price to charge is a function of exogenous variables:

$$P_i^* = Z_i^P \delta + u_i \qquad (9)$$

where Z_i^P is the vector of exogenous variables for community i (defined in Table 1), $u_i \sim N(0, \sigma_u^2)$, and δ is a vector of parameters to be estimated.

We do not observe the optimal price. We observe only the user fee that is charged by each community (P_i):

$$
\begin{aligned}
P_i &= P_i^* & &\text{if } P_i^* > 0 \\
P_i &= 0 & &\text{otherwise.}
\end{aligned}
\qquad (10)
$$

We use the standard Tobit model to estimate Eq. (10).[14]

---

[13] Cities with multiple private haulers are excluded; we wish to model the city's endogenous determination of price, not a competitive market determination of price.

[14] As an alternative, we estimated a censored regression model where the dichotomous decision is based on whether the optimal price P^* is above or below some "stochastic unobserved threshold" (Maddala [11, pp. 174–178]). A problem, however, is that such a model uses a Probit on the decision to implement a positive fee, the inverse Mills ratio to correct the estimation of P^* for those with a positive price, and the predicted optimal price $\hat{P}^*$ for all communities in the sample (with or without user fees) to replace the endogenous price in the garbage demand Eq. (6). That P^* may be quite high for a community that faces a high administrative cost and chooses not to implement that price. Yet households in (6) generate garbage in response to the actual price of zero, not the hypothetical high price P^*. The predicted $\hat{P}^*$ is very weakly correlated with actual price, and its use in (6) would not help determine household behavior. Instead, we need an instrument for both positive prices and zero prices, given that communities choose endogenously whether to implement a fee. Such an instrument is provided by the Tobit estimation of (10) which provides a prediction of the actual price, whether zero or positive. The correlation coefficient between the actual price and the predicted price generated from the Tobit estimation of (10) is 0.67.

Next, to obtain a consistent estimate of the effect of price in Eq. (6), we use the predicted price $\hat{P}_i$ calculated from (10) as an instrument for P_i.

2. *Results of the user fee Tobit.*   Results for the Tobit model are presented in Table 4. The coefficient on income is negative and significant, as a $1000 increase in per capita income reduces the optimal user fee by $.20. One explanation for this negative coefficient is that communities using property taxes to pay for garbage collection enable their residents to deduct those local taxes against Federal income tax. User fees are not deductible. Communities with high per capita incomes have more residents who itemize, and who face high income tax rates, so they find a user fee to be costly in terms of lost deductions.

Education is the only demographic variable that has a significant effect on the value of the user fee. We estimate that the optimal user fee increases by $.37 for a 10% increase in the percentage who are college graduates. Perhaps these communities find that educated individuals are less likely to engage in illegal dumping. Education might raise the opportu-

TABLE 4

Tobit Estimation of the Optimal User Fee
(Dependent Variable: P (Price per Bag of Garbage))

Variable	Coefficient	Standard error
CONSTANT	-8.0053	(18.61)
INCOME	-0.1955***	(0.0452)
RETIRE	0.0182	(0.0272)
FAM SIZE	0.0564	(0.7183)
EDUCATION	0.0368**	(0.0125)
OWNER	0.0115	(0.0111)
DENSITY	-0.1060	(0.1433)
DENSITY SQUARED	-0.0001	(0.0158)
I^{YW} (yardwaste ban)	1.8391***	(0.4733)
I^{DR} (deposit refund)	0.2863	(0.3548)
P_T (tipping fee)	0.0345***	(0.0084)
I^{SH} (state helps)	0.4909	(0.5253)
I^{SB} (state buys)	4.2700	(18.50)
Q (quota)	-8.6695***	(1.845)
QTIME	0.3634***	(0.1012)
$Q \times$ QTIME	0.3604	(0.4004)
I^{SL} (state law on recycling)	-0.7995	(0.5802)
I^{PT} (property tax limit)	0.2022	(0.4307)
I^{MUN} (municipal collection)	0.4756**	(0.2237)
Inverse Mills ratio	1.1212***	(0.1208)
Sample size	909	

Note. *, **, and *** indicate significance at the 0.10, 0.05, and 0.01 level, respectively.

nity cost of time, and thus raise the fee necessary to induce behavioral changes, but this regression controls for income (another proxy for wage rate).

A user fee might generate more illegal burning and dumping. This response may be greater in areas with very low population density (where garbage can be dumped in the woods) and with very high density (where garbage can be dumped in commercial dumpsters). Knowing this, the community may think that household dumping in response to the implementation of a user fee is a non-linear function of the population density.[15] Results do not substantiate this hypothesis, since the coefficients on density and density-squared are insignificant. Either communities are not worried about illegal dumping when they consider the implementation of a user fee, or we have a weak proxy for the household "price" of illegal disposal.

Many have conjectured that the optimal user fee increases with the tipping fee. Our results support this conjecture; a $10 increase in the regional tipping fee (per ton at the landfill) is estimated to increase the local user fee by $0.35 per bag. Also, the user fee is predicted to increase in states that ban yardwaste from landfills. Lastly, the significant effect of a quota and $QTIME$ are difficult to explain.[16]

Results in Tables 3 and 4 provide the necessary instruments for estimation of household demands, but they also provide an interesting analysis of local policy making. These results show how local government decisions respond to state mandates, demographic variables such as education, and economic variables such as income.

III. THE EFFECTS OF POLICY ON GARBAGE AND RECYCLING

In the last stage of this process, we use Eq. (6) to regress aggregate garbage or recycling quantities on the exogenous variables in X_i and on the predicted values of the curbside recycling variable from (8) and user fee variable from (10).

A. Estimating the Demand for Garbage Collection

The garbage regressions use only 756 towns without "subscription" programs and with complete data on garbage. The first column of Table 5a presents estimates from the endogenous choice model (two-stage least squares). The coefficient on the user fee ($P2$) is negative and significant at

---

[15] Fines for littering and the level of enforcement could also play a role in determining the costs of household dumping, but we were not able to obtain data on these variables.

[16] Indeed, using the coefficients on $QUOTA$ and its interactive term (and using the mean of $QTIME$), we calculate that a higher recycling quota decreases the optimal user fee.

the 1% level.[17] By these estimates, the change in price from zero to one dollar would reduce garbage per person per year by 412.37 pounds.

To better interpret the magnitude of this price coefficient, we provide three calculations of the price elasticity of demand. We assume the mean price (0.075) and quantity of garbage (911.7) are on one point along a linear demand curve with slope −412.37. The price elasticity at this point is only $(-412.37)(0.075/911.7) = -0.034$, because the average price (0.075) is very low. Most towns in our sample had not implemented a user fee program and thus charged a price of zero. Among towns *with* user fee programs, the average price charged is 0.999 (i.e., one dollar). Evaluated at this point on the same linear demand curve, the price elasticity is $(-412.37)(1/530.17) = -0.778$. Finally, the arc-elasticity resulting from an increase in price from 0 to $1.00, which is the same as the point-elasticity at a price of 50 cents, is −0.28. This final calculation is perhaps the one that is most appropriate to compare with elasticity estimates provided by the previous literature, but our estimate of −0.28 is larger than most of these previous estimates.[18]

The last two columns of Table 5a present OLS estimates from a model of the type used in the previous literature. These OLS estimates do not account for the possible endogeneity of the user fee or recycling dummy variables. The coefficient on the user fee is negative and significant, but the point estimate provided by the OLS model is only −275.08. Thus, consideration of endogenous choice raises the absolute value of the estimated coefficient by 50% (from 275 to 412). A test of the null hypothesis that these two coefficients are equal is rejected with 90% confidence. Therefore, we conclude that the OLS model underestimates the true impact of the implementation of a user fee.

Our introduction outlines two opposing possible sources of bias. Results here tend to reject the idea that an omitted variable such as "environmental awareness" increases the user fee and decreases the garbage amount. Instead, results here suggest that the bias may be the result of unobserved variables that jointly make a community more likely to implement a user fee and that also increase the amount of garbage. Or, the bias may be attributable to community self-selection. Communities with large per capita

---

[17] Most packages correct the standard errors for the use of a fitted value on the right-hand side, but this model mixes fitted values from both Probit and Tobit on the right-hand side. Thus the standard errors may be biased, and significance tests may be misleading.

[18] Using household data for one town's change in price from zero to 80 cents, Fullerton and Kinnaman [4] find an arc-elasticity of −0.075. Others have estimated the point-elasticity of demand for garbage to be −0.12 (Jenkins [7]), −0.15 (Wertz [24]), −0.26 and −0.22 (Morris and Byrd [13], in two communities), −0.14 (Skumatz and Breckinridge [20]), and −0.42 (Podolsky and Spiegel [16]).

436   KINNAMAN AND FULLERTON

TABLE 5a

Determinants of the Annual Weight of Garbage

(Dependent Variable: G (Pounds of Garbage per Person per Year))

Variable	Endogenous choice		OLS	
	Coefficient	Standard error	Coefficient	Standard error
CONSTANT	732.70***	199.2	752.59***	196.3
I^R (curbside recycling)	83.551	135.7	−36.210	31.91
$P2$	−412.37***	110.9	−275.08***	50.67
INCOME	19.149***	5.171	21.160***	4.891
RETIRE	−0.2020	3.358	−0.0226	3.313
FAM SIZE	19.789	74.72	4.2845	72.43
EDUCATION	−7.7338***	1.899	−7.3566***	1.755
OWNER	1.9534	1.589	1.9128	1.551
DENSITY	2.2680	15.20	6.0992	14.06
DENSITY SQUARED	0.0773	1.063	0.0267	1.043
I^{YW} (yardwaste ban)	−29.273	40.18	−30.919	34.08
I^{DR} (deposit refund)	−52.404	38.79	−55.227	38.27
I^{MAN} (mandatory recycling)	−88.796*	45.67	−52.146	31.46
Sample size	756		756	
R^2	0.088		0.109	

Note. *, **, and *** indicate significance at the 0.10, 0.05, and 0.01 level, respectively.

quantities of garbage may be more likely to implement a user fee than communities with lower per capita garbage totals.[19]

The implementation of curbside recycling is estimated to *increase* garbage by 83.55 pounds per person per year. This estimate differs considerably from the OLS estimate of −36.21, but neither estimate is statistically different from zero. The fact that the data are not able to establish a significant negative effect of curbside recycling on garbage quantities is an interesting result in itself. Although the estimated effect of a curbside recycling program on garbage totals appears to vary rather dramatically across model specifications (OLS vs 2SLS), this difference is not statistically significant.

Other estimates in Table 5a are similar to those in previous studies. The coefficient on income is positive and significantly different from zero at the 1% level. The income elasticity calculated from this coefficient is

[19] A joint Hausman test for correlation between the error and the price variable and recycling dummy does not reject the null hypothesis that no correlation is present in the garbage equation ($F[2,741] = 0.481$) but does reject the null in the recycling equation ($F[2,643] = 11.662$) estimated below. Monte Carlo simulations have shown that the Hausman test has poor power (the probability of accepting a false null is high).

TABLE 5b

Estimated Responses to Policy Using Other Price Definitions
(Dependent Variable: G (Pounds of Garbage per Person per Year))

Specification	Variable	Endogenous choice		OLS	
		Coefficient	Standard error	Coefficient	Standard error
Include	I^R (curbside)	15.059	122.1	−50.111	31.63
subscription	$P2$ (user fee)	−172.35**	77.82	−105.28**	33.11
Include	I^R (curbside)	21.211	128.4	−54.492*	31.99
subscription	$P1$ (user fee)	−133.98**	63.07	−62.578**	26.92
Use only	I^R (curbside)	**18.895**	**116.5**	−43.872	32.91
subscription	$P2$ (user fee)	**−22.669**	**73.85**	−1.7768	42.43
Use only	I^R (curbside)	**65.662**	**125.5**	−43.788	33.20
subscription	$P1$ (user fee)	**−61.722**	**61.89**	−1.4089	31.34
Exclude	I^R (curbside)	131.37	142.7	−37.592	31.97
subscription	$P1$ (user fee)	−443.39***	114.3	−249.35***	48.02

Note. Table 5b omits the estimated coefficients on all variables other than the two policy variables.

$0.262.$[20] Households with high income not only have more waste material to remove, but they also face a high opportunity cost of time spent recycling or dumping. Therefore, these households throw out more garbage. Also, the quantity of garbage decreases significantly with education. Better educated citizens may have greater preference for a clean environment, switching some of their disposal from regular garbage to recycling (as seen in the next section).

We also estimate the impact of state policies on garbage totals, but most are not significant. Communities in states that mandate household recycling ($I^{MAN} = 1$) generate 89 fewer pounds per person per year.[21]

Table 5b tests alternative specifications. First, we provide estimates of the effect of a user fee on garbage amounts using additional observations for communities that have implemented "subscription" programs. Recall that subscription programs require households to pay extra for a second

---

[20] Others have estimated this income elasticity to be 0.242 (Richardson and Havlicek [19]), 0.279 and 0.242 (Wertz [24]), 0.2 (Petrovik and Jaffee [15]), 0.41 (Jenkins [7]), 0.049 (Hong, Adams, and Love [5]), 0.22 (Reschovsky and Stone [18]), 0.57 (Podolsky and Spiegel [16]), and 0.05 (Fullerton and Kinnaman [4]).

[21] Some variables in Z^R and Z^P are excluded from X (every variable in Table 3 or 4 that is not in Table 5). To check for overidentification, we test the null hypothesis that the coefficients on these variables are jointly equal to zero, but we cannot reject the null. Therefore, the model does not appear to be overidentified.

can each week, but each household must pre-commit to a number of cans and is charged for those cans whether empty or full. Thus the true cost to the household for a marginal increase in garbage may be zero. Since "bag and tag" programs provide better marginal incentives, Nestor and Podolsky [14] predict that subscription programs are less effective at reducing garbage. The first panel of Table 5b reports estimated coefficients of the curbside recycling and user fee variables when subscription programs are included in the sample. The effect of price ($P2$) falls from -412.37 (Table 5a) to only -172.35 (Table 5b). The bold-faced values of Table 5b report estimated coefficients among *only* those communities that have implemented subscription programs. The effect of price on garbage disappears. Thus we find that "bag and tag" programs reduce garbage more than "subscription" programs.

Second, we test the specification of price. Table 5b also shows a separate set of estimations using $P1$ (the price of the *first* bag of garbage) in place of $P2$. The final row is comparable to the results in Table 5a where "subscription" programs are excluded from the sample. The estimated coefficient on price is fairly robust to the specification of price (-443.39 compared to -412.37).

B. Estimating the Demand for Recycling

The first column of Table 6a corrects for possible endogeneity in the town's choices about whether to collect recycling and whether to charge a price for garbage. The second column provides OLS results for comparison. In this regression, we used all 658 observations for communities with complete data on recycling quantity (and without "subscription" programs).

The implementation of a user fee ($P2$) is estimated using the endogenous choice model to increase the quantity of recycling by 30 pounds per person per year. This coefficient is not significantly different from zero, but it is almost exactly the same size as the significant coefficient in the OLS regression. Given this similarity of coefficients, the OLS estimate may not be biased. According to this estimate, the cross-price arc-elasticity of demand for recycling collection is 0.220 (evaluated at $P2$ equal to 50 cents).[22]

The implementation of a curbside recycling program in the endogenous choice model increases the quantity of curbside recycling by an average of 195.64 pounds per person per year, 81 pounds more than is estimated by the OLS model. Given the small standard errors, these two estimates are statistically different from one another at the 1% confidence level. Thus the OLS-estimated impact of curbside recycling may be biased downward.

---

[22] The U.S. EPA [23] estimates this cross-price elasticity to be 0.49, 0.48, and 0.06 for various different communities. Browne [2] finds it to be 0.102 for glass and cans, and -0.02 for paper recycling. Fullerton and Kinnaman [4] find 0.074 for all recycling.

TABLE 6a

Determinants of the Annual Weight of Recycling

(Dependent Variable: R (Pounds of Recycling per Person per Year))

Variable	Endogenous choice		OLS	
	Coefficient	Standard error	Coefficient	Standard error
CONSTANT	−121.46**	49.50	−147.96**	45.13
I^R (curbside recycling)	195.64***	28.26	114.63***	7.860
P2	30.221	26.08	28.974**	12.16
INCOME	−0.8818	1.279	−0.6275	1.148
RETIRE	1.1461	0.8351	1.5386**	0.7553
FAM SIZE	26.330	17.89	26.947*	16.48
EDUCATION	0.2656	0.4744	0.8215**	0.4124
OWNER	0.6527*	0.3877	0.7925**	0.3546
DENSITY	−6.2523*	3.767	−2.0681	3.267
DENSITY SQUARED	0.2742	0.2569	0.1454	0.2343
I^{YW} (yardwaste ban)	−8.6427	10.24	14.362*	7.978
I^{DR} (deposit refund)	−11.727	10.00	−11.689	9.211
I^{MAN} (mandatory recycling)	−9.4474	9.623	2.2907	7.260
Sample size	658		658	
R^2	0.294		0.401	

Note. *, **, and *** indicate significance at the 0.10, 0.05, and 0.01 level, respectively.

Again, this bias seems not to be caused by omitting a variable such as "environmental awareness" (which would increase both recycling and the probability of free curbside collection). Instead, the bias could be caused by unobservable variables that jointly decrease the quantity of recycling and increase the probability that a community implements curbside recycling. We cannot think of examples of such variables. More likely, then, this bias may be the result of community self-selection. Communities with low recycling amounts prior to curbside recycling may be more likely to implement a curbside program. Officials in these communities probably see the potential for large benefits from the implementation of curbside recycling.

Notice that the estimated increase in recycling attributable to a user fee (30 pounds per person per year) does not match the estimated decrease in garbage attributable to a user fee (412 pounds per person per year). In fact, an estimated 382 pounds per person per year has seemed to disappear. In response to the user fee, households may increase their other disposal options such as source reduction, composting, burning, or illegal dumping. These data do not allow us to determine which of these methods is used.[23]

[23] Using other data, Fullerton and Kinnaman [4] estimate the reduction of garbage at the curb attributable to a user fee, and that dumping may account for 28 to 43% of it.

The estimated increase in recycling brought on by a curbside collection program (196 pounds) exceeds the decrease in garbage (84 pounds in Table 5a). In response to a curbside recycling program, perhaps households begin to recycle an extra 112 pounds per person per year that were previously dumped or burned in the absence of the curbside recycling program.

We expect various offsetting effects of income on aggregate recycling amounts. First, if an increase in income leads to more consumption, it could generate more waste material for disposal in all three forms, including more recycling. Second, a higher wage increases the opportunity cost of time spent recycling, so it could decrease aggregate recycling. Third, the higher wage increases the opportunity cost of time spent illegally dumping waste, so the net effect on recycling could depend on which type of disposal is more time-intensive. The estimated coefficient on income in Table 6a is negative (but insignificant), suggesting that the second effect could be slightly stronger than the others.

Demographic characteristics also play a role in determining aggregate recycling quantities. At least in the OLS model, significantly more recycling per person is generated in communities where households are older, larger, more educated, and own more of their own homes. Retired individuals may have more time to separate and store recyclable waste. Educated individuals may be more aware of recycling opportunities and may also have greater taste for a clean environment. Owner-occupants may generate more waste and therefore recycle more, especially if they have more room to store and separate recyclable material. Population density has a significant negative effect on recycling per person, but again the square term is not significant.

Table 6b shows the results of regressions with alternative specifications. As in Table 5b, the results are robust to the specification of price ($P1$ vs $P2$). Also, "bag and tag" programs increase recycling more than "subscription" programs.

IV. CONCLUSION

Using original data and correcting for endogenous local policy choices, this paper contributes to the empirical literature estimating the effects of policies designed to reduce solid waste and increase recycling. We have learned that endogeneity does matter. That is, policy making appears to be a "purposeful action, responsive to economic and political conditions" (Besley and Case [1]). Estimation linked these policy choices to various observable exogenous variables.

We have also learned that the previous empirical literature may have underestimated the impact of these local programs by assuming the policy variables to be exogenous. It seems that the likelihood that a community

TABLE 6b

Estimated Responses to Policy Using Other Price Definitions
(Dependent Variable: R (Pounds of Recycling per Person per Year))

Specification	Variable	Endogenous choice		OLS	
		Coefficient	Standard error	Coefficient	Standard error
Include	I^R (curbside)	176.95***	24.94	113.18***	7.723
subscription	$P2$ (user fee)	15.008	23.56	24.078**	10.02
Include	I^R (curbside)	171.90***	26.32	113.79***	7.760
subscription	$P1$ (user fee)	20.649	23.75	18.310**	9.123
Use only	I^R (curbside)	167.18***	24.70	108.08***	7.702
subscription	$P2$ (user fee)	− 133.33	92.32	9.5832	17.08
Use only	I^R (curbside)	173.45***	24.60	108.31***	7.730
subscription	$P1$ (user fee)	− 63.392	53.00	2.5586	14.20
Exclude	I^R (curbside)	182.59***	28.82	114.77***	7.859
subscription	$P1$ (user fee)	43.686*	25.89	26.467**	11.38

Note. Table 6b omits the estimated coefficients on all variables other than the two policy variables.

implements a user fee or curbside recycling increases with the quantity of garbage. Ignoring this possibility produces biased estimates.

Finally, we estimated that the implementation of a $1 user fee could decrease the quantity of garbage by 412 pounds per person per year but increase recycling by only 30 pounds per person per year. Where did the extra garbage go? The difference could be explained partly by waste reduction at the source, or by composting, but it also could be explained partly by other less-attractive alternatives like burning or dumping. Towns are turning increasingly to user fees to help reduce garbage, but the advisability of this policy depends crucially on the unestimated extent of illegal dumping. Thus this paper points to the importance of future research on the methods of reducing garbage at the curb.

REFERENCES

1. T. Besley and A. Case, "Unnatural Experiments? Estimating the Incidence of Endogenous Policies," *Econ. J.*, in press.
2. A. G. Browne, "Experience with Residential Recycling and Volume-Based Fees for Trash Disposal in Western Massachusetts," unpublished manuscript (1994).
3. F. Efaw and W. N. Lanen, "Impact of User Charges on Management of Household Solid Waste," Cincinnati Municipal Environmental Research Lab, prepared by Mathtech, Inc., Princeton, NJ (1979).

442   KINNAMAN AND FULLERTON

4. D. Fullerton and T. C. Kinnaman, Household responses to pricing garbage by the bag, *American Economic Review*, **86**, 971–984 (1996).
5. S. Hong, R. M. Adams and H. A. Love, An economic analysis of household recycling of solid wastes: The case of Portland, Oregon, *Journal of Environmental Economics and Management*, **25**, 136–146 (1993).
6. International City Managers Association, "Special Data Issue Number 23: Residential Solid Waste Collection Programs," Washington, D.C. (1991).
7. R. Jenkins, "Municipal Demand for Solid Waste Disposal Services: The Impact of User Fees," unpublished manuscript (1991).
8. R. Jenkins, "The Economics of Solid Waste Reduction: The Impact of User Fees," Edward Elgar Publishing, Brookfield, VT (1993).
9. T. C. Kinnaman and D. Fullerton, How a fee per-unit garbage affects aggregate recycling in a model with heterogeneous households, *in* "Public Economics and the Environment in an Imperfect World" (A. L. Bovenberg and S. Cnossen, Eds.), Kluwer Academic Publishers, Dordrecht, The Netherlands (1995).
10. T. C. Kinnaman and D. Fullerton, "Garbage and Recycling in Communities with Curbside Recycling and Unit-Based Pricing," National Bureau of Economic Research Working Paper, No. 6021 (1997).
11. G. S. Maddala, "Limited-Dependent and Qualitative Variables in Econometrics," Cambridge University Press, New York (1983).
12. M. L. Miranda, J. W. Everett, D. Blume, and B. A. Roy, Market-based incentives and residential municipal solid waste, *Journal of Policy Analysis and Management*, **13**, 681–698 (1994).
13. G. E. Morris and D. Byrd, "The Effects of Weight or Volume-Based Pricing on Solid Waste Management," prepared for the U.S. Environmental Protection Agency (1990).
14. D. V. Nestor and M. J. Podolsky, "Implementation Issues in Incentive-Based Environmental Policy: A Comparative Assessment of Two Programs for Reducing Household Waste Disposal," unpublished manuscript (1996).
15. W. M. Petrovic and B. L. Jaffee, Measuring the generation and collection of solid waste in cities, *Urban Affairs Quarterly*, **14**, 229–244 (1978).
16. M. J. Podolsky and M. Spiegel, Municipal waste disposal: Unit-pricing and recycling opportunities, *Public Works Management and Policy*, **3**, 27–39 (1998).
17. R. Repetto, R. C. Dower, R. Jenkins, and J. Geoghegan, "Green Fees: How a Tax Shift Can Work for the Environment and the Economy," World Resources Institute, Washington, D.C. (1992).
18. J. D. Reschovsky and S. E. Stone, Market incentives to encourage household waste recycling: Paying for what you throw away, *Journal of Policy Analysis and Management* **13**, 120–139 (1994).
19. R. A. Richardson and J. Havlicek, Jr., Economic analysis of the composition of household solid wastes, *Journal of Environmental Economics and Management*, **5**, 103–111 (1978).
20. L. Skumatz and C. Breckinridge, "Handbook for Solid Waste Officials, Volume 2," U.S. Environmental Protection Agency, 530-SW-90-084B (1990).
21. R. Steuteville and N. Goldstein, State of garbage in America: 1993 nationwide survey, *Biocycle*, **34**, 42–50 (1993).
22. N. Tawil, "On the Political Economy of Municipal Curbside Recycling Programs: Evidence from Massachusetts," unpublished manuscript (1995).
23. U.S. Environmental Protection Agency, "Charging Households for Waste Collection and Disposals: The Effects of Weight or Volume-Based Pricing on Solid Waste Management," Washington, D.C. (1990).
24. K. L. Wertz, Economic factors influencing households' production of refuse, *Journal of Environmental Economics and Management*, **2**, 263–272 (1976).

[7]

Explaining household demand for the collection of solid waste and recycling

Thomas C. Kinnaman[*]

I. Introduction

Recent increases in solid waste disposal costs have encouraged many local governments to design more efficient solid waste management plans. Rather than just picking up garbage at the curb every week, 6000 towns and cities across the United States have implemented curbside recycling programs (Steuteville, 1996) and over 3000 have begun pricing garbage by the bag. These recent changes in solid waste policy have increased the need to estimate the amount of garbage and recycling generated by households, and to estimate how these generation rates depend on income and household demographic characteristics.

This chapter makes two important empirical contributions to the understanding of household disposal practices. First, using original household data, household demands for garbage collection and recycling services are estimated as functions of the per-bag price of garbage collection, household income, and demographic characteristics. These data provide rare insight into the disposal practices of households. These data are used by Fullerton and Kinnaman (1996) to estimate the *change* in garbage and recycling attributable to the implementation of a per-bag price for garbage collection, and are used here to estimate the *levels* of garbage and recycling collection demanded by households.

Second, this chapter employs questionnaire responses and observed garbage quantities to examine critically household reactions to the implementation of a per-bag pricing program. Households may reduce garbage and increase recycling, but they may also engage in composting, source reduction, or other forms of disposal.

Section II describes efforts made to gather these original data, and it presents the econometric model used in the estimation. Results are provided in Section III. Finally, in Section IV, household responses to a questionnaire are used to evaluate household reactions to the implementation of a per-bag pricing program.

II. The data and econometric specification

To test the model described below, data were obtained by directly measuring the garbage and recycling of 75 households over an eight-week period in Charlottesville, Virginia. Each household's garbage and recyclable materials were weighed early in the morning over four weeks before and four weeks after the implementation of a per-bag pricing program.[1] The number of cans of garbage presented by each household were also measured. The four observations were averaged to obtain a measure of the average quantity of garbage and recycling with, and without, a per-bag pricing program. Following this measurement period, each household completed a questionnaire that reported each household's size, ages, income, marital status, education, and other information that could be expected to influence the generation of garbage or recyclable materials.

Table 1 provides summary statistics for each of the variables observed. For better comparison with the literature, all continuous variables have been divided by the number of individuals in the household to get per-person measures (rather than per-household). As presented in Table 1, the average individual disposes of 10.14 pounds of garbage and 3.97 pounds of recyclable materials in an average week. The average person also put out an average of 0.60 cans of garbage per week. According to responses to the questionnaire, nearly 85 per cent of households in the sample own their home, 47 per cent of individuals in the sample work full time, and income is about $20 000 per person per year.

Table 1   Description of variables

Dependent variables: Mean (Standard Deviation)		
WEIGHT	10.14 (7.15)	Pounds of household garbage per person per week
VOLUME	0.60 (0.38)	Number of cans of household garbage per person per week
RECYCLE	3.97 (3.68)	Pounds of recyclable material per person per week
Independent variables: Mean (Standard Deviation)		
PRICE	0.40 (0.40)	The price paid by households for one can or bag of garbage
INC	4.63 (2.66)	The household annual income level is:
		1 – Less than £20 000
		3 – Between $20 000 and $40 000
		6 – Between $40 000 and $80 000
		9 – Greater than $80 000
OWN	0.85 (0.35)	1 – The occupants own the house
		0 – The occupants rent the house
WORK	0.47 (0.36)	The fraction of household members that work full time
COLLEGE	0.75 (0.44)	1 – Head of household has attended some college
		0 – Head of household has not attended some college
INFANT	0.03 (0.10)	The fraction of household members less than the age of 3
TEEN	0.03 (0.09)	The fraction of household members between 13 and 17
RETIRE	0.20 (0.35)	The fraction of household members over the age of 65
MARRY	0.65 (0.50)	1 – An adult married couple lives in the household
		0 – No married couple
HHSIZE	2.77 (1.32)	Number of individuals in the household
INCPER	2.07 (1.58)	*INC/HHSIZE*

The quantities of garbage and recycling are independently estimated as functions of exogenous variables described below. Since two measures of garbage quantity are observed, three separate estimation procedures are conducted (for garbage weight, garbage volume, and recycling weight).[2] The panel data set includes 75 households over two regimes, the periods of time before and after the implementation of the per-bag pricing program.

Let Y_{it} denote the per-capita weight of garbage (or volume of garbage, or weight of recyclable materials, depending on the equation) presented for collection over an average week by household i ($i = 1, \ldots, 75$) during regime t ($t = 1, 2$). Assume Y_{it} is a linear function of the price of garbage collection during regime t (P_t), exogenous income and demographic variables for that household (X_i) and an error term. The error term is comprised of two components: unobserved variables that may vary across households but not across time, such as preferences for the environment (denoted by μ_i), and unobserved variables that vary across time and households (ε_{it}). The three demand equations can then be represented by

$$Y_{it} = \beta_0 + P_t \beta_1 + X_i \beta_2 + \mu_i + \varepsilon_{it} \qquad (1)$$

Assume μ_i and ε_{it} are distributed independent of the variables in X_i.[3] Also, assume $E[\mu_i] = 0$, $E[\varepsilon_{it}] = 0$, $\mathrm{Var}[\mu_i] = \sigma_\mu^2$, $\mathrm{Var}[\varepsilon_{it}] = \sigma_\varepsilon^2$, and $\mathrm{Cov}[\varepsilon_{it}, \mu_i] = 0$. Therefore, $\mathrm{Var}[\varepsilon_{it} + \mu_i] = \sigma_\varepsilon^2 + \sigma_\mu^2$ and $\mathrm{Corr}[\varepsilon_{it} + \mu_i, \varepsilon_{is} + \mu_i] = \sigma_\mu^2/(\sigma_\varepsilon^2 + \sigma_\mu^2)$. Estimates of the parameters β_0, β_1, β_2, σ_ε^2, and σ_μ^2 are given below.

Because of the appearance of μ_i, the error term for a particular household will be correlated across regimes.[4] Since OLS estimates of β_0, β_1, and β_2 will be inefficient, GLS estimates are obtained. These estimates are provided in Table 2.

III. Results

Garbage weight
The first column of Table 2 provides GLS estimates of the effect of exogenous variables on the per-capita weight of garbage presented by households for collection each week. The coefficient on price is negative and significantly different from zero at the 5 per cent confidence level. Using this coefficient, the price elasticity of demand for the collection of garbage, measured in pounds, at mean levels of price and weight is equal to -0.076. This estimate is somewhat closer to zero than in previous studies.[5]

The coefficient on the income variable is slightly positive, but the standard error is large. Thus, the data here suggest that household income plays no significant role in explaining garbage totals. Rich households put out roughly the same quantity of garbage as poor households. The income elasticity generated from this coefficient is 0.062, at mean levels of income and garbage weight. Thus, even if it were statistically significant, this measure would be smaller than what other studies have found.[6]

Controlling for other differences, owner-occupied households present 5.48 more pounds per person per week than renters. Homeowners may generate more waste than renters by conducting more repairs and maintenance. They might also have more space to store recyclable material. An individual who works full time presents 6.33 fewer pounds of garbage each week. Individuals in these households are away from home more of the time, and therefore may generate less waste at home. Households with a member that has attended some college produce an average of 3.63 fewer pounds of garbage per week than households without a college attendee.

Table 2   GLS estimates of garbage and recycling quantities

Independent Variable	Dependent Variable		
	WEIGHT	*VOLUME*	*RECYCLE*
CONSTANT	19.442***	1.2505***	5.8497***
	(3.352)	(0.1455)	(1.773)
PRICE	−1.9118**	−0.3370***	0.7263**
	(0.758)	(0.0442)	(0.3246)
INCPER	0.3017	−0.0189	0.3348
	(0.6069)	(0.0263)	(0.3214)
OWN	5.4805**	0.2443**	2.8306**
	(2.353)	(1.018)	(1.246)
WORK	−6.3344**	−0.2072*	−2.7240**
	(2.528)	(0.1093)	(1.339)
COLLEGE	−3.6262**	−0.0634	−0.3211
	(1.800)	(0.0779)	(0.9531)
INFANT	−1.6123	−0.3126	−2.4687
	(7.279)	(0.3148)	(3.854)
TEEN	9.5113	0.3054	3.6235
	(8.294)	(0.3587)	(4.392)
RETIRE	−2.9622	−0.0602	−0.9887
	(2.877)	(0.1244)	(1.523)
MARRY	−2.4242*	−0.1913***	−1.1268
	(1.498)	(0.0648)	(0.7930)
HHSIZE	−2.2491***	−0.1469***	−1.0345***
	(0.7306)	(0.0316)	(0.3869)
σ_ε^2	20.23	0.060	4.241
σ_μ^2	22.29	0.030	6.963
$\rho = \sigma_\mu^2/(\sigma_\varepsilon^2 + \sigma_\mu^2)$	0.524	0.333	0.621
R^2	0.284	0.458	0.287

Notes:
Number of observations = 150.
All variables are defined in Table 1.
*, **, and *** indicate significance at the 10%, 5% and 1% levels.
σ_ε^2 and σ_μ^2 are estimates of the variances of the two components of the error term.
ρ estimates the correlation between ε and μ.

The household size variable is used to test for economies of scale within the household. The negative and significant coefficient on this variable indicates that larger households produce fewer pounds per person than smaller households. Using this coefficient, an increase in household size by one individual is estimated to reduce the weight of garbage by 2.25 pounds per person.

The variances of the error terms are provided in the final rows of Table 2. Roughly half of the variance in the error term is attributable to individual effects that are constant across regimes.

Garbage volume

The data allow for estimations of demands for collection of both weight and volume of garbage presented each week by households. The second column of Table 2 provides GLS estimation of the per-capita volume of garbage as a function of the same set of independent variables. Other than for income, which is not significant, the sign of each coefficient in the volume equation is identical to that in the weight equation. In both equations the coefficient on income is small and insignificant.[7]

The price arc-elasticity of demand, measured in volume, at mean levels of price and volume is –0.225. By comparing this price elasticity to the one for weight given in the previous section, we see that individuals respond to the unit-based pricing program by reducing the volume of garbage in greater proportions than they reduce the weight of garbage. This result is not surprising since, after all, the price is charged for the number of bags of garbage rather than for the weight.

Weight of recyclable materials

The third column of Table 2 provides estimates of the demand for the collection of recyclable materials, measured by weight. In these data, households respond to a price for garbage by increasing their recycling by 0.73 pounds per person per week. The implied cross-price arc-elasticity is 0.073 at mean levels.[8] Household income, however, does not appear to influence recycling amounts.

Other demographic variables influence the quantity of recycling. Homeowners produce 2.83 pounds of recycling per week more than renters, and full-time workers present 2.72 fewer pounds of recycling per week. Finally, recycling per person decreases significantly with household size.

IV. Unobserved methods of garbage removal

As households are made to face a positive marginal cost for garbage collection, they have several options available to reduce the amount of garbage they present for collection. These may include (1) recycling, (2) composting, (3) demanding less packaging at stores, or a host of 'other' means such as the use of garbage disposal, or possibly illegal methods.

Each household was asked on the questionnaire to reveal methods it had used to reduce garbage in response to the per-bag fee. Each household could indicate that it (1) did not attempt to reduce its garbage, or that it had (2) recycled more, (3) composted more, (4) demanded less packaging at stores, or (5) used 'other' means to reduce its garbage. Ideally, the survey might ask whether households disposed of garbage in some illegal fashion, but households may not respond to such a direct question if they are reluctant to admit illegal behavior. Since the first four options would seem to cover all possible legal alternatives, the 'other' option may signify the use of illegal disposal such as burning, littering, or using commercial dumpsters.[9]

Since the weight of each household's garbage and recyclable material are observed, comparisons can be made between responses on the questionnaire and actual behavior. Table 3 shows the change in the weight of garbage, the change in the volume of garbage, and the change in the weight of recyclable material for households choosing each method of garbage reduction in the questionnaire.[10]

For households indicating they 'did not reduce' their garbage, the actual weight of garbage fell by only 0.67 pounds per person per week. This amount is substantially lower than the 1.91 pounds average reduction per person observed overall. This subset did reduce their volume of garbage by 0.31 containers per person per week, so they may have devoted some effort to increase garbage density.

For households indicating they 'recycled more', actual recycling increased by 0.88 pounds per person per week. This amount is somewhat greater than (but not statistically different from) the increase of 0.73 pounds observed from all households, but it exceeds more substantially the increase of 0.35 pounds per person per week observed from the households that did not indicate they 'recycled more'. In addition, households may indicate more than one of the four methods of reducing garbage. For households indicating they 'composted more', the weight of garbage fell by 2.81 pounds per person per week. Little of this amount reappears as additional recycling, so that garbage does seem to have been removed from the waste stream.

For households that indicate they 'demanded less packaging at stores', the weight of garbage and of recycling both *increased*, by 1.58 ponds and by 0.08 pounds per person per week, respectively. That they were unable to reduce garbage is not entirely surprising, given the short time period of the study.

Finally, for households indicating they use 'other' means, actual garbage falls by 6.38 pounds per person per week. This fall in garbage is more than twice the amount in any other column of Table 3, and it is more than three times the average fall in garbage. In fact, several of these households present no garbage at all following the implementation of unit pricing. Moreover, the last column of Table 3 shows that those who reported 'other' methods reduced their recycling as well, whereas recycling rises in every other column of the table, and it rises by an average of 0.73 pounds per person – an amount that is significantly different from zero.

How could an increase in the price of garbage collection induce these folks to decrease their recycling? Kinnaman and Fullerton (1995) suggest that this outcome could be explained if illicit dumping has a fixed cost, such as the cost of finding an appropriate dump site. That fixed cost may keep most households from dumping at all, but an increase in the cost of legal garbage collection may be enough to outweigh that fixed cost for some households who then dump all of their waste, both garbage and recyclable material. Thus recycling at the curb actually falls.

In other words, these data may suggest that households are taking garbage to dumpsters or to discard at the side of the road. See Fullerton and Kinnaman (1996) for a more elaborate discussion of illegal dumping.

Table 3   Change in per-capita garbage and recycling for households that indicate each method of reduction[a]

	All households	Households indicating				
		Did not reduce	Recycled more	Composted more	Demanded less packaging	Used other methods
Percentage	100	25.3	65.3	30.7	17.3	10.7
Change in garbage weight in pounds (Standard Error)	−1.9118** (0.8320)	−0.6743 (3.554)	−2.2029 (1.620)	−2.8092 (1.909)	1.5838 (1.738)	−6.3815* (3.688)
Change in garbage volume in cans (Standard Error)	−0.3370*** (0.0458)	−0.3149* (0.1750)	−0.3133*** (0.0844)	−0.3283** (0.1235)	−0.1492 (0.0961)	−0.4375** (0.1737)
Change in recycling weight in pounds (Standard Error)	0.7263* (0.3767)	0.5092 (1.269)	0.8778 (0.9897)	0.0915 (1.305)	0.0829 (1.706)	−0.9957 (1.291)
Change in total weight in pounds (Standard Error)	−1.1855 (1.197)	0.4417 (4.214)	−1.3251 (2.276)	−2.7178 (2.682)	2.4123 (2.938)	−7.3772* (4.123)

Notes:
a.   This table shows the change in weights and volumes per person per week. Households were allowed to indicate more than one method of reduction, in response to the question: 'Since the sticker program was implemented on July 1, 1992, which of the following means have you used to reduce the amount of garbage you have collected each week?'.
Standard errors are in parentheses.
*, **, and *** indicate significance at the 10%, 5%, and 1% level.

V. Conclusion

Using measured garbage and recycling totals and responses to questionnaires, this chapter estimates household demand for garbage and recycling collection services. Households respond to an increase in the per-bag price by reducing garbage and increasing recycling. A number of other relationships between garbage and recycling quantities and household demographic characteristics are also uncovered by the data. For example, income is estimated to have no significant effect on garbage and recycling totals. For communities faced with increasing costs of disposing solid waste, the results of this chapter may provide valuable assistance in the design and understanding of solid waste management plans.

Notes
*   The author wishes to thank Don Fullerton, Phil Heap, Catherine O'Connor and Steve Stern for assistance.
1. See Fullerton and Kinnaman (1996) for a careful description of the data gathering effort. Charlottesville already provided voluntary curbside recycling of several materials for all of its residents. Containers of recyclable materials were collected each week on the same day as regular garbage collection. In December 1991, the city decided that in July 1992 it would start charging residents for each bag of garbage collected. This program would require residents to place a sticker, costing $0.80, on each 32-gallon can or bag of garbage for collection. The city would not collect garbage without a sticker.
2. The three equations could be estimated together using seemingly unrelated regressions, but results are unaffected since all equations use the same right-hand variables.
3. A Hausman test could not reject the null hypothesis that μ_i and ε_{it} are independent of X_i.
4. The Breusch and Pagan Lagrange multiplier test rejected the null hypothesis that $\sigma_\mu^2 = 0$ for all three equations, at the 1 per cent level. Therefore, either a random or fixed effects model is necessary to obtain efficient estimates of the parameters. The fixed effects model is not appropriate here because of the very few time periods and the lack of variation in the X_i across regimes, so the random effects model is used.
5. An arc-elasticity is measured since price is only zero or 80 cents. Using aggregate data, others have estimated the price elasticity to be –0.12 (Jenkins, 1991), –0.15 (Wertz, 1976), –0.26 and –0.22 (Morris and Byrd, 1990, in two communities), and –0.14 (Skumatz and Breckinridge, 1990).
6. Other studies have used aggregate data sets to estimate this income elasticity. For example, Hong et al. (1993) estimate 0.049, Richardson and Havlicek (1978) estimate 0.242, Wertz (1976) estimates 0.279 and 0.242 in two different samples, Petrovic and Jaffee (1978) estimate 0.2, and Jenkins (1991) estimates 0.41.
7. This negative coefficient on income in the volume equation may be attributable to the method used to measure volume (counting the number of garbage containers each morning). High-income households often use large, sturdy garbage containers with wheels. They are also more apt to use garbage compactors. Low-income households typically use plastic bags and may find it more difficult to compact garbage. They therefore are more likely to carry two light plastic bags to the curb instead of wheeling one heavy container. Perhaps one long-run result of a per-bag pricing program is that households may purchase larger containers with wheels to decrease volume, in order to decrease disposal costs.
8. Using only two observations from each community, US EPA (1990) estimates this cross-price elasticity for Perkasie, PA (0.49), Illion, NY (0.48), and Seattle (0.06 in 1985–86 and 0.10 in 1986–87).
9. The questionnaire did not include an option for putting more food through an in-sink garbage disposal, but the *change* in this behavior is likely to be small.
10. A multinomial probit model was employed to estimate the effects of demographic variables on the chosen method of disposal. Very few of the variables were statistically different from zero.

References
Fullerton, Don and Kinnaman, Thomas C. (1996), 'Household Responses to Pricing Garbage by the Bag', *American Economic Review*, 86(4), September 1996, 971–84.
Hong, Seonghoon, Adams, Richard M. and Love, H. Alan (1993), 'An Economic Analysis of Household Recycling of Solid Wastes: The Case of Portland, Oregon', *Journal of Environmental Economics and Management*, 25(2), September 1993, 136–46.

Jenkins, Robin (1991), 'Municipal Demand for Solid Waste Disposal Services: The Impact of User Fees', unpublished manuscript, University of Maryland.

Kinnaman, Thomas C. and Fullerton, Don (1995), 'How a Fee Per-unit Garbage Affects Aggregate Recycling in a Model With Heterogeneous Households', in *Public Economics and the Environment in an Imperfect World*, Bovenberg, Lans and Cnossen, Sijbbren (eds), Boston: Kluwer.

Morris, Glenn E. and Byrd, Denise (1990), 'The Effects of Weight or Volume-based Pricing on Solid Waste Management', unpublished report, US EPA, January.

Petrovic, William M. and Jaffee, Bruce L. (1978), 'Measuring the Generation and Collection of Solid Waste in Cities', *Urban Affairs Quarterly*, 14, December 1978, 229–44.

Richardson, Robert A. and Havlicek, Joseph, Jr. (1978), 'Economic Analysis of the Composition of Household Solid Wastes', *Journal of Environmental Economics and Management*, 5(1), March 1978, 103–11.

Skumatz, Lisa and Breckinridge, Cabell (1990), *Handbook for Solid Waste Officials, Volume 2*, Washington DC: EPA 530-SW-90-084B, June.

Steuteville, Robert (1996), 'The State of Garbage in America', *Biocycle*, 37(5), May, 54–61.

US Environmental Protection Agency (1990), *Charging Households for Waste Collection and Disposals*, Washington DC: EPA 530-SW-90-047.

Wertz, Kenneth L. (1976), 'Economic Factors Influencing Households' Production of Refuse', *Journal of Environmental Economics and Management*, 2(3), May 1976, 263–72.

[8]

EXPLAINING THE GROWTH IN MUNICIPAL RECYCLING PROGRAMS
The Role of Market and Nonmarket Factors

THOMAS C. KINNAMAN
Bucknell University

The implementation of thousands of municipal recycling programs in the United States has increased recycling's portion of solid waste from 10% to 30% over the past decade. But the lack of accurate data has spurred a debate over whether the growth in recycling can be attributed to market or nonmarket factors. To address this issue, this article conducts a benefit-cost analysis of a municipal recycling program. Results suggest recycling is costly. So why, then, does it remain popular? This article suggests that local governments could be responding to households that perceive a benefit from recycling services. These benefits are estimated with a contingent valuation survey.

The portion of municipal solid waste that is recycled in the United States has steadily increased from approximately 10% in 1989 to 30% in 1997. This trend can be attributed primarily to the implementation of more than 8,000 municipal curbside and drop-off recycling programs over this period (Glenn, 1998). Currently, 46% of Americans have access to curbside recycling, and many more have local access to drop-off facilities. Clearly, the rapid growth in municipal recycling programs can be considered one of the more significant environmental policy movements over the past decade.

An interesting policy question is the extent to which this recent growth in municipal recycling programs can be attributed to market factors. Casual evidence supports such a link. First, recycling is most common in the northeast region of the United States where solid waste disposal costs (tipping fees) exceed those in other regions of the country. Second, the growth in recycling has come on the heels of increases in solid waste transportation costs that began when municipalities started to shift garbage disposal from local town dumps to remote regional landfills.[1] However, the original data employed by this article to estimate the market benefits and costs of operating a municipal recycling program show that costs to collect and process recyclable material exceed the benefits from selling the collected materials and from taking less garbage to the landfill. Therefore, if recycling is indeed expensive, then nonmarket factors must have also played a role in the past decade's growth in recycling. One potential nonmarket factor could be a reduction in the external costs of traditional garbage disposal attributable to the extra recycling. Garbage disposal is a messy practice: Landfills emit foul odors and threaten area ground water supplies, and incineration produces air pollution and toxic ash. But these disposal

AUTHOR'S NOTE: The author wishes to thank participants at the workshop on Economic Policy and Public Finance at the University of Chicago and at the annual meetings of the Pennsylvania Economic Association. Nada Gray (Borough Manager of Lewisburg) and Shawn McLaughlin (environmental planner and recycling coordinator of Union County) were helpful in providing essential data. Chaffee Pham and Peter Coughlin provided very able research assistance.

PUBLIC WORKS MANAGEMENT & POLICY, Vol. 5 No. 1, July 2000 37-51
© 2000 Sage Publications, Inc.

practices increasingly occur in rural settings at some distance from the municipality (see Note 2). Municipal governments might not worry about these environmental costs if garbage is "exported" to surrounding regions.

Because neither market nor environmental factors seem to fully explain the growth in recycling, this article suggests and tests a third factor. Municipal recycling programs, like other municipal services such as parks and recreational facilities, could provide some kind of direct benefits to local residents. Local governments may have implemented recycling programs in response to these benefits; if households benefit, the program need not pay for itself. Results from a contingent valuation survey of local households support this claim.

The Benefit-Cost Data

Recall that the first contribution of this article is to estimate the market benefits and costs of municipal recycling programs. If market benefits exceed costs, then the growth in recycling could be attributed to such factors. But reliable benefit-cost data are difficult to obtain by either of two available strategies. The first strategy takes advantage of the fact that some state government recycling offices keep cost records for all of their state's recycling programs to award municipalities grants to reimburse their recycling expenses.[2] Each of these records could be combined to form a cross-sectional data set of recycling costs. But municipalities differ over procedures used to budget recycling expenses. Some local governments include the capitalized cost of unused landfill space, whereas others do not. Some local governments include the cost of garbage collection when the same truck collects garbage and recycling, whereas others do not. A few include the opportunity cost to employ municipal resources to store recyclable materials, but most do not. Based on survey responses from 102 municipal solid waste officials, Savas (1979) estimates that actual solid waste collection costs are 30% higher than municipal accounts indicate. Folz (1999) also reports a considerable variation in how municipalities estimate their own recycling costs. For these reasons, a cross-sectional data set may prove unreliable for an accurate estimate of the market costs and benefits of recycling.[3]

A second and perhaps more accurate method of obtaining benefit-cost data is to collect it directly from individual communities. This case study approach has been employed in studies done by trade associations within the solid waste industry such as the Solid Waste Association of North America (SWANA) (1995). The SWANA study finds that the market costs of curbside recycling in six communities in the United States average $74 per ton more than the cost of traditional landfill disposal. Hanley and Slark (1994) conducted a benefit-cost analysis in a single town in Scotland. They estimate the quantifiable market and nonmarket benefits of newspaper recycling exceed the market costs. Therefore, little consensus has been reached on estimating the costs of municipal recycling programs within the economics literature.

This study utilizes the case study approach to gather data but adds considerable detail to existing efforts. Original data are gathered to estimate virtually all of the direct program costs and benefits of operating a single recycling program. Intensive interviews were conducted with local officials. Several on-site visits and inspections of every step of the recycling process took place. Government account ledgers were reviewed when necessary, but total costs were estimated using economic rather than accounting principles. As should become apparent below, many of the benefits and costs of recycling included in this study would be impossible to measure without such a thorough data-gathering process. Thus, one contribution of this article is the provision of more accurate recycling benefit-cost data.

The data were gathered in Lewisburg, Pennsylvania, a municipality located along the Susquehanna River in the central part of the state. Lewisburg has operated a drop-off facility for several materials since the early 1980s. In 1988, the municipality voluntarily implemented a curbside recycling program in which newspapers and aluminum were collected each month from households. Thus, Lewisburg's program was fairly mature in 1996 when cost data were gathered.

Table 1:   A Statistical Comparison of Lewisburg to the State and Nation

	Income[a]	Education[b]	Education[c]	Density[d]
Lewisburg	26,123	83.7	34.2	5,785
Pennsylvania				
Urban	24,859	75.2	20.1	
Urban fringe	26,541	81.0	24.3	
Small towns[e]	21,234	73.4	14.2	
Nation				
Urban	25,381	76.6	22.6	
Urban fringe	27,607	81.6	25.5	
Small Towns[e]	20,959	70.8	14.6	
Pittsburgh				6,652.5

NOTE: Data are from the 1990 U.S. Census.

a. Among year-around full-time workers.

b. Percentage high school graduates among those older than 25.

c. Percentage college graduates among those older than 25.

d. Persons per square mile.

e. Places with populations between 2,500 and 9,999.

In 1991, Lewisburg was required by the commonwealth of Pennsylvania to pass a local ordinance making the recycling of certain materials mandatory for households and businesses.[4]
Because of this law, households in Lewisburg are now required to recycle glass as well as newspaper and aluminum. Curbside collection of these materials is provided once per month at no fee
to households,[5] but enforcement of the ordinance is weak: Garbage handlers simply periodically inspect the contents of garbage and refuse to collect material that contains recyclables.[6]
Lewisburg also provides drop-off facilities that accept bi-metal cans, magazines, and 1-gallon
plastic milk jugs and 2-liter plastic beverage containers. No curbside collection of these materials is provided. Residents and firms in Lewisburg recycled a total of 334.46 tons of material in
1995, representing 11.59% of the total waste stream.[7]

Although a small town, Lewisburg's demographic characteristics resemble to some extent
those of larger cities and (especially) their suburbs. Using U.S. Census data, Table 1 compares
the income and education level of an average individual older than 25 years of age in Lewisburg
with the average individual older than 25 residing in other types of communities. The average
full-time worker in Lewisburg makes $26,123 dollars per year, which compares favorably to the
average full-time worker in an urban suburb (termed "urban fringe") and is more than $5,000
more than the average person in other small towns across the country. Similar comparisons can
be made with education levels. The percentage of individuals older than 25 years of age in
Lewisburg with a high school (83.7%) or college (34.2%) degree resembles most the education
levels attained in an urban fringe area.[8]

Lewisburg's population density is also somewhat unique among small towns. Because
Lewisburg's housing stock is composed of Victorian town homes located adjacent to one
another, the population density of 5,785 per square mile resembles the density of Pittsburgh's. If
the cost of collecting recyclable material is a function of the population density, then cost data
gathered in Lewisburg could also be useful to estimate costs in larger communities.[9] However,
larger communities could enjoy economies of scale (Bohm, Folz, & Podolsky, 1999).

The Market Benefits and Costs of Municipal Recycling

The market benefits of Lewisburg's municipal recycling program are (a) the revenue earned
from the sale of the recycled materials and (b) reductions in garbage collection and disposal
costs. The market costs of the program include costs to collect, process, store, and deliver the
materials to secondary markets. Market costs also accrue to recycling firms and households.
Each of these benefits and costs are estimated and discussed separately below.

40   PUBLIC WORKS MANAGEMENT & POLICY / July 2000

TABLE 2: The Net Operating Cost Differential of Recycling

	Amount (dollars)
Direct program benefits	
Reduced disposal costs (334.46 tons times $47 per ton)	15,719.62
Reduced solid waste transportation costs	1,539.03
Sale of recycled materials (see Table 3 for prices and quantities)	9,125.90
Total	26,384.55
Direct program costs	
Collection/delivery costs	
Curbside collection from households[a]	4,080.00
Processing costs	
Labor cost to receive corrugated boxes and office paper	2,080.00
Labor cost to receive aluminum, glass, bi-metal cans, plastic	2,320.00
Routine maintenance for glass shredder	370.00
Storage costs	
Rent on tractor trailer to store corrugated boxes and office paper	3,600.00
Rental cost for storage space for plastic	1,650.00
Rental cost for storage space for magazines	325.00
Opportunity cost of municipal warehouse to store glass and aluminum	1,740.00
Transportation costs	
Cost to ship glass to market	2,750.00
Cost to ship aluminum to market	1,645.11
Cost to ship plastic and bi-metal cans to market	960.00
Administrative costs	
Three hours per week devoted to recycling by borough manager	2,500.00
Advertising costs	1,303.76
Capital costs	
Original purchase price of glass crusher (at $2,750.00)	
Original purchase price of newspaper shredder (at $49,171.00)	
One-time upgrade to newspaper shredder[b] (at $22,196.00)	
Annual rental cost of capital (5% of $74,117.00)	3,705.85
Total	29,029.92
Net operating cost differential	–2,645.37

a. This cost was estimated using market data for collection costs.
b. Buyer of newspaper needed upgrades to make shredding and bailing of newspaper more efficient.

MARKET BENEFITS TO THE MUNICIPAL GOVERNMENT

Market benefits that accrued to Lewisburg's economy in 1995 from the implementation of the recycling program are provided in Table 2. A significant benefit of the recycling program was the reduction in disposal costs paid at the landfill. The municipality saved $15,719.62 (334.46 tons recycled times the local tipping fees of $47 per ton). If the landfill internalizes the scarcity value of landfill space (Hanley & Slark, 1994), then the tipping fee reflects the cost of purchasing new land once the current landfill is full. If the tipping fee does not reflect the costs of new land (which is likely for publicly owned landfills), then the private cost of garbage disposal is underestimated by the tipping fee.

A second benefit arose from taking fewer deliveries of solid waste to the landfill. Municipal garbage trucks made 432 trips (delivering 2,917.02 tons of garbage) over the year prior to mandatory recycling and 345 trips (delivering 2,631.55 tons) over the year following its implementation, saving 87 trips. Based on the average gas mileage of garbage trucks, the municipality saved an estimated $11.99 for each 30-mile roundtrip, implying total savings of $1043.13 in 1995. The drivers were salaried, so labor costs did not decrease; nor did the municipality enjoy lower insurance rates on garbage trucks. But the 20% reduction in the number of trips to the landfill may have imposed less wear and tear on the garbage trucks. Trucks of similar size rented for $0.19 per mile in a competitive truck-renting market. Using this figure to estimate the depreciation to a truck from an additional mile, $5.70 per trip ($495.90 per year) was saved.

Table 3:   Prices and Quantities of Each Material Recycled

Material	Price^a in $ (per pound)	Household Quantity (in pounds)	Firm Quantity (in pounds)	Extra Services Included in Price
Corrugated boxes	0	3,884	193,703	Transportation and processing
Mixed office paper	0	0	24,907	Transportation and processing
Magazines	0	27,268	30	Transportation and processing
Aluminum	0.54	5,740	353	None
Glass	0	—	12,198^b	Transportation and processing
Brown	$.015	47,900	—	None
Green	$.015	25,940	—	None
Clear	0.0225	204,340	—	None
Newspaper	0	88,000	0	Transportation
Bi-metal cans	0.0085	15,345	0	None
PET plastic (milk jugs)	0	10,691	0	None
HDPE plastic (coke bottles)	0	7,035	0	None

a. Denotes price received by the municipality.
b. Data for glass collected from businesses by private haulers does not specify color. Private haulers market this glass directly.

A third direct program benefit of curbside recycling was the provision of recycled materials to the economy. In competitive markets, the economic value of each material is estimated by its price.[10] The price paid to the municipality for each material is provided in the second column of Table 3. The material was purchased by either an intermediate or final buyer.[11] Any extra services provided by an intermediate buyer are listed in the fifth column of Table 3. The costs of providing these extra services do not need to be estimated separately because they are incorporated (or internalized) into the lower price paid to the municipality for the materials.

An estimate of the value of all recycled material is obtained by multiplying the price received by the municipality for each material by the quantity of each material recycled. A total of $9,125.90 worth of materials was sold. The summation of the market benefits from reduced disposal costs, reduced trips to the landfill, and the sale of recycled materials amounted to $26,384.55. These benefits will be compared with the market costs of recycling described in the next sections.[12]

MARKET COSTS TO THE MUNICIPAL GOVERNMENT

The recycling process required (a) the collection of recyclable materials from the curbs of households, (b) the processing and storage of these recyclable material at the municipal recycling center, and (c) the transportation of these materials to final markets. Administrative resources were also required to oversee the process. The costs of each of these steps are also given in Table 2 and discussed below.

The municipality paid a hauling firm $4,080 in 1995 to collect glass, aluminum, and newspaper once per month from households. Glass and aluminum were processed and stored in a 560 square foot warehouse owned by the municipality. Although the municipality does not pay rent for the use of this warehouse, it foregoes the opportunity to rent the warehouse space to others. The competitive rental cost of comparably sized storage space was $1,740 per year (and several storage companies were sold out of lots this size).

Dropped-off materials must also be received and stored. Plastics dropped off by households were stored at a separate facility not owned by the municipality at a cost of $1,650 per year. A tractor-trailer bed was rented at an annual cost of $3,600 to receive and store corrugated boxes and office paper dropped off by businesses and households. Magazines were stored separately at a cost of $325 per year. The cost of labor necessary to monitor the drop-off facilities and receive materials amounted to $4,400 per year.[13]

The municipality chose to crush glass and aluminum to reduce transportation costs. This light processing occurred in the municipality-owned warehouse described above. The municipality initially paid $2,750 for a crusher and paid an average of $370 each year to maintain it.[14] The crushed glass, crushed aluminum, plastic, and other materials were transported to final buyers at a cost of $5,355.11.

Newspaper is shredded separately for use as animal bedding by local farmers. The municipality agreed to purchase a newspaper shredder for a large local farm at a cost of $71,367. In exchange, the farm agreed to collect the newspaper from the recycling center each month and to pay all routine maintenance involved with the shredder.

The costs of the glass crusher and the paper shredder comprise the only significant fixed costs of the recycling program. The $74,117 used to pay these up-front costs could have been invested. Assuming a potential 5% real rate of return, the capital costs amounted to $3,705.85 per year. Administrative costs consisted of the value of 3 hours per week allocated by the borough manager to recycling and advertising expenses paid to promote the program each year.

According to these data, the total costs of the recycling program amounted to $29,029.37. Thus, the market costs of the municipal recycling program exceeded the benefits by $2,645.37. The market cost to recycling firms and households will be added to this figure below.

MARKET COSTS TO RECYCLING FIRMS

If local ordinances require firms to recycle certain materials, such as corrugated boxes and mixed office paper, these costs should be factored into the benefit-cost calculus. Many of the municipal recycling programs in operation in this country (including Lewisburg's) contain such local ordinances. And whether these materials are taken to a drop-off location in the borough by businesses themselves or taken away by a private hauler, the mandate to recycle involves the use of resources that have been ignored by previous estimates of recycling costs. Municipal government officials facing reelection could internalize these costs if local firms vocalize their displeasure with the municipal recycling program or if local consumers complain after facing the resulting higher prices.

Three private haulers competed in Lewisburg for the delivery of recyclable materials. Two of the three haulers provided price information, and both charged $20 per delivery for a large pick-up load (about 6 square yards). The municipal government documented each of the 362 deliveries of commercial recyclables in 1995. Assuming competition in the collection industry (where price is equal to marginal cost), the value of economic resources allocated to deliver recyclable material amounted to $7,240.

Most businesses self-delivered recyclable materials to the recycling center. According to government records, 866 self-deliveries were made in 1995. The value of each firm's resources devoted to the self-delivery of recyclable materials is not observed. However, it can be assumed that delivery costs must have been less than $20 per trip or these firms would have hired one of the three private haulers to take delivery. Assuming an average cost of $10 per trip implies the total cost of self-delivering recyclable materials is $8,660. Thus, the cost to local firms is estimated at $15,900.[15]

MARKET COSTS TO RECYCLING HOUSEHOLDS

Recycling also involves the use of scarce household resources (such as time and storage space) that could have been allocated to other uses. Jakus, Tiller, and Park (1996) use survey responses to estimate that it takes an average of 36 seconds to recycle newspaper and 54 seconds to recycle glass. Schaumberg and Doyle (1995) assume households take 5 minutes per week to prepare all recyclable material. Assuming a cost of labor of $7.50 per hour, this cost amounts to $60 per ton. Reschovsky and Stone (1994) find that households reporting adequate storage space are much more likely to report on a mail survey that they recycle.

Table 4: Values of Disposal Fee, Price Index of Recycled Materials, and Recycling Costs That Allow Recycling to Be Cost-Effective

Recycled Materials Price Factor[b]	Necessary Value of Disposal Fee With:[a]			
	Current Program Costs	10% Cost Reduction	20% Cost Reduction	30% Cost Reduction
1.00	102.45	89.01	75.58	62.15
1.25	95.63	82.19	68.76	55.33
1.50	88.81	75.37	61.94	48.50
1.75	81.98	68.55	55.12	41.68
2.00	75.16	61.73	48.30	34.86

NOTE: This table reads as follows. If recycling costs were to decrease by 10%, and if prices of all recycled materials increased by 25% (price factor of 1.25), then the recycling program would be cost-effective if the disposal fee were to rise to $82.19 per ton.
a. Current disposal fee is $47.00.
b. Current price factor is 1.00. Simply multiply the price factor by current prices of recycled materials to get threshold prices. Current price of aluminum is $0.54 per pound; current price of clear glass is $45 per ton. The current price of bi-metal cans is $17 per ton.

These costs are not included in the benefit-cost analysis here because they will be incorporated indirectly in the responses obtained by the contingent valuation study below. For example, if a household reports that it is willing to pay $5 per quarter for municipal recycling services, then this household can be assumed to enjoy the recycling program by at least $5 more than their resource costs or they would have declined the offer to pay that amount. The results of the survey are described more carefully below.

AN ANALYSIS OF THE MARKET BENEFITS AND COSTS

Combining the $2,645.37 paid by the Lewisburg municipal government in 1995 with the $15,900 paid by local firms for delivery implies the local economy's total out-of-pocket expenses amounted to $18,545.37 (an average of $10.35 per Lewisburg household). When broken down by tons, the Lewisburg economy paid an average of $102.45 per ton to recycle the material—$55.45 per ton more than the cost of disposing that material in the landfill. These costs would not have accrued to the economy in the absence of the recycling program.

Two general points can be made based on this result. First, recycling is a costly local service. Waste removal costs could decrease by utilizing the lower-cost landfill rather than operating a recycling program. Second, this cost estimate almost doubles the $10,106 "reimbursement" grant received by Lewisburg from the commonwealth of Pennsylvania's recycling office. The value of that grant was based on the quantity of each type of material recycled, not on actual costs. Given the thoroughness of this study's data collection effort, state-generated cross-sectional cost data may be inaccurate, providing added argument for the need to gather data on a case-by-case basis.

Could recycling ever pay for itself? Perhaps, but the value of at least one of the variables used in the analysis above would need to change for the costs of municipal recycling to equal zero. For example, benefits would increase if the tipping fee or the prices paid for recycled materials were to increase. Costs of collecting, processing, storing, and transporting recyclable material might also fall. Table 4 provides threshold values of the tipping fee, a price index of recycled materials, and program costs that would allow the recycling program to finance itself. At current prices and program costs, the tipping fee would have to roughly double to $102.45 per ton for curbside recycling to pay for itself. The tipping fee would have to rise to only $62.15 if collection costs fell by 30%. An increase in the price of materials could also make recycling cost-effective. For example, if prices increased by 50% (a price index of 1.50), the recycling

44   PUBLIC WORKS MANAGEMENT & POLICY / July 2000

program would pay for itself without a change in collection costs if the tipping fee increased to $88.81. A number of other combinations provided in Table 4 could also allow the out-of-pocket recycling expenses to equal zero. At the current tipping fee of $47 per ton, prices of materials would have to double (price factor of 2.00) and collection costs would have to decrease by 20%.

Many of these changes may be difficult to achieve. The highest state-averaged tipping fee in the country is $61 per ton in New Jersey (Glenn, 1998). Material prices have increased but have not sustained their higher levels. Increases in the technology of collecting and processing recycled materials could decrease costs, and many advocates of curbside recycling emphasize these possibilities. But with the recent fall in tipping fees in the northeastern United States, prospects appear dim for the self-financing of municipal recycling.

Note that a significant component of the costs of the program is the delivery of corrugated boxes and office paper by commercial establishments to a drop-off center. The commonwealth government of Pennsylvania (as well as a handful of other states in the northeast) mandates such activity. As illustrated in Table 3, 118.33 tons of Lewisburg's recycling efforts (35%) was based on the involuntary recycling efforts of local firms. If the mandatory ordinance requiring participation among firms were eliminated, direct costs to the local government would fall by $5,680 (because the municipality would no longer need to receive or store corrugated boxes and office paper). Direct costs to local firms would fall by the previously estimated $15,900. Direct benefits would also fall by an estimated $6,296.73, because those previously recycled materials would have to be instead transported and disposed in the landfill. Thus, the entire cost of the program would fall from $18,545.37 to only $3,262.10—only $1.82 per household per year. Possible policy implications are (a) states eliminating the requirement that firms recycle or (b) municipalities engineering a more efficient method to collect those materials.

Alternative Explanations for the Growth in Recycling

Although the economics literature has yet to reach a consensus on a single cost estimate of recycling, nearly all studies suggest recycling is costly. Why, then, does municipal recycling remain popular if local economies are in fact losing money from operating these programs? This section provides alternative explanations.

First, local and state policy officials may be pursuing policy objectives with incomplete information. Perhaps once local and state officials are aware of the full costs of these programs, they will slowly begin to eliminate them. Some casual data supports this claim. The District of Columbia had recently temporarily suspended its recycling programs, citing higher than expected costs. Eleven states have also reported a decrease in the number of curbside recycling programs in 1997 (Glenn, 1998), perhaps due to updated information on the costs. But the general trend toward recycling is still one of growth. The state of Ohio recently reported 86 new municipal programs began operation in 1997, and three other states reported the addition of more than 20 programs, bringing the nation's total to nearly 9,000 programs. Clearly, 9,000 municipal governments haven't miscalculated the market benefits and costs of recycling.

Second, perhaps local policy officials have implemented municipal programs to satisfy an objective other than the pursuit of market benefits. Municipal recycling programs are expected to produce environmental benefits, and local governments are surely aware of this. Increases in recycling are expected to reduce the external costs associated with landfill disposal and incineration, both as well as air and water pollution.[16] According to Franklin Associates (1994), the use of recycled over virgin inputs in manufacturing is estimated to reduce 10 types of air emissions and 8 types of water effluents, even accounting for the extra emissions from curbside collection and processing practices. The greatest reductions would occur for carbon dioxide, methane, particulate matter, nitrogen oxides, and sulfur oxides. Using those estimates, Lewisburg's recycling activities are estimated to decrease carbon dioxide emissions by 434 tons and sulfur dioxide emissions by 2 tons.

As indicated in the introduction, however, the citizens of a community that is considering the implementation of a recycling program do not enjoy these external benefits. Most municipalities dispose garbage in regional landfills located several miles away, and the reduction in air and water pollution occurs in manufacturing regions in other parts of the state or country. In fact, only the environmental costs of municipal recycling services such as extra congestion and truck pollution are local to the community. Individuals far from the municipality enjoy the environmental benefits. Local governments cannot be expected to voluntarily incur local environmental problems to produce such benefits for others.

Perhaps because of this logic, seven state governments have passed legislation requiring all communities to implement curbside recycling programs; another 15 provide financial incentives (Glenn, 1998). These laws are often accompanied by state grants designed to finance local recycling efforts. An example of such a law is Act 101, passed in 1991 by the commonwealth of Pennsylvania. This law has had a tremendous impact on the number of municipal recycling programs operating in the state. Prior to Act 101, 245 towns recycled only 414,000 tons in Pennsylvania. By 1993, after the full effects of the law were realized, 755 curbside recycling programs were recycling 1,710,000 tons of material.[17]

Perhaps, then, the growth in municipal recycling is not a function of local decisions but of the implementation of these state laws with the accompanying grants. For example, Lewisburg's grant of $10,106 exceeded the market costs of recycling to the municipality ($2,645.37). Indeed, 5,221 of the 8,937 municipal curbside programs nationwide (58.4%) operate in states with such laws and grant programs (Glenn, 1998). These laws and grants provide a powerful descriptor for the national trend. But what drove the local decisions of the other 3,500 communities and the portion of the 5,221 communities that chose to implement a recycling program prior to the implementation of any state law? A final explanation given in this article for the growth in municipal recycling programs relates to local government responses to the preferences of their citizens. The next section explores this option.

Nonmarket Benefits to Households

Could households directly value the ability to recycle? If so, then political benefits could accrue to local politicians that adopt recycling programs (West, 1990). Municipal governments could devote resources to recycling programs to satisfy the demands of their citizens, just as they do with other municipal services such as parks and recreational facilities.

But how do residents benefit directly from recycling services? Households may altruistically dislike contributing garbage. These tastes could arise either from some endowed sense of civic duty or to avoid the perception of harming the environment.[18] Households endowed with such preferences can be expected to devote scarce resources to recycling even in the absence of a legal or economic incentive. Indeed, Fullerton and Kinnaman (1996) find that 73.3% of households lacking such incentives regularly participate in a recycling program. Because a municipal recycling program simplifies the household's recycling effort, the household would encourage its government to implement one.[19]

A contingent valuation study was conducted in Lewisburg to estimate the household's value (willingness to pay) for the municipal recycling program described above. A sample of households was randomly selected from the local directory.[20] These households were telephoned and told that a $5 donation would be made to a local charity of their choice if they responded to a few questions about recycling. The response rate was nearly 83%.[21]

The questions and results of the survey appear in the appendix. Seventy-five percent of households surveyed indicated they normally participated in the curbside recycling program. Most households recycled because they believed recycling was good for the environment rather than through a sense of civic duty, though 33% of households could not choose between these two options. A majority of households also believed that storing material was the most difficult aspect involved with recycling. Difficulty in cleaning and separating materials and remembering the correct day to produce materials at the curb were problems identified by a smaller percentage of households.

162   The Economics of Household Garbage and Recycling Behavior

Responses to Question 6 are important for the estimation of nonmarket benefits to households. Households previously paid $31.35 each quarter for regular garbage collection. Each household was asked whether it would prefer to pay an extra amount that could be added to the quarterly waste bill (either $2, $3, $5, $10, or $20, determined randomly) or abandon the recycling program.[22] All but one of the households presented with the $2 fee was willing to pay the extra fee, whereas 17 of 20 presented with a $3 fee would pay it. But only 12 of the 20 households would pay a $20 fee.[23]

A maximum likelihood procedure developed by Cameron and James (1987) was used to estimate the household's willingness to pay for the recycling program based on the "yes"/"no" responses to Question 6. Assuming a normal distribution, the average willingness to pay is estimated at $23.12 per quarter (with a standard error of $14.48), or $92.48 per year.[24] As described above, logic indicates that this figure is net of any household resource costs incurred while recycling.[25]

Because contingent valuation surveys are based on responses to hypothetical questions, some question their validity. Other forms of evidence are provided here to support the notion that households value (and would be willing to pay for) the ability to recycle. First, private firms have profited from providing private curbside recycling services in towns without a municipal collection program. For example, private recycling firms (with clever names such as "Paper Chase" and "Trash Rehash") were relatively successful in several Virginia cities in the early 1990s before the implementation of free (to the household) municipal programs drove these firms out of the industry. Second, several municipalities have presented households the option of paying a recycling surcharge in their garbage bills in exchange for the collection of recycled materials. Officials from the City of Richmond, Virginia, report than more than half of their residents agreed to pay $2.00 per month for optional recycling services. Third, evidence for these benefits can be gathered by assessing the value of resources employed by households to voluntarily transport recyclable material directly to markets or drop-off centers in the absence of a municipal collection program. Empirical evidence suggests this amount is not zero.[26] Finally, Tawil (1995) and Kinnaman and Fullerton (in press) both use large cross sections of municipalities to estimate the probability that a municipality chooses to implement curbside recycling. Tawil (1995) finds that the probability is based not only on financial costs but also on the percentage of the local population with membership in environmental organizations. Kinnaman and Fullerton (in press) find that market and nonmarket variables (such as the average education level of local residents) affect the likelihood of municipal recycling. These various sources all support the notion that households value the ability to recycle and are willing to pay for such services. Municipal governments might be responding to these preferences by implementing curbside programs.

Policy Implications and Concluding Remarks

This article first conducted a careful investigation of the direct benefits and costs of recycling in a single municipality to test whether market factors could contribute to the growth in municipal recycling programs. The direct costs of operating a municipal recycling program are estimated to exceed the benefits by roughly $55.44 per ton, or $10.35 per household per year. Although representative of just one municipality, this estimate is perhaps the most thoroughly researched in the literature and further confirms the notion that recycling is a costly government service.

Unknown to many economists is why governments continue to implement such programs in the face of their costliness. Alternative reasons requiring local governments to either be misinformed or altruistic are unconvincing. This article tested a third factor: The growth in recycling can be attributed to local government's response to the preferences of households. The results of a contingent valuation survey indicated that households on average are willing to pay $92.48 each year for the municipal recycling program. Other sources of evidence confirm this notion. Perhaps the decisions of local governments are made partly to address these preferences.

Orthodox practitioners of benefit-cost analysis could argue that the results of this study suggest that municipal recycling programs are efficient because the nonmarket benefits to the average household (estimated here at $92.48 per year) exceed the market costs to the average household ($10.35 per year). In essence, the provision of municipal recycling services benefits society by more than the cost of resources required. But others might question the inclusion of such intangible benefits to households in the benefit-cost calculus because households' willingness to pay seems to be based on altruistic preferences. How were households endowed with such preferences? Economists rarely dwell into such issues and instead prefer to accept preferences as given. But critics of municipal recycling programs argue that households may have based such preferences on incomplete information that arose from a perceived national shortage of disposal space.[27] These critics also point to the fact that garbage disposal space has nearly doubled over the past decade, and household preferences could change once they become aware of this fact. Hence, the intangible benefits to recycling households estimated by this study may be short-term phenomena and should not be used to shape environmental policy.

Such debates should probably remain with policymakers. The point of this study is to explain the trend in recycling, not justify or criticize it. And although the intangible benefits to households may be questionable to critics of recycling, they are quite real to the elected officials of the local government contemplating the implementation of a recycling program. Residents have demanded municipal recycling services, and governments seem to have responded.

Of course, municipal recycling could still pass an overall benefit-cost criterion even if the nonmarket benefits to households measured above are excluded from the analysis. Households located near rural dumping sites and manufacturing centers do face the external costs of garbage disposal. The environment in the vicinity of these households would benefit directly from reductions in garbage brought on by municipal recycling programs. Additional research could determine the value of such benefits. If the value of these more tangible benefits exceeds the direct costs measured here, then curbside recycling could be justified on benefit-cost principles.

Appendix:
The Questionnaire With Mean Responses

Hello. My name is Peter Coughlin. I am a student at Bucknell University. We are doing a survey on how people feel about recycling in Lewisburg. Bucknell University will make a $5 donation to a local charity if you agree to answer a few questions about recycling. The survey should take no longer than 3-4 minutes and your responses will be held confidential. Do you have a few minutes?

IF NO: May I call you back at a more convenient time?

1] Would you prefer the $5 donation be given to
_____ The William Cameron volunteer fire department   [60%]
_____ Lewisburg Evangelical hospital   [23%]
_____ The local chapter of the United Way   [17%]

2] The Borough of Lewisburg collects newspaper, glass, and aluminum cans from your curb on the first Saturday of every month. Would you say you normally participate in this recycling program?
_____ Yes   [75%]   (Go to Question 3a)
_____ No   [25%]   (Go to Question 3b)

3a] Would you say the main reason you recycle is because it is good for the environment, or because it is your civic duty?
_____ It is good for the environment   [53%]
_____ It is my civic duty   [13%]   [33% did not answer]

3b] In your opinion, is recycling good for the environment?
_____ Yes   [96%]
_____ No   [4%]

LIVERPOOL JOHN MOORES UNIVERSITY
LEARNING & INFORMATION SERVICES

4] Which of the following would you consider the most difficult part of recycling?
_____ It is hard to clean and separate the material   [17%]
_____ It is hard to find a storage place in your house   [57%]
_____ It is hard to remember the right day   [18%]   [7% did not answer]

5] As you may know, the Borough of Lewisburg also provides a drop-off facility on 5th Street for you to take your tin cans, plastic bottles, and cardboard boxes. Would you say you normally take some of these materials to 5th Street?
_____ Yes   [54%]
_____ No   [46%]

6] Please think carefully about your answer to this next question. You currently pay $31.35 per quarter for disposal service. If it was found that the municipality needed to increase your quarterly bill by $2, $3, $5, $10, or $20 to NEW VALUE to keep recycling available in Lewisburg, would you be willing to pay it? Or would you prefer the recycling program be abandoned?

	$2	$3	$5	$10	$20
_____ Pay the extra fee	19/20	17/20	18/18	17/22	12/20
_____ Abandon the recycling program	1/20	3/20	0/18	5/22	8/20

7] (Only for people that said YES to Question #2) If curbside recycling were not available in Lewisburg, do you think you would take newspaper, glass, and aluminum to the 5th Street drop-off center?
_____ Yes   [83%]
_____ No   [17%]

Now, I have a few final questions about yourself

8] Do you own or rent your home?
_____ Own   [64%]
_____ Rent   [36%]

9] How many individuals live in your household?_____[2.39]

10] What year were you born in?_____[average age: 52 years]

11] Do you hold a college degree?
_____ Yes   [60%]
_____ No   [40%]

12] Would you say your household income is
_____ Less than $20,000   [19%]
_____ $20,000-$40,000   [31%]
_____ More than $40,000   [40%]   [10% did not answer]

Thank you very much for your time spent answering these questions. A $5 donation will be made to the _____. Have a nice evening.

13] Sex of respondent:_____ male[32%]
                        _____ female[68%]

Notes

1. Subtitle D of the Resource Conservation and Recovery Act (RCRA) of 1976 is partly responsible for the shift to more distant landfills. This law imposed technology-based standards on the construction, operation, and closure of solid waste landfills. Old town dumps were often out of compliance and forced to close (the number of landfills operating in this country decreased rapidly from about 8,000 in 1988 to slightly more than 2,500 in 1997). But the sizes of most newly constructed landfills increased to reduce average costs (based on data reported by Glenn, 1998, the nation's average disposal capacity doubled from just 9 years in 1988 to roughly 20 years in 1997). Land costs and organized NIMBY

(not in my backyard) groups near population centers have discouraged these new larger landfills from locating in populated areas.

2. Grants in the amount of $183 million were provided by 34 state governments in 1997 to offset some of the costs of setting up and operating recycling programs (Glenn, 1998).

3. Carroll (1997) used such a cross section of towns in Wisconsin to estimate that it costs between $140 and $240 per ton to recycle. Market benefits are not estimated. Folz (1999) used self-reported survey-based cost data to estimate that recycling costs an average of $85 per ton. Franklin Associates (1994) used data based on national cost averages to simulate the costs of adding a curbside program in a city of 500,000 people. Recycling is estimated to increase solid waste management costs by $9.52 to $16.53 per ton. Finally, Palmer, Sigman, and Walls (1997) did not measure costs directly but used elasticity estimates to conclude that recycling up to a rate of 7.5% of total waste can be beneficial if a deposit-refund policy (the lowest cost policy) is used by the community to encourage recycling. Recycling beyond this threshold is costly.

4. Act 101, passed in July of 1988, requires all communities with populations above 5,000 in Pennsylvania to implement curbside recycling programs. The act also provides grants to offset recycling expenses.

5. Nor do households in Lewisburg face a unit-based pricing program for regular garbage collection.

6. Duggal, Saltzman, and Williams (1991) found that communities that enforce recycling laws with fines experience no more recycling than towns without such enforcement.

7. Industrial waste and recycling is omitted from the analysis. Very little industrial production occurs in Lewisburg. The local government does not manage any industrial waste that is produced.

8. Lansana (1993) found differences in recycling attitudes and behavior between urban and suburban areas.

9. Dubin and Navarro (1988) found that an increase in the population density by 100 persons per square mile decreases the average cost per ton of collected materials by $1.62. Kinnaman and Fullerton (1999) estimated that an increase of 100 persons per square mile increases the likelihood that a community will adopt curbside recycling by 0.39%.

10. The price of recyclable material will provide a biased measure of the marginal benefit of recycling if the extraction of virgin material is federally subsidized. Without a reliable estimate of the cross-price elasticity of demand for recycled materials with respect to a change in the price of virgin material, the effect of this bias cannot be controlled for.

11. An intermediate buyer often provides processing and transportation services for the municipality and, therefore, pays a lower price for the material.

12. Another potential benefit to the municipal government is garbage collection costs attributable to the extra recycling. Data limitations prevent including this benefit in the analysis.

13. Although the municipal recycling program provides local jobs to unskilled laborers, the additional jobs would be considered a benefit only during periods of underemployment. Unfilled job vacancies for unskilled labor have been common in the Lewisburg economy throughout the 1990s. Thus, labor is treated here as a cost of recycling and not a benefit.

14. The glass shredder needs new knives twice per year, a new conveyor belt every 2 years, and a new chute every 3 years.

15. Klein and Robison (1993) studied the impact of garbage costs on commercial recycle behavior.

16. Roberts, Douglas, and Park (1991) used contingent valuation to estimate a willingness to pay $227 per household per year to avoid the siting of a landfill near their community.

17. Little is currently known about the desirability of such state laws. A state law requiring the implementation of recycling programs by all communities could be beneficial if the external benefits of a better environment experienced by all state citizens exceeded the summation of the costs to all municipalities required to recycle. An extensive benefit-cost study would be necessary to estimate the external benefits of recycling to other members of the state or country. With a simplifying assumption, cost data gathered in Lewisburg can be used to provide a point estimate of the total out-of-pocket costs of the state law. Recall that Lewisburg's recycling program cost $18,545.17 to recycle 334.46 tons of material, amounting to $55.44 per ton more than regular disposal. If the cost per ton to recycle in other parts of Pennsylvania is the same as in Lewisburg, the total cost of recycling the additional 1,296,000 tons brought on by the state law is estimated at $71.85 million, or $15.98 per household. If households value the external benefits by more than this value, the state law could be welfare improving. This estimate assumes the cost of disposal and the prices of recyclable materials are not affected by the implementation of the state law requiring municipal recycling programs.

18. Combining nine survey-based studies, DeYoung (1996) found that individuals derive intangible payoffs from engaging in either frugal or conservation activities.

19. Households could instead be endowed with tastes for a clean environment and would recycle if they believe their efforts would improve the overall quality of the environment. But because the number of households in the economy is large, each household has the incentive to free-ride off of the recycling activities of others.

20. One unfortunate weakness of this survey technique is that residents with unlisted phone numbers are systematically excluded from the sample.

21. Of the 177 households telephoned, 19 lines were disconnected and 37 were not home after three attempts. Of the 121 that answered, 21 refused to respond to the survey. The size of the sample was defined primarily to satisfy research budget constraints. A larger sample would have increased the likelihood that the sample was representative of the population.

22. This procedure is an example of a "closed-ended" contingent valuation survey. Other survey methods include an "open-ended" procedure, a "sequential bids" procedure, the "response card" approach, and the "open-ended with follow-up" procedure. The primary advantage to the approach used in this study is that it is easy on the survey respondents

50   PUBLIC WORKS MANAGEMENT & POLICY / July 2000

(perhaps increasing the response rate) and the pricing scenario mimics an actual market decision (Cameron & Huppert, 1991). A weakness is that the sample size must be very large to capture efficient estimates of the average willingness to pay. The literature is rich with examples of each method. See Cameron and Huppert (1991) for a sample.

23. Households also identified their income and demographic characteristics. As identified in the appendix, 83% of households in the sample were owner occupied, the average household size was 2.39, and the average age was about 52 years. Sixty percent held at least a bachelors degree, 40% earned more than $40,000 per year, and 68% of the respondents were women. Conventional survey wisdom indicates that women are more likely to pick up the phone than are men. Young adults were also more likely to be away from home in the early evening while the survey was taken.

24. A nonparametric procedure developed by Kristrom (1990) was also used to derive a point estimate of the household's average willingness to pay for the recycling program. Using this method, the mean willingness to pay for the municipal recycling program is estimated at $24.83 per quarter, or $99.32 per year.

25. Households that chose to abandon the recycling program in Question 6 (rather than pay the fee) may hold a negative net willingness to pay. The resource cost to recycle to these households could be greater than any utility gained from the program. But these households are only made worse off by the program if they are forced to participate. Although the municipality has passed a mandatory participation ordinance, it is rarely enforced on households. Assume, then, that no households are made worse off by the program.

26. Tiller, Jakus, and Park (in press) apply CVM to estimate that a suburban household is willing to pay $11.74 per month for drop-off recycling. Jakus, Tiller, and Park (1996) use surveys and travel-cost data to estimate that a household is willing to pay $5.78 per month ($69.36 per year) on average for the ability to recycle newspaper and glass.

27. This perception may have been the result of the media's elaborate coverage of the garbage barge Mobro's storied attempts to unload (unsuccessfully) garbage along the east coast of the United States in 1987 (Bailey, 1995).

References

Bailey, J. (1995, January 19). Waste of a sort: Curbside recycling comforts the soul, but benefits are scant. *The Wall Street Journal*, p. A1.

Bohm, R. A., Folz, D. H., & Podolsky, M. J. (1999). *Cost and economies of scale in the provision of recycling services* (Working paper). University of Tennessee.

Cameron, T. A., & Huppert, D. D. (1991). Referendum contingent valuation estimates: Sensitivity to the assignment of offered values. *Journal of the American Statistical Association, 86*(416), 910-918.

Cameron, T. A., & James, M. D. (1987). Efficient estimation methods for "close-ended" contingent valuation surveys. *Review of Economics and Statistics, 69*, 269-276.

Carroll, W. (1997). *The costs and performance of residential recycling programs: Evidence from Wisconsin* (Working paper). Eau Claire: University of Wisconsin.

DeYoung, R. (1996). Some psychological aspects of reduced consumption behavior, the role of intrinsic satisfaction and competence motivation. *Environment and Behavior, 28*(3), 358-409.

Dubin, J. A., & Navarro, P. (1988). How markets for impure public goods organize: The case of household refuse collection. *Journal of Law, Economics, & Organization, 4*(2), 217-241.

Duggal, V. G., Saltzman, C., & Williams, M. L. (1991). Recycling: An economic analysis. *Eastern Economic Journal, 17*(3), 351-358.

Folz, D. H. (1999). Municipal recycling performance: A public sector environmental success story. *Public Administration Review, 59*(4), 336-345.

Franklin Associates. (1994, September). *The role of recycling in integrated solid waste management to the year 2000* (Report prepared for Keep America Beautiful, Chap. 6, Appendix I). Stamford, CT: Keep America Beautiful.

Fullerton, D., & Kinnaman, T. C. (1996). Household responses to pricing garbage by the bag. *American Economic Review, 86*(4), 131-148.

Glenn, J. (1998, April). The state of garbage in America. *Biocycle*, pp. 32-43.

Hanley, N., & Slark, R. (1994). Cost-benefit analysis of paper recycling: A case study and some general principles. *Journal of Environmental Planning and Management, 37*(2), 189-197.

Jakus, P. M., Tiller, K. H., & Park, W. M. (1996). Generation of recyclables by rural households. *Journal of Agricultural and Resource Economics, 21*(1), 96-108.

Kinnaman, T. C., & Fullerton, D. (in press). Garbage and recycling in cities with unit-based pricing. *Journal of Urban Economics.*

Klein, Y. L., & Robison, D. (1993). Solid waste disposal costs, product prices, and incentives for waste reduction. *Atlantic Economic Journal, 21*(1), 56-65.

Kristrom, B. (1990). A non-parametric approach to the estimation of welfare measures in discrete response valuation studies. *Land Economics, 66*(2), 135-139.

Lansana, F. M. (1993). A comparative analysis of curbside recycling behavior on urban and suburban communities. *Professional Geographer, 45*(2), 169-179.

Palmer, K., Sigman, H., & Walls, M. (1997). The cost of reducing municipal solid waste. *Journal of Environmental Economics and Management, 33*(2), 128-150.

Reschovsky, J. D., & Stone, S. E. (1994). Market incentives to encourage household waste recycling: Paying for what you throw away. *Journal of Policy Analysis and Management, 13*(1), 120-139.

Roberts, R. K., Douglas, P. V., & Park, W. M. (1991). Estimating external costs of municipal landfill siting through contingent valuation analysis: A case study. *Southern Journal of Agricultural Economics*, pp. 55-165.

Savas, E. S. (1979). How much do government services really cost? *Urban Affairs Quarterly, 15*, 23-41.

Schaumberg, G. W. Jr., & Doyle, K. T. (1995). *Wasting resources to reduce waste: Recycling in New Jersey* (Policy Analysis No. 202). Washington, DC: Cato Institute.

Solid Waste Association of North America. (1995). *Integrated municipal solid waste management: Six case studies of system costs and energy use* (Summary report).

Steuteville, R. (1996). The state of garbage in America. *Biocycle, 37*(5), 54-61.

Tawil, N. (1995). *On the political economy of municipal curbside recycling programs: Evidence from Massachusetts* (Working paper). Washington, DC: Congressional Budget Office.

Tiller, K. J., Jakus, P. M., & Park W. M. (in press). Household willingness to pay for dropoff recycling. *Journal of Agricultural and Resource Economics*.

Varian, H. R. (1984). *Microeconomic analysis* (2nd ed.). New York: Norton.

West, J. P., et al. (1990). The implementation of local solid waste policies in Florida. *Journal of Environmental Systems, 20*, 71-90.

[9]

Environmental Levies and Distortionary Taxation: Comment

By DON FULLERTON*

With no revenue requirement, or where government can use lump-sum taxes, Arthur C. Pigou (1947) shows that the first-best tax on pollution is equal to the marginal environmental damage. Consumers then pay the social marginal cost of each item, the direct cost of resources, plus the indirect cost of pollution.

Suppose government needs more revenue, however, and cannot use lump-sum taxes. In this second-best world, our intuition might tell us to raise all tax rates: the tax on any "clean" commodity should be raised above its first-best level of zero, and the tax on a "dirty" good should be raised above its first-best Pigovian level (the marginal environmental damage). Despite this intuition, a recent paper by A. Lans Bovenberg and Ruud A. de Mooij (1994 p. 1085) claims to "... demonstrate that, in the presence of preexisting distortionary taxes, the optimal pollution tax typically lies below the Pigovian tax... ."

This note argues that nothing is necessarily wrong with the intuition that all taxes should be raised. Nothing is wrong with the Bovenberg and de Mooij model either, but the above quote could be misinterpreted. I generalize their model to reconcile these opposing views.

Earlier writers have expressed several versions of the "double-dividend hypothesis."[1]

These views are discussed more below, but a strong version of this hypothesis might claim that a revenue-neutral switch toward a tax on the dirty good and away from taxation of clean goods can improve environmental quality *and* reduce the overall cost of tax distortions. By implication, this view might suggest that any additional revenue requirements should be met by raising the tax on the dirty good by more than taxes on clean goods. The important and correct result of Bovenberg and de Mooij is that this strong view is flawed.[2] Even if the pollution tax helps solve an environmental problem, it likely worsens other tax distortions. Thus, the tax on the dirty good should rise by less than the tax on the clean good. Bovenberg and de Mooij focus on the *differential* between the tax rates on the clean and dirty goods, but they never quite say so. They assume the tax on the clean good is always zero, so their dirt tax *is* the differential. With this choice of normalization, starting with the dirt tax at the Pigovian rate, additional revenue would be raised by the labor tax while the dirt tax (differential) would fall.

However, other normalizations are equally valid and sometimes preferable. In their model, the extra labor tax is equivalent to a uniform tax on both goods. Thus, from the same starting point with the dirt tax at the Pigovian level, an equivalent policy would raise both the commodity tax rates. The total tax on the dirty good would then exceed the Pigovian level.

Bovenberg and de Mooij clearly understand this point, but their readers might not. Therefore, the first purpose of this note is just to clarify the interpretation of their results. The

* Department of Economics, University of Texas, Austin. TX 78712 (e-mail: dfullert@eco.utexas.edu). I am grateful for financial assistance from National Science Foundation grant SBR-9413334 and Environmental Protection Agency grant R824740-01, and for helpful suggestions from Lans Bovenberg, Larry Goulder, Gib Metcalf, Ian Parry, Ronnie Schöb, Pete Wilcoxen, Jay Wilson, Ann Wolverton, and two anonymous referees. This paper is part of the National Bureau of Economic Research's research program in Public Economics. Any opinions expressed are those of the author and not those of the National Science Foundation, the Environmental Protection Agency, or the National Bureau of Economic Research.

[1] Examples include David Terkla (1984), Dwight R. Lee and Walter S. Misiolek (1986), and Wallace E. Oates (1991).

[2] Other recent literature that refutes the strong view includes Bovenberg and F. van der Ploeg (1994), Ian W. H. Parry (1995), and Bovenberg and Lawrence H. Goulder (1996). Further discussion is provided by Oates (1995) and by Goulder (1995), who distinguishes weak and strong forms of the double-dividend hypothesis.

second purpose is to explore the role of "normalization" in a model with tax rates on both goods and on labor. Any one tax rate can be set to zero, as a conceptual matter, but implementation of some taxes might be easier than others as a practical matter.

In fact, I later reinterpret the model of Bovenberg and de Mooij to describe a case where production requires both a clean input and "emissions." This dirty input is difficult to monitor, because it is not purchased on the market. Enforcement is difficult, if midnight dumping is easy. Yet any one of these tax rates can be set to zero. Thus, the emissions tax can be entirely replaced by the equivalent combination of a subsidy to all clean inputs plus an additional tax on output. This "two-part instrument" provides the same changes in all relative prices, and thus the same outcome, as the emissions tax. And both parts apply to market transactions, with invoices to substantiate the tax due or the subsidy requested.

I. The Model

Bovenberg and de Mooij use a linear production technology where a unit of time can be retained as leisure V, or it can be supplied as labor L to produce the dirty good D, the clean good C, or government consumption G. The number of individuals is N, and labor productivity is h. They define units such that all unit production costs are one. Thus:

$$(1) \qquad hNL = NC + ND + G.$$

Their second-best optimum may involve a tax on the dirty good at rate t_D and on labor at rate t_L. Here, I add the possibility of a tax on the clean good at rate t_C. The procedure is to look at a revenue-neutral change that leaves G unaffected. Differentiate (1), use $dG = 0$, and divide by N:

$$(2) \qquad hdL = dC + dD.$$

Household utility depends on choices of private goods, given the public good G and the level of environmental quality E. Thus, households maximize:

$$(3) \qquad U = u(C, D, V, G, E)$$

subject to their budget constraint:

$$(4) \qquad hL(1 - t_L) = C(1 + t_C) + D(1 + t_D).$$

Environmental quality is a function of the output of the dirty industry, $E = e(ND)$, where $e' < 0$. Define τ as the dollar cost of environmental damage per unit of the dirty output:

$$(5) \qquad \tau = -\frac{\partial u}{\partial E} e' N / \lambda.$$

Each household's consumption of D imposes cost on the utility of N households, converted into dollars when divided by λ, the marginal utility of income. As will be confirmed shortly, this τ at the first-best optimum is the Pigovian tax rate.

In general, the government's second-best problem is to maximize utility by its selection of tax rates t_C, t_D, and t_L. At that second-best optimum, given the revenue requirement ($dG = 0$), there is no change that can raise utility. Totally differentiate the utility function (3), use $dV = -dL$, and set dU equal to zero:[3]

$$(6) \qquad dU = 0 = -\frac{\partial u}{\partial V} dL + \frac{\partial u}{\partial C} dC$$

$$+ \frac{\partial u}{\partial D} dD + \frac{\partial u}{\partial E} e' N dD.$$

Then use household first-order conditions,[4] the definition of τ in (5), and the production frontier (2) to get:

$$(7) \qquad 0 = ht_L dL + t_C dC + (t_D - \tau) dD.$$

Consider three special cases. First, suppose $t_L = t_C = 0$. Either government has some other lump-sum source of revenue, or, by happy coincidence, the Pigovian tax collects just

---

[3] I set $dU = 0$ to characterize the second-best optimum, whereas Bovenberg and de Mooij use dU to discuss the effect on utility of reducing t_D below the first-best Pigovian level. Both methods reveal whether t_D lies below τ, the marginal environmental damage, but the actual value of τ may depend on which point is evaluated. I am grateful to Gib Metcalf for pointing this out.

[4] First-order conditions imply $\partial u / \partial C = \lambda(1 + t_C)$, $\partial u / \partial D = \lambda(1 + t_D)$, and $\partial u / \partial V = \lambda h(1 - t_L)$.

enough revenue to finance G. Then, (7) implies $t_D = \tau$. This first-best outcome confirms that τ in equation (5) is indeed the first-best Pigovian tax.

Second, consider the case of Bovenberg and de Mooij, where $t_C = 0$ and the revenue requirement means $t_L > 0$. Then, (7) implies:

$$(8) \qquad t_D - \tau = -ht_L \frac{dL}{dD}.$$

Thus, the sign of dL/dD is crucial, and their paper devotes an entire section to it. In order to get definitive results for the change in L, they assume that a subutility function for consumption goods $Q(C, D)$ is homothetic and weakly separable from leisure.[5] They consider a small revenue-neutral change that would raise t_D and lower t_L. In brief, they note that any added tax on D is a partial consumption tax that raises the overall cost of consumption and reduces the real wage. It therefore affects the labor/leisure choice as well as the mix of C and D. The added t_D must exceed the fall in t_L, to collect the same revenue. Because it is more distorting, they argue, the increase in t_D affects actual labor supply more than the equal-revenue reduction in t_L. Thus, both D and L fall.

For present purposes, let us just accept the argument that dL/dD is positive. In this case (where $t_C = 0$), equation (8) means the second-best pollution tax lies below the marginal environmental damage ($t_D < \tau$).

Third, however, the same equation (7) can be employed to show the case where $t_L = 0$. In this case, t_C is used to raise the necessary revenue, and:

$$(9) \qquad t_D - \tau = -t_C \frac{dC}{dD}.$$

Assuming no perverse revenue effects, and $t_L = 0$, revenue neutrality requires that an increase in t_D be accompanied by a fall in t_C. Thus, dC/dD clearly is negative. As long as revenue needs mean that t_C is positive, then

$t_D > \tau$, and the second-best pollution tax exceeds the marginal environmental damage. This result confirms the intuition that the dirt tax can help raise revenue.

More generally, equation (7) implies:

$$(10) \qquad t_D < \tau \qquad \text{iff} \qquad t_C < -ht_L \frac{dL}{dC}.$$

In the ongoing example, a revenue-neutral shift from labor tax toward dirt tax is likely to reduce D and increase C, but also reduce labor supply. Thus, dL/dC is negative, and the critical threshold for t_C is positive. Bovenberg and de Mooij choose a value ($t_C = 0$) that lies below this threshold, so their second-best pollution tax lies below the marginal environmental damage. But the result could have gone either way. If the preexisting t_C happens to equal $-ht_L dL/dC$, by coincidence, then the second-best pollution tax could exactly match τ.

II. Interpretations

The simple explanation for these results is that the labor tax is equivalent to a uniform tax t on both C and D. The budget constraint in (4) is the same whether labor income is multiplied by $(1 - t_L)$, or all expenditures are multiplied by $(1 + t)$, as long as $(1 + t) = 1/(1 - t_L)$. Government revenue also is unaffected by this switch. Start from the Bovenberg and de Mooij solution with $t_L > 0$, $t_C = 0$, and $t_D < \tau$. Then with no effect on any outcome whatsoever, any portion of the labor tax can be replaced by raising both t_C and t_D, until t_D matches or exceeds the marginal environmental damage.[6]

The alternative normalization can be used to help clarify Bovenberg and de Mooij. In equation (9), where $t_L = 0$, the result was $dC/dD < 0$ and, therefore, $(t_D - \tau) > 0$. Thus, under this normalization, the dirt tax is indeed used to raise revenue. Bovenberg and de Mooij show that labor supply falls, however, so the production frontier means dC/dD is smaller than one (in absolute value). Thus, from (9),

---

[5] In addition, to focus on the relevant externality and taxes, the framework assumes away any other distortions such as imperfect competition or government regulation.

[6] Ronnie Schöb (1997) makes a similar point.

the revenue-raising *component* of the dirt tax $(t_D - \tau)$ is less than t_C. The reason is that while both taxes distort the labor-leisure choice, the already-higher t_D also distorts the consumption mix.

In personal correspondence, Bovenberg says:

> To avoid confusion, we probably should have said that "optimal tax differentiation is less than the Pigovian rule would suggest." Our point is perhaps clearer in a model in which intermediate inputs pollute. In that case, the optimal pollution tax is always below the Pigovian tax, since the optimal tax on clean intermediate inputs is always zero. (Bovenberg and Goulder, 1996)

Another interpretation is provided by an equation in Agnar Sandmo (1975) that can be slightly rewritten to express the total tax on the dirty good as a weighted average of a revenue-raising Ramsey term (R) and the marginal environmental damage (τ):

$$(11) \qquad t_D = \left(1 - \frac{1}{\eta} \right) R + \frac{1}{\eta} \tau,$$

where η is the marginal cost of public funds. With distorting taxes in the economy, a marginal dollar of revenue has a social cost that is more than a dollar ($\eta > 1$). Thus, the environmental component (τ/η) is less than the Pigovian rate (τ). Interestingly, an increase in the government revenue requirement means an increase in the distortionary effects of taxes, a higher η, more weight on the revenue-raising term, and less weight on the marginal environmental damage.[7]

Because Bovenberg and de Mooij set $t_C = 0$, they use the labor tax to acquire additional revenue. The revenue-raising term in (11) is zero, so $t_D = \tau/\eta < \tau$. With this normalization,

if government needs more revenue, the labor tax would rise while the dirt tax actually would fall.

If, instead, the labor tax were zero, then R in (11) may be large and $t_D > \tau$. With this normalization, both t_C and t_D are raised to acquire more revenue. Thus, the intuition described in my introduction just uses a normalization different from that of Bovenberg and de Mooij.

What about the double-dividend hypothesis? Early writers used partial equilibrium models and often were not explicit about the experiment under consideration. In some cases, they had in mind a reform that would replace command and control regulation with a Pigovian tax. If this switch provides the same environmental protection, with the same effect on product prices, it would raise revenue that could be used to reduce distorting labor taxes. Bovenberg and de Mooij agree this reform would raise welfare.[8] In other cases, early writers may have had in mind an initial point that was suboptimal. If some taxes are more distorting than others, then a reform might well be able to increase a pollution tax, reduce a highly distorting tax, and raise welfare. Bovenberg and de Mooij also do not intend to refute this general proposition. Instead, their main point is that the early use of partial equilibrium models often did not recognize that additional environmental taxes can raise product prices in a way that exacerbates labor-supply distortions.

In this sense, early writers were correct to think that the tax on the dirty good could be increased in some circumstances, even perhaps above the marginal environmental damage, but wrong to think that it would necessarily be less distorting than other taxes.

---

[7] This interpretation, as suggested by a referee, appears in Bovenberg and van der Ploeg (1994). The higher marginal cost of public funds (η) means that all public goods are more expensive, including protection of the environment. Thus, the tax system is used less for the environment and more to try to raise revenue efficiently.

[8] In the terminology of Goulder (1995) and Parry (1995), this reform would have only the positive "revenue-recycling" effect of reducing other distorting taxes, without the negative "tax-interaction" effect of reducing the real net wage. This reform is equivalent to the "weak" version of the double-dividend hypothesis: if an uncorrected externality is subjected to initial taxation, then welfare is higher if the revenue is used to reduce other distorting taxes than if it is returned to consumers lump sum.

III. The Equivalence of Environmental Taxes and Subsidies

Finally, alternative normalizations are useful as a practical matter. Some countries may have large labor taxes (where the normalization of Bovenberg and de Mooij would be relevant), while others rely more on commodity taxes (where t_L is low and $t_D > \tau$). Also, in terms of reform, some instruments are easier to implement than others. Indeed, many tax-rate combinations can achieve the same second-best optimal quantities.

A. *No Need to Tax the Dirty Good*

In the first interpretation, as above, $Q(C, D)$ is a subutility function over two market goods. Suppose, however, that political constraints or administrative costs prevent the authorities from taxing the dirty good at all, so $t_D = 0$. No problem. By equation (7), just set:

$$(12) \qquad t_C = \tau \, \frac{dD}{dC} - ht_L \, \frac{dL}{dC}.$$

To shift consumption away from D, this tax on C must be negative.[9] This solution works like an implicit deposit-refund system, or withholding tax. If the dirt tax is unenforceable (t_D must be zero), just raise the labor tax and give part of it back as a subsidy on clean consumption.[10]

This observation leads to one more refutation. One other version of the double-dividend hypothesis might claim that an environmental tax always leads to higher welfare than an environmental subsidy, because the revenue from a tax can be used to reduce other dis-

torting taxes in the economy, while the environmental subsidy must be funded by *raising* other distorting taxes. Not so. This model shows that the two tax systems are equivalent. The tax on the dirty good raises its price, which reduces the real net wage and offsets the cut in the labor tax. Symmetrically, the subsidy to the clean good reduces its equilibrium price, which raises the real net wage and offsets the needed increase in the labor tax. Thus, the tax system with the subsidy to the clean good plus higher labor tax is equivalent in all respects to the tax system with the higher dirt tax and lower labor tax.

B. *No Need to Enforce Against Dumping*

In a second interpretation, $Q(C, D)$ represents the "technology" of household disposal. Then Q is a single consumption good, C represents the amount going into clean forms of disposal such as recycling or sanitary landfill, and D is the amount dumped illegally.[11] Instead of describing indifference curves between C and D, the $Q(C, D)$ function describes isoquants that show different combinations of clean disposal and dumping that are feasible and consistent with any given level of consumption Q; the rest of the model is unchanged. A difficult problem for policy makers (and for economists using enforcement models) is how to set the level of costly enforcement, the probability of detection, and the penalty for dumping (t_D). Results here suggest this problem can be entirely circumvented. An equivalent outcome can be achieved by adding a tax on all output Q (or equivalently, on labor) and a subsidy to proper disposal. This solution is an explicit, second-best deposit-refund system.

---

[9] To have the same effect on relative prices as the earlier tax on D, this solution must subsidize C. In the earlier case, denoted here by asterisks, the budget constraint was $hL(1 - t_L^*) = C + D(1 + t_D^*)$. Divide through by $(1 + t_D^*)$ and call the result $hL(1 - t_L) = C(1 + t_C) + D$. Then the new t_L must be $(t_L^* + t_D^*)/(1 + t_D^*)$, and $t_C = -t_D^*/(1 + t_D^*)$.

[10] Labor L can be taken to represent all resources that can be sold in the market or retained for use at home. Then t_L needs to tax all income to be a withholding tax on all spending.

[11] Fullerton and Thomas C. Kinnaman (1995) use such a function to solve for the optimal tax on output and subsidy to clean disposal (deposit-refund system) in a first-best model. Results here show equivalence in a second-best model. In this case, the units convention means that it costs a dollar to purchase *and dispose of* one unit in the form of C, or a dollar to purchase and dispose of one unit in the form of D. If clean disposal is more expensive, a dollar on C yields less consumption.

C. No Need to Monitor Emissions

In a third interpretation, $Q(C, D)$ is a constant returns-to-scale production function. Utility depends on consumption of Q, but the optimizations above simply substitute into that utility function the firm's production of Q, which uses a clean input C and emissions D. These emissions may be solid, liquid, or gaseous. The firm buys each unit of C on the market for a dollar (or $1 + t_C$, gross of tax). Each unit of emissions also entails some private cost for removal, transport, and disposal. By the units convention above, a unit of emissions is defined as the amount that costs a dollar (or $1 + t_D$, gross of tax). The utility function also could be amended to add other goods that are produced using only the clean input (labor).

Suppose the economy starts with a labor tax to raise revenue. The additional Pigovian tax would apply to emissions, and Bovenberg and de Mooij show that the second-best emissions tax t_D is less than marginal environmental damage τ. This emissions tax has an ''output effect'' that raises the cost of production, reducing demand for the good, and a ''factor substitution effect'' that induces the firm to cut emissions per-unit output. But emissions are not a purchased input with an invoice to help monitor and enforce the tax. An equivalent ''two-part instrument'' would provide a tax on output (to get the output effect) and a subsidy to clean inputs (to get the factor substitution effect). Both of these apply to market transactions, with invoices. Since labor is already subject to tax, however, this ''subsidy'' to the clean input really just means a lower tax here than in other nonpolluting industries. The combination (t_L, t_D) can be replaced by a system with a lower rate of tax on clean inputs used in Q, plus an excise tax on Q.

IV. Conclusion

Bovenberg and de Mooij obtain the correct analytical results with their normalization where the tax on the clean good is zero, but they leave the impression that the tax on the dirty good always lies below the Pigovian rate. Other normalizations have no effect on the equilibrium outcome, but they are very useful

to help interpret these results. First, if the labor tax were zero, the total tax on the dirty good could exceed the Pigovian rate. It is the difference between the tax on the dirty good and the tax on the clean good that is less than the Pigovian rate. Second, even if the dirt tax were zero, the same second-best optimum can be achieved using a higher tax on labor and a subsidy to clean consumption. Finally, this last normalization is useful to show that a tax system with an environmental subsidy may be no different from one with an environmental tax—even in terms of revenue—since they can achieve the exact same equilibrium. A waste-end tax may be difficult to enforce, because of illegal dumping, and it raises product prices in a way that reduces the real net wage. A subsidy to proper disposal can achieve the same incentives, and it reduces product prices in a way that *offsets* the effect of the extra labor tax needed to pay for it.

REFERENCES

Bovenberg, A. Lans and de Mooij, Ruud A. ''Environmental Levies and Distortionary Taxation.'' *American Economic Review*, September 1994, *84*(4), pp. 1085–89.

Bovenberg, A. Lans and Goulder, Lawrence H. ''Optimal Environmental Taxation in the Presence of Other Taxes: General-Equilibrium Analyses.'' *American Economic Review*, September 1996, 86(4), pp. 985–1000.

Bovenberg, A. Lans and van der Ploeg, F. ''Environmental Policy, Public Finance and the Labour Market in a Second-Best World.'' *Journal of Public Economics*, November 1994, *55*(3), pp. 349–90.

Fullerton, Don and Kinnaman, Thomas C. ''Garbage, Recycling, and Illicit Burning or Dumping.'' *Journal of Environmental Economics and Management*, July 1995, *29*(1), pp. 78–91.

Goulder, Lawrence H. ''Environmental Taxation and the Double Dividend: A Reader's Guide.'' *International Tax and Public Finance*, August 1995, *2*(2), pp. 157–83.

Lee, Dwight R. and Misiolek, Walter S. ''Substituting Pollution Taxation for General Taxation: Some Implications for Efficiency in Pollution Taxation.'' *Journal of Environ-*

mental Economics and Management, December 1986, *13*(4), pp. 338–47.

Oates, Wallace E. "Pollution Charges as a Source of Public Revenues." Discussion Paper QE92-05, Resources for the Future, Washington DC, 1991.

———. "Green Taxes: Can We Protect the Environment and Improve the Tax System at the Same Time?" *Southern Economic Journal*, April 1995, *61*(4), pp. 915–22.

Parry, Ian W. H. "Pollution Taxes and Revenue Recycling." *Journal of Environmental Economics and Management*, November 1995, *29*(3), pp. S64–77.

Pigou, Arthur C. *A study in public finance*. London: Macmillan, 1947.

Sandmo, Agnar. "Optimal Taxation in the Presence of Externalities." *Swedish Journal of Economics*, March 1975, *77*(1), pp. 86–98.

Schöb, Ronnie. "Environmental Taxes and Preexisting Distortions: The Normalization Trap." *International Tax and Public Finance*, 1997 (forthcoming).

Terkla, David. "The Efficiency Value of Effluent Tax Revenues." *Journal of Environmental Economics and Management*, June 1984, *11*(2), pp. 107–23.

[10]

The case for a two-part instrument: presumptive tax and environmental subsidy

Don Fullerton and Ann Wolverton[*]

I INTRODUCTION

Economists have long noted that many types of pollution can be controlled efficiently by placing a price or tax directly on the polluting activity (Pigou, 1932). This incentive can induce the household or firm to find the cheapest possible way to reduce waste, whether by recycling, installing new equipment, switching fuels, using labor-intensive methods, or perhaps just reducing production of the offending good. Still, few such taxes are ever employed by policy makers. Most environmental policies in the US and other countries are command and control regulations, and most environmental taxes are labeled as environmental only because the resulting revenues are spent on clean-up, not because the tax applies per unit of a polluting activity.[1]

Perhaps the major reason that taxes on polluting activities are rare is that wastes are hard to monitor and the taxes are difficult to enforce. Practical policy requires that the tax apply to an observable market transaction like the purchase of petroleum or chemical inputs, rather than to the 'spilling of oil' or the 'dumping of chemical wastes.' These polluting activities can be prohibited by law, and controlled through the required use of certain technologies, but they are hard to measure for the application of a waste-end tax.

The point of this paper is that the desirable incentive effects of a waste-end tax can be matched exactly, without the measurement and enforcement problems, by the use of a two-part instrument. To see this equivalence, one must first view the generation of waste as an input to production, with its own marginal product, just like labor, capital, and materials.[2] Then the tax does not need to apply directly to the unobservable wastes. Identical changes in relative prices can be achieved with a tax on an observable transaction such as the purchase of the output, in combination with a subsidy to other observable transactions like the purchase of all other inputs to production except waste.

32

The intuition is fairly simple, and follows from the idea that the waste-end tax has two intended incentive effects. First, it raises production costs and makes the good more expensive, so the output effect reduces production and therefore consumption of the good. Second, it makes the waste more expensive relative to other inputs, so the substitution effect reduces waste per unit of the remaining amount of the output that still gets produced. By analogy, the two-part instrument accomplishes the same effects separately. The first part imposes a tax on the output, reducing production and consumption of the good. This tax on output is equivalent to a tax at the same rate on all inputs to production, including labor, capital, materials, and waste. The second part subsidizes all non-waste inputs, which makes waste relatively more expensive and reduces waste per unit of output.

We refer to the first part of the two-part instrument as a presumptive tax; it is imposed under the presumption that all production uses a dirty technology or that all consumption goods become waste. The second part is an environmental subsidy; it is provided only to the extent that production uses clean technology or that consumption goods are recycled. The obvious practical example of a two-part instrument is a deposit-refund system: the consumer pays a deposit under the presumption that the item will be discarded improperly, and gets a refund only with proper performance (when the item is recycled). When litter or other illegal disposal cannot be taxed directly, the deposit-refund system can accomplish the same goals (Bohm, 1981; Stavins, 1991; Cropper and Oates, 1992). A subsidy to the form of disposal with lower social costs provides the substitution effect, shifting disposal away from socially-costly dumping, but that subsidy implicitly makes consumption cheaper and *encourages* purchase of the good. An output tax corrects this latter effect.

The literature does not use the term presumptive tax to refer exclusively to the first part of a two-part instrument. Gunnar Eskeland (1994) defines it as a tax that exploits the presumed relationship between the good to be taxed and the pollution to be regulated, but he does not require that it be paired with a subsidy.[3] Using this definition, any indirect tax that acts as a proxy for the direct taxation of emissions can be called a presumptive tax. For example, a gasoline tax is a presumptive tax on emissions, because one presumes that gasoline use is related to emissions. The tax on gasoline is more practical than a tax on vehicle emissions, but it is not a perfect proxy because it does not provide incentives to fix a car's broken pollution control equipment or to buy a car with lower emissions per gallon of gasoline.

In this paper, to avoid categorizing any indirect tax as a presumptive tax, we will refer to a presumptive tax only in combination with an environmental subsidy. The above gasoline tax is an indirect tax on emissions, but we refer to it as a presumptive tax only if it is coupled with a subsidy to the repair of all vehicles' broken pollution control equipment, or a subsidy to the purchase of vehicles with lower emissions per gallon of gasoline. The two-part instrument thus improves the aim of policy at the desired behavioral targets.[4]

The main advantage of the two-part instrument is that both parts apply to market transactions with invoices to help ensure compliance. In contrast, a Pigovian tax may apply to the firm's own measure of an input that is not purchased on the market and therefore does not have an invoice. The two-part instrument puts the information requirements where they can be met most cheaply and efficiently. It shifts the burden of proof. The firm must measure its own clean inputs and provide the evidence necessary to receive the subsidy.

Discussions in the literature of the tax-subsidy combination largely have been limited to deposit-refund systems in which the deposit and the refund are explicitly linked, and in which the deposit and the refund are equal to one another.[5] No such restrictions are made here. The refund may be paid to an individual or firm other than the one who paid the deposit, and the optimal refund may be a different amount than the original deposit. The tax and subsidy may even apply to different commodities altogether.

Current deposits and refunds do apply to particular consumer items such as beverage containers, car hulks, oil, and batteries, but we wish to emphasize that this concept has much wider applicability and may provide a promising alternative to widely-used command-and-control (CAC) policies.[6] In a broad sense, the United States income tax system operates on a deposit-refund principle. An individual pays a presumed amount of tax directly out of his or her paycheck each month, and a refund is given at the end of the fiscal year if the individual files a proper tax return with proof of overpayment. The same approach can be used in an environmental context. Thus, instead of limiting ourselves to a discussion of a deposit and refund, we want to think more generally about how a simple excise tax on a given consumption good can be coupled with a subsidy per ton of recycled material used in production. If markets work, this subsidy can be passed on to suppliers of recycled goods.

We begin in section II by outlining two simple general equilibrium models to demonstrate the equivalence between a Pigovian tax on emissions and a presumptive tax–environmental subsidy combination. This equivalence is shown to hold even when one agent pays the tax on a good or factor and a different agent receives the subsidy, possibly on a different good or factor. In the first model, the deposit always equals the refund. In the second model, however, this is not necessarily the case. Section III examines some practical advantages and disadvantages of using a presumptive tax–subsidy combination to elicit the optimal solution. Section IV provides a review of how this idea of a two-part instrument has been used in actual policy implementation. Finally, we conclude in section V that the presumptive tax coupled with a performance subsidy is a broader and more useful policy instrument than commonly thought.

II   THEORETICAL EQUIVALENCE TO A PIGOVIAN TAX

A   The Simplest Possible Model

To illustrate the equivalence between the Pigovian tax and the two-part instrument, we build a simple general equilibrium model in the tradition of Baumol and Oates (1988).[7] In the simplest possible model, the economy is a closed one with linear production and only one jurisdiction. We also assume perfect information, no transactions costs, and no pre-existing distortions.

In this simple model, the society consists of n identical households. Each household owns one unit of 'resources,' which may include a fixed amount of labor, capital, land or any other resource that can be sold in the market or used at home. The household sells some of this resource and uses the income to buy a clean good c and a dirty good d. It retains some of these resources to produce a household good h, which can be interpreted either as leisure or as household production. We define the units in our model such that the marginal rate of transformation is equal to 1. Thus, given these assumptions, the resource constraint is simply: $h + c + d = 1$. Utility of the household u depends positively on each of these three goods and negatively on the total amount of the dirty good present in society, $D = nd$. Throughout this chapter, lower case letters denote individual household amounts, while upper case letters denote aggregates for the society.

The social planner maximizes the utility of a representative household, subject to the resource constraint, recognizing the effect of each household's consumption of the dirty good d on the total amount of D. Thus, the optimization problem is:

$$\max u(c,d,h,nd) + \lambda(1 - h - c - d) \tag{3.1}$$

with respect to c, d, and h. This yields the first order conditions:

$$u_c = \lambda \tag{3.2a}$$

$$u_d + nu_D = \lambda \tag{3.2b}$$

$$u_h = \lambda \tag{3.2c}$$

where a subscript denotes a partial derivative, and λ is the social marginal value of the resource. These first order conditions state that the marginal utility from an additional unit of c, d, or h equals the marginal social cost, λ.

In the private market with perfect competition, the individual household maximizes utility subject to its budget constraint:

36   *Environmental economics*

$$\max u(c, d, h, D) + \gamma[(1 - h)(1 - t_r) - c(1 + t_c) - d(1 + t_d)] \quad (3.3)$$

where prices are normalized to one, t_c is the tax per unit of c, t_d is the tax per unit of d, and t_r is the tax per unit of resources supplied in the market. A household does not take into account the effect of its own use of d on the total amount of the dirty good D in society. Thus, it maximizes utility with respect to c, d, and h but takes D as given. The first order conditions from the individual household's problem are:

$$u_c = \gamma(1 + t_c) \quad (3.4a)$$

$$u_d = \gamma(1 + t_d) \quad (3.4b)$$

$$u_h = \gamma(1 - t_r). \quad (3.4c)$$

The solution strategy is to find tax rate combinations where the market (equations 3.4a–3.4c) is induced to match the social optimum (equations 3.2a–3.2c). We first examine the case where $t_c = t_r = 0$. From (3.2a) and (3.4a), we then find that $\lambda = \gamma$; the social utility from one more unit of income (or time) is equal to its private utility. Using this relationship and combining (3.2b) with (3.4b) reveals that the optimal tax on d is:

$$t_d = -(nu_D/\gamma) \quad (3.5)$$

This result is a simplified version of the Pigovian tax derived in Baumol and Oates (1988). It is the total, for all n households, of the marginal disutility from another unit of d, converted into dollars when divided by the marginal utility of income. Since n and γ are positive, a negative externality u_D yields a positive tax t_d. The tax discourages consumption of d, inducing households to reach the social optimum.

Suppose, however, that t_d cannot be used as a policy instrument, either because it is difficult to enforce or because d is hard to measure. We can still obtain the same first-best outcome by using the two other instruments: t_c and t_r. With a non-zero tax on c, however, λ is no longer equal to γ. Using (3.2a) and (3.4a), we find that $\lambda = \gamma(1 + t_c)$. Also, from (3.2c) and (3.4c), we have $\lambda = \gamma(1 - t_r)$. Using these two expressions for λ, it must be the case that $t_c = -t_r$. As a consequence, one of these 'taxes' will in fact be a subsidy.

Next, with $t_d = 0$, (3.4b) states that $\gamma = u_d$. If we substitute $\lambda = \gamma(1 - t_r)$ into (3.2b) and solve for t_r, we have:

$$t_r = -(nu_D/\gamma). \quad (3.6)$$

Given that $\gamma \geq 0$ and $u_D \leq 0$, t_r is a positive tax. This tax applies to all earnings. As previously established, t_c is the negative of this result. This subsidy is a rebate on all spending *except* spending on the dirty good.[8]

Thus, even a very simple model can be used to demonstrate the equivalence of the two-part instrument with the standard Pigovian tax. The deposit still equals the refund, but otherwise this tax-subsidy combination does not resemble the standard deposit-refund system because the tax applies to labor or capital income while the subsidy is on an entirely different commodity.

This presumptive tax can be part of the income tax collected by the government each year, while a separate subsidy applies to c. As a practical matter, this subsidy can appear simply as a sales tax that is lower on c than on all other goods. Thus, the consumer may not even notice the connection between the tax and the subsidy, despite the fact that together they induce the optimal behavior.[9]

B   A Model with Production and Emissions

A second general equilibrium model illustrates the usefulness of the two-part instrument for controlling a firm's emissions from production. As in the previous model, we make the standard assumptions of no transaction costs, perfect information, no pre-existing distortions, a closed economy, and perfectly competitive markets. Again, the society consists of n identical households. Each household's utility u is a function of one good d, household production h, and the total amount of waste in the society $W = nw$. Thus,

$$u = u(d,h,W) \tag{3.7}$$

where $u_d \geq 0$, $u_h \geq 0$, and $u_W \leq 0$.

The good d is produced using the following constant returns to scale production function:[10]

$$d = f(r_d, w). \tag{3.8}$$

where r_d is the direct use of resources r in the production of d. Production cannot occur without the generation of waste w. This waste requires the use of some private resources for removal and disposal r_w, in the amount $r_w = \alpha w$. The household good h is produced using only one input r_h, the amount of the resource retained at home. Thus, $h = r_h$. With a fixed total resource r, the resource constraint for the model is $r = r_d + r_h + r_w$.

The social planner maximizes utility subject to production and resource constraints as well as $r_w = \alpha w$. Substituting these constraints into the planner's problem yields:

$$\max \quad u[\,f(r_d, w), r_h, nw] + \lambda[r - r_d - r_h - \alpha w]. \tag{3.9}$$

The planner maximizes utility by choosing r_d, w, and r_h, explicitly taking into account the effect of production waste on utility. This gives the following first order conditions:

$$u_d f_{r_d} = \lambda \tag{3.10a}$$

$$u_d f_w + nu_W = \alpha\lambda \tag{3.10b}$$

$$u_h = \lambda \tag{3.10c}$$

where f_{r_d} is the partial of f with respect to r_d, and f_w is the partial of f with respect to w. Intuitively, these first order conditions state that the marginal social benefit from a particular use of the resource is equal to the marginal social cost.

In the private market, the consumer maximizes utility with respect to d and r_h subject to a budget constraint:

$$\max \quad u(d, r_h, W) + \gamma[(r - r_h) - d(p_d + t_d)] \tag{3.11}$$

where t_d is a tax on the consumption of d, and the resource r is the numeraire. The individual consumers have no control over the total amount of waste being produced by firms. However, they are still affected by its generation; thus, $u_W \leq 0$. The first order conditions are:

$$u_d = \gamma(p_d + t_d) \tag{3.12a}$$

$$u_h = \gamma. \tag{3.12b}$$

Producers of d maximize profits by their choice of inputs r_d and w. Thus, the firm's problem is:

$$\max \quad p_d f(r_d, w) - (1 + t_r) \cdot r_d - (\alpha w + t_w w) \tag{3.13}$$

where t_r is a tax on the use of resources r_d, and t_w is a possible tax on waste emissions. The first order conditions yield two important relationships:

$$p_d = (1 + t_r)/(f_{r_d}) \tag{3.14a}$$

$$p_d = (\alpha + t_w)/(f_w). \tag{3.14b}$$

In this model, from (3.12b) and (3.10c), we again have $\lambda = \gamma$. When both t_r and t_d are zero, the government has only t_w available to induce the private market to match the social optimum. We set (3.14a) equal to (3.14b) and use the result along with (3.10a) and (3.10b) to find the Pigovian tax:

$$t_w = -(nu_W/\gamma). \tag{3.15}$$

However, this tax on emissions does not apply to a market transaction and may therefore be difficult to monitor. In the case where emissions cannot be taxed directly ($t_w = 0$), both t_r and t_d can be used to arrive at exactly the same first-best socially optimal solution. This combination may be easier to implement, since it involves a tax on the output of a market good d, and on the input of a market resource r.

We begin by solving for t_d. Substituting (3.14b) into (3.12a) and then into (3.10b), we find that:

$$t_d = -(nu_W/\gamma f_w) \tag{3.16}$$

Since consumers derive negative utility from W, and firms have a positive marginal product from w, t_d is a positive tax on consumer purchases of d. It can be rewritten as the marginal external damage from w (the Pigovian tax on firms in (3.15)) divided by the marginal product of w. Thus, intuitively, t_d can be interpreted as the increase in the price of d that would have occurred with a tax on waste.

Now we solve for t_r by substituting (3.10a), (3.14a) and (3.16) into (3.12a):

$$t_r = (nu_W f_{r_d})/(\gamma f_w). \tag{3.17}$$

Since $u_W \leq 0$, we know t_r is negative. This subsidy is the marginal external damage from w multiplied by the ratio of the marginal products. This latter ratio is the slope of the isoquant, the trade-off between units of the dirty input and the clean input. Thus, if the relative price of r_d is high (α low), then the subsidy must also be high to generate the necessary substitution from w to r_d. The subsidy would not exceed 100 percent, however. The optimal subsidy per unit of clean input, t_r, can also be interpreted as the damage per unit of dirty input multiplied by the number of dirty inputs per clean input.

The use of t_d with t_r constitutes a two-part instrument that yields the same efficient results as the standard Pigovian tax on waste. Thus, the equivalence between the two tax systems still holds in a model where producers have a choice regarding emissions per unit of output. In this model, the equivalency between the Pigovian tax and the two-part system holds even though the Pigovian tax is placed on the firm, while the presumptive tax is placed on the purchases made by consumers. As in the previous model, the tax and subsidy are not explicitly linked; the tax is on the output while the subsidy is on the clean input. In addition, the deposit is no longer required to equal the refund.[11]

The tax-subsidy combination is useful particularly when a tax directly on emissions is difficult to enforce. Because emissions are not observed in a market transaction, a presumptive tax is placed instead on the output, which is easily observed in the market. Given a presumed relationship between output and emissions, the tax on output is a proxy for a direct tax on emissions. However, if producers can change emissions per unit of output, then this presumptive tax might not be a good proxy by itself. The firm's purchase of clean inputs such as labor or capital are also observed in the market, and can be subsidized by a reduction in other taxes that are normally collected on those inputs. The combination of a tax on output with a subsidy on clean inputs is a perfect proxy for an unenforceable tax on the dirty input.

III BEYOND THE MODEL: TWO-PART INSTRUMENT vs PIGOVIAN TAX

The two models above are simple, and yet they demonstrate cases where the two-part instrument is equivalent to a Pigovian tax. The results cannot be used to choose one such policy over another, however. To make the case for the two-part instrument, we must look outside the models at considerations such as feasibility, administrative costs, policy enforcement, and political perceptions. We also examine the possible effects of relaxing some of our models' assumptions.

A Practical Differences from a Pigovian Tax

First, consider feasibility. A Pigovian tax directly on the dirty input or emissions may not be possible, either because emissions cannot be measured or because the tax is not enforceable. For example, a tax on vehicle emissions is not yet technologically feasible (Harrington et al., 1994), and a tax on 'midnight dumping' is not enforceable. When the Pigovian tax is not viable, the equivalent two-part instrument has an obvious advantage. It still discourages the illegal disposal which is so costly to clean up and so hazardous to health.

Second, even when the Pigovian tax is feasible, the two-part instrument will often have lower total social costs of administration. The Pigovian tax requires one party, the government, to collect data on emissions of a different party, the polluter. In contrast, the two-part instrument places the data requirements on those with information. The shift in the 'burden of proof' leaves the individual consumer or firm to provide proof that proper disposal has taken place in order to obtain the subsidy. As argued by Russell (1988), these monitoring costs must be lower for the firm or consumer than for a government official who has less knowledge of the production or disposal process. Some of the reduced administrative cost of government may be offset by the increased compliance cost of firms and consumers, but the total is likely to be smaller since the firm's cost of monitoring its own amounts of each type of disposal is probably lower than the government's costs of monitoring those behaviors. The government needs only to set the deposit and the refund, and to check for the authenticity of a returned item or clean input (Stavins, 1991).

Third, consider enforcement problems. To enforce the Pigovian tax, the government must try to prevent illegal dumping by properly setting the rate of taxation, the rate of audit or inspection, and the rate of penalty. The Pigovian tax itself provides an incentive to hide taxable emissions. In contrast, the two-part instrument provides incentives to *reveal* data in order to qualify for the subsidy. In fact, the two-part instrument effectively taxes illegal dumping (by not returning the presumptive tax on amounts dumped), and so it can discourage dumping to the proper extent without any additional legal sanctions.[12]

The two-part instrument might provide doubled opportunities for cheating, since the presumptive tax on output is subject to evasion while the subsidies on clean inputs or on 'proper' disposal are subject to overstatement. The potential for cheating is relatively low for these market transactions, however, since each transaction involves an invoice for payment which is difficult to fabricate. In contrast, the single Pigovian tax on emissions or any less-desired type of disposal does not apply to a market transaction. The firm can make up its own records involving emissions, and it can dump illegally without records at all. No other party verifies the transaction. Two simple examples illustrate this risk. A tanker truck carrying liquid waste can enter a truck wash, start the washer sprays, and open the drain on the bottom of the truck effectively rinsing away the waste without paying the tax. Another example is of waste oil, which can be discarded on roadbeds of railroad lines in order to escape detection and the waste-end tax (Fullerton, 1996). The alternative is a simple tax on all purchases of oil, plus a subsidy on its proper disposal.

Any cheating that does occur under incentive-based policies is frequently due to asymmetric information. The firm or consumer often has more and better information than the government and this, while lending itself to the idea of shifting the burden of proof to the party that has better access to the information, also allows for the danger of falsifying the 'proof' (Russell, 1990). This proof does apply to a market transaction, as just discussed, but some degree of enforcement is necessary in order to ensure that this proof accurately reflects the true behavior of the consumer or firm. Thus, to optimize compliance on the part of the individual firm or consumer, the government must implement the proper mix of penalties and audits – not on emissions or dumping, but on properly reported output subject to a tax and on inputs eligible for a subsidy. Even this type of enforcement can be a difficult and rather inefficient task. Russell (1990) notes that auditing in the United States is infrequent and poorly performed, and thus does not act as sufficient inducement for accurate paperwork. Further complicating the ability of the government to audit a firm is the risk of infringing on the firm's constitutional protection against forced entry without reason. Under Pigovian taxation, audits often must be announced prior to arrival, allowing the firm to cover up any illegalities beforehand. Shifting the burden of proof to the firm under a tax-subsidy combination, on the other hand, means the government does not have to force entry. If the firm wishes to receive the subsidy, then it must open its own doors and provide proof to demonstrate eligibility.[13]

A fourth consideration is political appeal. The Pigovian tax may not be a popular action if it raises taxes on consumers or firms. At least in the case where the same individual or firm that pays the deposit has the opportunity to receive a refund, the deposit-refund system may be more popular with voters. If those who properly dispose of an item can receive a refund on the tax originally paid, then taxes increase only for those who refuse to participate. According to a GAO study (US Government Accounting Office, 1990), the bottle bill faces, on average, an 87 percent approval rating in states with a bottle bill, and a national bottle bill has a 70 percent approval rating with American citizens. For more general two-part instruments, political feasibility may be greater in the case where consumers get the rebate and producers pay the tax than in the case where producers get a subsidy and consumers pay the tax.

A second reason for its potential political appeal, according to the literature, is that the deposit-refund system can be self-financing; the refund can be taken directly from funds generated by deposits (Russell, 1988). However, we wish to emphasize that the pairing of a presumptive tax with an environmental subsidy does not require that the funds gathered from the tax be set aside for the accompanying subsidy nor that the tax equal the subsidy. While this eliminates a potential political advantage, it can create another: flexibility in the use of funds. The two-part instrument can also provide the government with a possible source of revenue. This is not an advantage specific to the two-part instrument, however. As we have shown, the two-part instrument is equivalent to the Pigovian tax. Therefore the revenue from the presumptive tax must exceed the cost of the environmental subsidy by exactly the amount of revenue that would have been collected by the Pigovian tax.

Other attributes have been ascribed specifically to various incarnations of the deposit-refund system. For instance, the deposit on a beverage container does not need to be claimed by the original purchaser. In fact, the incentive to return the item is effectively transferred to anyone finding it (Bohm, 1981). Thus, while a busy person with a high time value might throw a bottle out of the car window, another person with a low time value might pick up bottles along the roadside in order to collect the refunds. This combination is efficient, and it helps to prevent litter.[14] Other argued advantages include: health savings due to a decrease in litter-related injuries; a decrease in roadside damage to bicycle tires and farm equipment; job creation due to an increased demand for truck drivers, sorters, and recyclers; and energy savings from the use of recycled rather than virgin materials.

B   A Relaxation of the Models' Assumptions

With several simplifying assumptions, the tax-subsidy combination works perfectly in the context of our general equilibrium models. These simplifying assumptions include: no transaction costs, perfect information, no pre-existing distortions, a closed economy, and perfect competition. When each of these assumptions is relaxed, complications may arise. Any of these complications might reduce the effectiveness of the two-part instrument; however, most of these problems apply equally to the usual waste-end or Pigovian tax. Such considerations are important to discuss.

First, transaction costs can contribute to the cost of compliance for the firm or consumer. A two-part instrument requires two collection or payment points: one at the time of purchase and another at the time of return. Also, a firm accepting the returned item often faces additional storage and transportation costs as well as the cost of providing the promised refund. With a large number of small transactions, the act of paying out a refund can be expensive. In fact, many times these transaction costs are so high that other policy instruments can reach the same goal much more cost-effectively. For these reasons, we emphasize that the two-part instrument need not operate as a strict deposit-refund system. The two-part system does not need to collect and return five cents on each aluminum can. Approximately the same incentives can be provided with substantially lower transaction costs by a simple sales tax or excise tax on beverages and a subsidy paid to recycling firms per ton of recycled aluminum. Without making the individual consumer stand in line to get the five cent refund, the subsidy per ton of recycled aluminum will affect market prices in a way that still induces stores to offer efficient service or some other inducement to consumers who bring in aluminum cans.

A second potential complication is the lack of perfect information. With imperfect measures of social costs, the government might set the wrong rate for the presumptive tax or subsidy. If so, then the two-part instrument will not induce the socially efficient mix of 'proper' disposal (such as recycling) and 'improper' disposal (such as litter). This imperfection can mean costly clean-up of improperly disposed waste, if the refund is too low, or it can signify unwarranted social costs from too much proper disposal, if the refund is too high.[15] This complication equally affects the Pigovian waste-end tax, however, since the authorities are required to know *a priori* what size tax is needed to induce optimal behavior. For the Pigovian tax, Baumol and Oates (1971) describe a system of 'standards and prices' that can be used to adjust the tax rate by trial and error, and the exact same argument applies to the two-part instrument. Once the authorities have set a target for quantities to be recycled, they can adjust the deposit and refund periodically until the desired quantity is reached. Thus, the element of trial-and-error is not particularly worse under a tax-subsidy combination.

A third potential pitfall relates to the theory of the second-best. Pre-existing distortions can affect the size of the tax or subsidy needed to balance two major objectives, namely, raising revenue and ensuring the desired amount of proper disposal. Bovenberg and De Mooij (1994) examine the case of a Pigovian tax with a pre-existing labor tax that distorts the consumer's choice between consumption and leisure. Thus, in the second-best world, neither the Pigovian tax nor the equivalent two-part instrument maximizes social welfare because they both exacerbate the labor-leisure distortion. As shown in Fullerton (1997), however, the two-part instrument and the Pigovian tax equally affect the labor-leisure choice. As a consequence, the same second-best correction applies. The properly modified rate of taxation on waste can still be replaced by equally modified rates for the presumptive tax and environmental subsidy.

Fourth, potential complications arise in relation to the assumption of a closed economy. If the two-part instrument operates as a presumptive tax on all output and a subsidy to all clean inputs, then it still serves as an effective tax on domestic pollution, even if the output is exported. For a deposit-refund system, however, the equivalence can be broken if the deposit is paid on goods before export, and subsequent recycling is not re-imported to receive the refund. Conversely, if the foreign firm pays the deposit on goods shipped to the US, and is then responsible for receiving and recycling its own goods, the extra transportation and transaction costs can operate as a type of non-price trade barrier. It may be easier for the foreign firm to arrange with a domestic firm for the collection, storage, and transportation of its disposed products such as bottles or other forms of packaging. Also, it may be easier to offer a refund to the consumer for the proper return of the product through domestic facilities. Otherwise, the foreign firm may have to set up recycling facilities in the US or transport its recycled products back to the originating country. If this is the case, the domestic firm may gain an advantage over the foreign producer. This argument may be important for products such as computers where many producers rely on a take-back system in order to re-use valuable components. However, in cases where the foreign producer is not responsible for recycling its own product, so that a domestic firm can collect the product for recycling, this advantage disappears.

Finally, imperfect competition or monopoly behavior in certain industries can complicate the model significantly. If a firm with market power has already restricted output below the socially optimal level, then a tax on output can induce a further restriction and decrease social welfare even more. In this case, even without the presumptive tax, a subsidy to proper disposal may reduce the overall cost of production and help offset the pre-existing market distortion (Baumol and Oates, 1988). In a simple monopoly model, the tax-subsidy combination is still equivalent to the emissions tax; it raises production costs and exacerbates the monopoly distortion. In a more complicated game-theoretic model of oligopoly, we hesitate to conjecture about this equivalence.

Though the models above are used to show where the two-part instrument is equivalent to the Pigovian tax, considerations beyond the model are reasons enough to give careful thought to the tax-subsidy combination. In many cases, the problems listed here are of a lesser degree for the two-part instrument than for the Pigovian tax, making the case even stronger for the pairing of a presumptive tax with a subsidy.

IV   POLICY EXPERIENCES

This section reviews actual experiences with two-part instruments in the United States as well as in other countries. Examples that are discussed include deposit-refund systems on bottles, waste oil, and car hulks. In many cases the relative success or failure of a deposit-refund system appears to be related to the ability of the government to set the appropriate deposit or refund to induce the desired behavior.

A   'Bottle Bills' for Beverage Containers

A two-part instrument has most often appeared as a deposit-refund system. A 'bottle bill' is one of its most common forms. This policy combines a deposit paid by the consumer at the time of purchase and a refund when the beverage container is properly returned.[16] Ten states in the US reportedly have bottle bills.[17] California's bottle bill differs from those in other states in that the distributors pay the deposit, while consumers receive the refund (Container Recycling Institute, 1992). Also, in most states the deposit does not equal the refund because of a handling fee.[18] Indications of the success of such policies are mixed. Evidence that suggests some degree of success includes reports of a high response rate by consumers, a reduction in solid waste, a decrease in litter, and high-quality recyclable inputs. Evidence is somewhat less convincing with respect to energy savings, job creation, and administrative, production, and distributive costs.

Return rates for bottles appear to be high in the US. Table 3.1 presents both the overall return rate and return rates by bottle type, if available, for each of the US states with bottle bills. Overall return rates range from 76.5 percent in New York to 93 percent in Michigan.[19] For specific bottle types, the lowest return rate is 50 percent for plastic containers in California, while the highest return rate is 95 percent for aluminum containers in Iowa. Such high return rates stand in marked contrast to non-bottle-bill items. For instance, Oregon boasts an overall return rate on aluminum, plastic and glass containers of 92.3 percent, whereas the overall return rate for non-bottle-bill containers is less than 30 percent (Wahl, 1995).

Table 3.1   Return rates for containers in bottle-bill states

State	Return rates (%)	
California	Aluminum	88
	Glass	76
	Plastic	50
	Overall	84
Connecticut	Cans	88
	Bottles	94
	Plastic	70–90
Delaware	Not available	
Iowa	Aluminum	95
	Glass	85
	Plastic	70–90
	Overall	91
Maine	Beer/Soda	92
	Wine/Spirits	80
	Juice	75
Massachusetts	Overall	85
Michigan	Overall	93
New York	Soda	66
	Beer	79
	Overall	76.5
Oregon	Aluminum	86.6
	Glass	94.1
	Plastic	92.5
	Overall	92.3
Vermont	Overall	85

Sources: Gupta (1996), NY Department of Environmental Conservation (1994), Wahl (1995), Iowa Department of Natural Resources (1996), and Container Recycling Institute (1992).

Reports also indicate that solid waste has seen a slight decrease due to the bottle bill. The GAO (1990) cites a 6 percent reduction by weight, and an 8 percent reduction by volume of the amount of solid waste being landfilled. However, opponents cite these small figures as a reason for repeal of bottle bills; the benefits are too small to justify the cost of implementing such a system. Bottle bills seem to have had a significant impact on litter, however. A GAO study (1990) finds a decrease in litter between 79 and 83 percent for nine states with bottle bills (excluding California). Because the bottle bills are so effective at decreasing litter, these states have experienced a significant decrease in damages and injuries due to broken bottles and other discarded beverage containers. For instance, injuries to children caused by broken bottles decreased 60 percent after the implementation of the bottle bill in Massachusetts (Friedland and Perry, 1995).

Critics of the bottle bill often argue that it deprives curbside recycling programs of a large potential source of revenue. A GAO study (1990) found the two policies to be complementary, however. While some consumers will return a bottle in order to receive the refund, others will not be willing to take the time to do so; these individuals may still find it easy to throw the bottle in the recycling bin for curbside pick-up. A Rhode Island study demonstrates that, while having both programs in place is more costly, having a bottle bill in addition to a curbside recycling program will divert an additional 17 to 35 percent from the waste stream (Naughton et al, 1990).[20]

Also, bottle bills provide higher-quality material than curbside recycling programs. Containers are more homogenous because they have been sorted; glass is often unbroken and sorted by color. The monetary incentive guarantees a steady supply of recycled beverage containers (Iowa Department of Natural Resources, 1996). For all of these reasons, firms that use recycled materials have demonstrated their preference for recycled glass and plastic from bottle-bill states. Two-thirds of glass and 98 percent of plastic recycled by firms are purchased from the nine bottle-bill states other than California (Friedland and Perry, 1995) whereas these states contain only 17 percent of the US population.

Questions about the cost of a deposit-refund system such as the bottle bill also have countered these seemingly impressive statistics. Production and distribution costs to the beverage industry have reportedly increased as a result of compliance with the bottle bill (GAO, 1990). The increase in cost is especially evident for firms responsible for collecting the bottles, distributing the refund, and storing the bottles after they are returned. The sheer number of small transactions that take place each day also cost the firm a great deal. In a report issued by the GAO (1990), the increase in cost is estimated to lie between 2.4 and 3.2 cents per container. Ackerman et al (1995) report that Massachusetts' firms face a cost increase of 2.3 cents per container.[21] When viewed by the ton, such costs are substantial. For steel cans, 2.3 cents per can translates into a cost of $320 per ton of waste reduced. For aluminum cans it is even higher: $1300 per ton.

Landfilling, in most cases, is a much cheaper disposal alternative. In weighing costs against benefits, several studies find that bottle bills – as they are currently run – may not in fact be economically efficient.[22]

According to the Project 88 report (Stavins, 1991), the design of a deposit-refund system is the primary determinant of its success or failure. For instance, a single-tiered system, where the refund is the same for all containers regardless of differences in recycling value, has lower transaction costs than a multi-tiered system, where different containers have refund values that depend on the material from which they are made. However, the single-tiered system is a poorer estimate of the true social cost (Jenkins and Lamech, 1992). Drop-off requirements can also affect the inconvenience costs to the consumer. In Oregon, for instance, a consumer can drop off beverage containers to any store that carries that brand, regardless of where the beverage was originally purchased. Retailers do not have to sort the containers because distributors have an agreement among themselves on collection and credit for containers.

Evidence also indicates that administrative costs decrease significantly for a more consolidated system. In California, for example, the deposit-refund system is run by the state instead of by the retail firms. In a 'standards and prices' approach[23] a minimum return rate of 80 percent is mandated, and the deposit-refund system is adjusted to reach that goal (Naughton et al., 1990). Redemption centers are jointly arranged by retailers within convenience zones of a halfmile radius (for example, at a centrally-located grocery store), so that retailers do not have to be directly involved in redeeming cans and bottles (Mrozek, 1995). The state also pays a handling fee to recycling centers to collect and process cans. Unclaimed deposits are used to pay for administration. Costs are much lower in California than in other states, approximately 0.2 cents per can. For steel cans, this translates into a decreased cost from $320 to $28 per ton of garbage reduced. For aluminum, the costs decrease from $1300 to $120 per ton (Palmer et al., 1997).[24]

B Deposit-Refund Systems for Other Items in the US

Deposit-refund systems in the United States have also been used to promote oil recycling through the return of used motor oil, and lead recycling through the return of lead-acid car batteries.[25] Two states that have battery deposit-refund systems are Rhode Island and Maine. Other states have unlegislated deposit-refund systems run by industry.[26] Most of the benefits as well as the criticisms listed above for bottles also apply here. The fact that both oil and lead are health hazards and costly to clean up means that a deposit-refund system may be more useful than other policy instruments. Sigman (1995b) examines the determinants of the illegal dumping of lubricating oil and finds evidence that a deposit-refund system is a useful method for decreasing illegal disposal; the availability of opportunities for the reuse of oil are found empirically to affect illegal dumping. Several problems specific to the return of car batteries and oil are noted throughout the literature. One such problem is the possibility that a refund that is set too high will induce individuals either to steal car batteries or to bring in a cheaper oil-like substance to get the offered refund. Thus, it is important to set both the deposit and the refund at an appropriate level.[27] Another problem discussed is the fact that refunds are often available only in large urban areas (Jenkins and Lamech, 1992). Rural populations (which may be significant, depending on the country) may not recycle oil or return car batteries if they have to drive into the city to return the product.

Evidence of other deposit-refund systems in the US is scattered. Idaho has a deposit-refund system in place for old tires (Dinan, 1993). In that state, a $1 up-front user fee is assessed on each new motor vehicle tire purchased. From these fees, retreaders are paid a $1 subsidy for each retreaded tire, and other end-users of old tires are paid $20 per ton (Idaho Department of Health and Welfare, 1996).[28] Also, Maine reportedly has a deposit-refund system in place for commercial pesticide containers (Stavins, 1991).

C   Experiences with Deposit-Refund Systems Outside the US

Deposit-refund systems have also been used outside the United States. Within the OECD, the number of deposit-refund systems in each country has grown 35 percent to 100 percent between 1987 and 1993; this growth is mainly caused by a concern for packaging waste (Barde and Opschoor, 1994). Table 3.2 provides the number of deposit-refund systems in existence in mainly OECD countries, and it shows the types of items covered under these systems. Sweden and the United States are reported to have four different types of deposit-refund systems in place. Norway, Austria, Germany, Canada, and Australia all have three deposit-refund systems in operation; the remaining countries have only one or two systems. The most commonly covered items under a deposit-refund system are metal cans, plastic and glass containers, and car hulks. Some of the more unusual items covered by a deposit-refund system include fluorescent light bulbs in Austria, and logging in Indonesia.

Japan has its own 'bottle bill' with a return rate of 92 percent (Rhee, 1994). Korea also has two main deposit-refund systems in place: one on glass bottles, and one on solid and toxic waste. The program for solid waste covers items such as televisions, washing machines, tires, and batteries. Evidence suggests that Korea's deposit-refund systems have not been successful. Proper disposal of toxic wastes has been extremely low; only 8 percent of firms paying the initial deposit receive a refund. In total for Korea, approximately US$ 16.9 million has been collected in deposits while only US$ 38000 has been returned as refunds. Taiwan also has a deposit-refund system for 12 different products. In 1992, the

return rate – at least for plastic PET bottles – rose substantially, to just under
80 percent. Before, however, it was 41 percent.

Table 3.2   Deposit-refund systems by country

Country	Number of D-R systems	Items affected
Australia	3	Metal cans, plastic containers, glass bottles
Austria	3	Plastic containers, glass bottles, fluorescent bulbs
Belgium	1	Glass bottles
Canada	3	Metal cans, plastic containers, glass bottles
Denmark	2	Plastic containers, glass bottles
Estonia	1	Glass bottles
Finland	2	Plastic containers, glass bottles
France	1	Glass bottles
Germany	3	Plastic containers, glass bottles, packaging
Greece	1	Car hulks
Iceland	2	Plastic containers, glass bottles
Indonesia	1	Logging
Japan	1	Beverage containers
Korea	2	Glass bottles, solid and toxic waste items
Netherlands	2	Plastic containers, glass bottles
Norway	3	Car hulks, plastic containers, glass bottles
Portugal	1	Metal cans, plastic containers, glass bottles
Sweden	4	Car hulks, metal cans, plastic and glass bottles
Switzerland	1	Glass bottles
Taiwan	1	12 product items
Turkey	1	Glass bottles
United States	4	Metal cans, plastic and glass bottles, car batteries

Sources: Barde and Opschoor (1994), and OECD (1994b).

One reason listed for Japan's success – and for the relative failure of bottle
bills in Taiwan and Korea – is the long history of deposit-refund systems run
by private industry in Japan prior to the government program (O'Connor,
1994). Also, in Korea, the government deliberately set the deposit and refund
too low because of a concern about inflation (Rhee, 1994).

A more creative use of the two-part instrument has been attempted in
Indonesia. This country has experimented with a deposit-refund system in
order to try to slow deforestation. Loggers pay an up-front fee before harvesting

trees and then receive a refund when the logged trees are replaced with saplings. However, initial findings show this scheme to be ineffective. Even with the subsidy, the net benefits of replanting are reported to be less than the net benefits from not doing so (O'Connor, 1994). Thus, little replanting actually takes place.

Many instances of deposit-refund systems appear in Europe, mostly on beverage containers.[29] Return rates are between 40 and 100 percent, depending on the country and the type of container. A few of these programs are discussed below in more detail.

Sweden has deposit-refund systems for items such as aluminum cans, other beverage containers, and car hulks. The Swedish government has attempted to enforce a mandatory return rate of 75 percent. Evidence regarding car hulks, however, is not encouraging. Due to a small refund of SEK 300, and 12 years without adjusting for inflation (at which point the refund was the equivalent of SEK 120), returns of car hulks have been low (OECD, 1994a). The promised refund cannot compete with alternatives to returning the car hulks, such as storing or selling the parts and then dumping the remaining hulk (OECD, 1989).

Norway also has a deposit-refund for car hulks. Contrary to its Swedish counterpart, Norway's deposit-refund system works quite well, mainly due to a higher refund. The return rate is estimated to be between 90 and 99 percent. The deposit is paid when a new car is purchased, and the refund is given when a car is taken to a scrapping facility. One criticism of the Norwegian deposit-refund system, however, is a lack of scrapping facilities in convenient locations (OECD, 1989).[30]

The Netherlands has private deposit-refund systems in place for PET and glass bottles. The 1992 government budget also provided for the obligatory return of batteries, refrigerators, aluminum cans, and oil in the event that the current industry system fails (OECD, 1994a). Failure is defined by the government as less than a 30 percent return rate (OECD, 1989).[31] Also, the Dutch literature has discussed the feasibility of a deposit-refund system for controlling polluting substances such as cadmium and nitrates. Any domestic or imported product containing the polluting substance would be subject to a deposit upon sale. Refunds would be provided once the item was properly disposed of or exported.[32]

So far, almost all of the policies reviewed here still relate to explicit deposit-refund systems with a particular link from the deposit to the refund. A major point of this paper, however, is that the two-part instrument can be defined more broadly and employed more widely. Indeed, virtually all governments already employ implicit two-part tax-subsidy combinations. For example, a sales tax or value-added tax is collected on the purchase of all items, while the collection of household waste is subsidized through the provision of free municipal garbage services. 'Proper' household disposal is subsidized by this curbside collection, since the city pays for the trucks, work force, and tipping fees. The alternative is a Pigovian waste-end tax that would collect the marginal social cost per bag of garbage put on the curb for collection. This Pigovian tax might work well in suburbs and small towns where illegal dumping is not prevalent, but it would not work well in rural or urban areas where the fee can easily be avoided by dumping garbage on deserted roads, vacant lots, or in commercial dumpsters (Fullerton and Kinnaman, 1995). This improper disposal is avoided by the free collection of garbage, and municipal solid waste budgets are often financed by a local sales tax. The resulting combination is a two-part instrument, whether intended or not.

V   CONCLUSION

This paper builds two relatively simple general equilibrium models to demonstrate the equivalence between the Pigovian tax and the combination of a presumptive tax and performance subsidy. These models also help demonstrate the flexibility of this two-part instrument. To analyse the usefulness of the tax-subsidy combination, we review conceptual problems with its implementation and practical problems with the actual use of the tax-subsidy combination throughout the world. While the tax-subsidy combination is increasingly being used, in the form of a deposit-refund system, we argue that more flexible interpretations are important to explore. The two parts of such a policy do not have to apply to the same side of the market. Enactment might be easier, for example, if firms pay the tax while consumers receive the subsidy. The tax and subsidy do not have to equal one another, and they can apply to different goods altogether. Compared to a Pigovian tax, a two-part instrument may be easier to enforce, may be easier to enact, and can still force the market to recognize the social cost of disposal.

NOTES

*   We are grateful for financial assistance provided by EPA grant R824740-01-0. A special thanks to Gunnar Eskeland, Gib Metcalf, Arvind Panagariya, Bob Schwab, Hilary Sigman, Rob Stavins, Margaret Walls and Sarah West for helpful comments and suggestions. This paper is part of the NBER's research program in Public Economics. Any opinions expressed are those of the authors and not those of the Environmental Protection Agency or the National Bureau of Economic Research.
1.   The US Internal Revenue Service identifies four 'environmental taxes': (1) petroleum, for the Oil Spill Liability Trust Fund and for Superfund; (2) chemical feedstocks, for Superfund; (3) ozone-depleting chemicals, for the general fund; and (4) motor fuels, for the Leaking Underground Storage Tank (LUST) fund. These taxes apply to useful petroleum and chemical inputs, not to waste by-products or emissions (Fullerton, 1996).
2.   One can think of labor, capital, and materials as inputs to the production of a good output and a bad output (such as waste). Then the production function can be rearranged algebraically

by moving waste to the other side of the equation, so that the good output is a function of capital, labor, materials, and waste.

3. The presumptive tax-subsidy combination is not excluded from his analysis, but it is not his primary focus. Eskeland simply defines presumptive taxation more broadly to include taxes unaccompanied by subsidies. Eskeland and Devarajan (1996) show how different combinations of instruments can be used to approach the effect of an ideal Pigovian tax.

4. Actually, the two-part instrument might be difficult to implement perfectly for vehicle emissions because driving is not a market commodity which can be taxed in a way that will mirror the subsidy for clean inputs to driving. Certain kinds of heterogeneity also can be a problem for the two-part instrument, as discussed below.

5. Several papers compare this restricted deposit-refund system to other policies such as an advanced disposal fee or a virgin materials tax. Sigman (1995a) uses a partial equilibrium framework to analyse lead recycling, while Miedema (1983) uses a general equilibrium context to compare solid waste policy options. Dinan (1993) finds that, since a deposit-refund system is equivalent to a waste-end tax, it is more efficient than a virgin materials tax. Palmer et al. (1997) build a partial equilibrium model and run simulations in which the deposit is assumed to equal the refund, but where the deposit is paid by producers while the refund is given to recyclers. Swierzbinski (1994) uses a partial equilibrium, game-theoretic approach that allows the deposit to differ from the refund, but he requires that they apply to the same firm.

6. The two-part instrument may not be such a promising alternative, however, in cases where emissions are already being measured cheaply and effectively. Air emissions such as SO_2, for instance, are already monitored effectively by the EPA with installed continuous emissions monitoring (CEM) systems; firms are fined at the end of the year if actual emissions exceed the amount allowed. The two-part instrument may be more important in cases with many small polluters, where expensive emission monitoring equipment would be required for each.

7. Another model, similar to this one, is applied to the specific problem of household disposal in Fullerton and Kinnaman (1995).

8. We can generalize this result to an n good model in which a Pigovian tax on one good can be mimicked by taxes and subsidies on the remaining $n - 1$ goods. This follows from the fact that supply functions are homogenous of degree zero in prices, and demand functions are homogenous of degree zero in prices and income.

9. A simple modification to the model can introduce the idea of a 'bottle bill' explicitly by making utility a function of $q(c,d)$ where q is the quantity of drinks consumed, c is the clean disposal of those bottles through recycling and d is the dirty disposal alternative. The two-part instrument would then be to tax q and subsidize c, which effectively taxes the use of d without actually applying a direct tax to this disposal alternative.

10. Because of constant returns to scale, all of these variables can be expressed in amounts per household.

11. Note that if two or more unobservable pollutants are used as inputs to production, this scheme will not work unless the Pigovian solution were to tax these pollutants at the same rate.

12. In fact, this argument suggests that any further legal sanctions on dumping are not only unnecessary, but also undesirable. If the firm pays a presumptive tax on all output that is equal to the social external cost of dumping, and then receives a subsidy on all activities except dumping, it already pays the marginal social cost of that dumping. Then the chosen amount of dumping is the socially optimal amount of dumping, and any additional legal sanction would overcorrect the externality and reduce social welfare!

13. See Swierzbinski (1994) for a partial equilibrium game-theoretic approach to this problem. His model allows the firm the opportunity to request an audit, in order to get refunds, but such an audit still requires the government officials to measure the emissions.

14. The waste-end tax might be just as efficient, if high-time-value individuals can get their trash sorted by paying low-time-value individuals, but the waste-end tax would not directly subsidize low-time-value individuals to pick up litter along the roadway. Also, the refund provides some incentive to clean up the existing stock of litter, while the waste-end tax applies only to new litter (Lee et al., 1992).

15. In the case where the refund level is too high, individuals may even try to bring in a stolen or substitute item in order to receive the refund.
16. A beverage container is usually defined as 'any sealable bottle, can, jar, or carton which is primarily composed of glass, metal, plastic, or any combination of those materials and is produced for the purpose of containing a beverage' (Massachusetts Executive Office of Environmental Affairs, 1989).
17. These ten states include California, Connecticut, Delaware, Iowa, Maine, Massachusetts, Michigan, New York, Oregon, and Vermont. The system in California is sometimes called a deposit-refund system and is sometimes referred to as an advanced disposal fee.
18. According to Jenkins and Lamech (1992), the handling fee in most states is 20 percent of the deposit.
19. Porter (1983) finds a slightly higher return rate for Michigan of 95 percent.
20. A Massachusetts study also finds that the bottle bill actually helps the recycling programs in that state, since a bottle bill is often a cheaper option in locations where curbside collection is expensive to implement. Also, restaurants and businesses are usually excluded from curbside recycling and can use a bottle bill to recycle containers. This can mean a substantial increase in a state's total recycling; 80 percent of the beverage containers collected in Massachusetts come from commercial sources (Friedland and Perry, 1995).
21. These costs do not include administrative costs to government or political rent-seeking costs to firms.
22. Porter (1978) concludes that in Michigan, for a five cents per container average time cost, the average benefit received from proper disposal must be greater than $12.48 per person annually (in 1974 dollars) in order for the deposit-refund system to be considered economically worthwhile. Using Porter's framework, Naughton et al. (1990) estimate the average inconvenience costs in California of returning aluminum, non-refillable glass and plastic containers. Per container, estimates ranged from 29 to 57 cents.
23. See Baumol and Oates (1971) for more on the 'standards and prices' approach.
24. Technology can also play an important role in making the deposit-refund system more efficient. One such technology is the reverse vending machine. It can be installed in a grocery store where consumers then load their beverage containers into the machine. The items are placed on a conveyor belt where each is scanned to distinguish valid containers from invalid ones, as well as type (if the refund differs by type) of container. The machine then either prints out a voucher or pays the proper refund to the consumer. Thus, the store need not dedicate extra personnel to the task of refunding money or sorting containers (Pang, 1996).
25. Nationally, 'do-it-yourselfers' apparently account for 50 percent of the illegal dumping of oil, while they only account for 5 percent of the recycling of oil (Stavins 1991). Thus, a deposit-refund system that creates incentives to discourage littering and illegal dumping is a promising policy tool. Also, reportedly 80 percent of lead consumption in the United States is attributable to lead-acid batteries (Sigman, 1995a). Therefore, concentrating on lead-acid batteries when formulating policy seems justified.
26. Such lead-acid battery deposit-refund systems reportedly exist in Arizona, Arkansas, Connecticut, Idaho, Michigan, Minnesota, New York, and Washington (Sigman, 1995a).
27. Analogous rebates are offered in programs that buy up old cars. Alberini et al. (1994) note several potential problems with this type of program. Individuals might be induced to let their cars deteriorate more than otherwise, or they may bring old cars into the jurisdiction in order to get the rebate.
28. Waste tires are principally used as a fuel supplement. The Idaho tax-subsidy combination for tires was scheduled to end by 1 July 1996.
29. Andersen (1994) states that a system of fees coupled with subsidies is appealing relative to an emissions tax for the countries he focuses on – Denmark, France, Germany, and the Netherlands – for reasons of political acceptability.
30. The Estonian deposit-refund system on glass bottles also functions poorly due to a lack of return locations (OECD, 1994b).
31. Again, the 'standards and prices' approach in Baumol and Oates (1971) is being used; a standard of 30 percent is set, and then a pricing mechanism, in the form of the deposit-refund system, is adjusted to attain the standard.

32. Tax-subsidy combinations are also suggested in the literature for the recovery of CFCs from refrigerators and air conditioners (Fisher et al., 1995), as well as for the recovery of sulfur dioxide from the air (Bohm, 1981).

REFERENCES

Ackerman, Frank, Dmitri Cavander, John Stutz and Brian Zuckerman (1995), *Preliminary Analysis: The Costs and Benefits of Bottle Bills*, Draft Report to USEPA/Office of Solid Waste and Emergency Response, Boston: Tellus Institute.

Alberini, Anna, David Edelstein, Winston Harrington and Virginia D. McConnell (1994), 'Reducing Emissions from Old Cars: The Economics of the Delaware Vehicle Retirement Program', Discussion Paper, no. 94-27, Washington, DC: Resources for the Future.

Andersen, Mikael Skou (1994), *Governance by Green Taxes: Making Pollution Prevention Pay*, Manchester: Manchester University Press.

Barde, Jean-Phillippe and Johanes Baptist Opschoor (1994), 'From Stick to Carrot in the Environment', *OECD Observer*, **186**, 23–7.

Baumol, William and Wallace Oates (1971), 'The Use of Standards and Prices for Protection of the Environment', *Swedish Journal of Economics*, **73**, 42–54.

Baumol, William and Wallace Oates (1988), *The Theory of Environmental Policy*, Second Edition, New York: Cambridge University Press.

Bohm, Peter (1981), *Deposit-Refund Systems*, Washington, DC: Resources for the Future.

Bovenberg, Lans and Ruud de Mooij (1994), 'Environmental Levies and Distortionary Taxation', *American Economic Review*, **84**, 1085–9.

Container Recycling Institute (1992), *Beverage Container Deposit Systems in the United States*, Washington, DC: Container Recycling Institute.

Cropper, Maureen and Wallace Oates (1992), 'Environmental Economics: A Survey', *Journal of Environmental Literature*, **30**, 675–740.

Dinan, Terry (1993), 'Economic Efficiency Effects of Alternative Policies for Reducing Waste Disposal', *Journal of Environmental Economics and Management*, **25**, 242–56.

Eskeland, Gunnar (1994), 'A Presumptive Pigovian Tax: Complementing Regulation to Mimic an Emissions Fee', *The World Bank Economic Review* **8**(3), 373–94.

Eskeland, Gunnar and Shantayanan Devarajan (1996), *Taxing Bads by Taxing Goods: Pollution Control with Presumptive Charges*, Washington, DC: World Bank.

Fisher, Brian, Scott Barrett, Peter Bohm, J.K. Mubazi, Anwar Shah and Robert Stavins (1995), 'An Economic Assessment of Policy Instruments to Combat Climate Change', *Report of Working Group III of the Intergovernmental Panel on Climate Change*, Switzerland.

Friedland, Shelly and Amy Perry (1995), *Many Happy Returns: A Retrospective of the Massachusetts Bottle Bill*, Massachusetts: MASSPIRG.

Fullerton, Don (1996), 'Why Have Separate Environmental Taxes?' in James M. Poterba (ed.), *Tax Policy and the Economy*, **10**, Cambridge: MIT Press for the National Bureau of Economic Research.

Fullerton, Don (1997), 'Environmental Levies and Distortionary Taxation: Comment', *American Economic Review*, **87**, 245–51.

Fullerton, Don and Thomas Kinnaman (1995), 'Garbage, Recycling, and Illicit Burning or Dumping', *Journal of Environmental Economics and Management*, **29**, 78–91.

Gupta, Ashok (1996), Letter, Albany: New York State Department of Environmental Conservation, March.

Harrington, Winston, Margaret Walls and Virginia McConnell (1994), 'Shifting Gears: New Directions for Cars and Clean Air', Discussion Paper, no. 94-26-REV, Washington, DC: Resources for the Future.

Idaho Department of Health and Welfare, Division of Environmental Quality (1996), *Idaho Waste Tire Disposal Annual Report to the Legislature*, Boise.

Iowa Department of Natural Resources (1996), *Beverage Container Law Overview*, Des Moines.

Jenkins, Glenn and Ranjit Lamech (1992), 'Market-Based Incentive Instruments for Pollution Control', *International Bulletin of Fiscal Documentation*, **46** (11), 523–38.

Lee, Dwight, Philip Graves and Robert Sexton (1992), 'Controlling the Abandonment of Automobiles: Mandatory Deposits vs. Fines', *Journal of Urban Economics*, **31**, 14–24.

Massachusetts Executive Office of Environmental Affairs (1989), *Provisions for Recycling of Beverage Containers*, Massachusetts.

Miedema, Allen (1983), 'Fundamental Economic Comparisons of Solid Waste Policy Options', *Resources and Energy*, **5**, 21–43.

Mrozek, Janusz (1995), 'Beverage Container Recycling: Incentives versus Attitudes as Explanations of Behavior', Working Paper, Atlanta: Georgia Institute of Technology.

Naughton, Michael, Frederick Sebold and Thomas Mayer (1990), 'The Impacts of the California Beverage Container Recycling and Litter Reduction Act on Consumers', *The Journal of Consumer Affairs*, **24**(1), 190–220.

New York Department of Environmental Conservation (1994), *Report on Unclaimed Beverage Container Deposits*, New York: Division of Solid Waste.

O'Connor, David (1994), 'The Use of Economic Instruments in Environmental Management: The East Asian Experience', in *Applying Economic Instruments to Environmental Policies in OECD and Dynamic Non-Member Countries*, Paris: OECD.

Organisation for Economic Cooperation and Development (1989), *Economic Instruments for Environmental Protection*, Paris: OECD.

Organisation for Economic Cooperation and Development (1994a), *Environment and Taxation: The Cases of the Netherlands, Sweden and the United States*, Paris: OECD.

Organisation for Economic Cooperation and Development (1994b), *Managing the Environment: The Role of Economic Instruments*, Paris: OECD.

Palmer, Karen, Hilary Sigman and Margaret Walls (1997), 'The Cost of Reducing Municipal Solid Waste', *Journal of Environmental Economics and Management*, **33**, 128–50.

Pang, Tanya (1996), 'Empty Bottles Fill Coffers of Norwegian Firm', *Reuter European Community Report*, 28 April.

Pigou, Arthur (1932), *The Economics of Welfare*, Fourth edition, London: MacMillan and Co.

Porter, Richard (1978), 'A Social Benefit–Cost Analysis of Mandatory Deposits on Beverage Containers', *Journal of Environmental Economics and Management*, **5**, 351–75.

Porter, Richard (1983), 'Michigan's Experience with Mandatory Deposits on Beverage Containers', *Land Economics*, **59** (2), 177–94.

Rhee, Ho-Saeng (1994), 'The Use of Economic Instruments in Environmental Protection in Korea', in *Applying Economic Instruments to Environmental Policies in OECD and Dynamic Non-Member Countries*, Paris: OECD.

Russell, Clifford (1988), 'Economic Incentives in the Management of Hazardous Wastes', *Columbia Journal of Environmental Law*, **13** (2), 257–74.

Russell, Clifford (1990), 'Monitoring and Enforcement' in Paul Portney (ed.), *Public Policies for Environmental Protection*, Washington, DC: Resources for the Future.

Sigman, Hilary (1995a), 'A Comparison of Public Policies for Lead Recycling,' *RAND Journal of Economics* **26** (3), 452–78.

Sigman, Hilary (1995b), 'Midnight Dumping: An Empirical Analysis of Illegal Waste Oil Disposal', Working Paper, University of California, Los Angeles.

Stavins, Robert (1991), *Project 88-Round II: Incentives for Action: Designing Market-Based Environmental Strategies*, Sponsored by Timothy Wirth and John Heinz, Washington, DC: US Senate.

Swierzbinski, Joseph (1994), 'Guilty Until Proven Innocent – Regulation with Costly and Limited Enforcement', *Journal of Environmental Economics and Management*, **27** (2), 127–46.

United States General Accounting Office (1990), *Trade-Offs Involved in Beverage Container Deposit Legislation*, Washington, DC: USGAO.

Wahl, Mary (1995), Letter to State Representative Lisa Naito, Oregon Department of Environmental Quality, Portland.

Name index

Ackerman, F. 4, 5, 17, 190
Adams, R.M. 34, 35, 38, 39, 40, 41, 105, 121, 122, 123, 138
Aldy, J.E. 25, 26, 42
Andersen, M.S. 197
Anderson, C. 99
Anderson, R.C. 16
Ashford, N.A. 42
Atri, S. 13
Auerbach, A.J. 109

Babcock, L. 88
Bailey, J. 5, 6
Barde, J-P. 192
Bauer, S. 42
Baumol, W.J. 53, 98, 107, 178, 187, 188, 197
Becker, A. 24, 37, 40
Beede, D.N. 15, 28, 42
Besley, T. 122, 141
Bingham, T.H. 16
Bloom, D.E. 15, 28, 42
Blume, D.R. 42, 95
Bohm, P. 103, 176, 185, 198
Bohm, R.A. 21, 23, 24, 155
Bovenberg, A.L. 63, 168, 169, 170, 171, 173, 187
Breckinridge, C. 89, 94, 121, 136, 151
Brisson, I.E. 8, 24
Browne, A.G. 122, 123, 139
Brueckner, J. 120
Butterfield, D.W. 24
Bynum, D.Z. 11
Byrd, D. 94, 151

Callan, S.J. 17, 25, 34, 35, 37, 40
Cameron, T.A. 162, 166
Cargo, D.B. 89
Carroll, W. 23, 24, 165
Case, A. 122, 141
Choe, C. 108, 112
Cointreau-Levine, S.J. 28
Cooley, P.C. 16
Copeland, B.R. 20, 50, 60, 65, 116
Coughlin, P. 153, 163
Criner, G. 34, 36
Cropper, M. 176

de Mooij, R.A. 168, 169, 170, 173, 187

De Young, R. 165
Devarajan, S. 196
Dinan, T.M. 10, 11, 12, 65, 192, 196
Dobbs, I.M. 11, 50, 75, 103
Douglas, P.V. 15, 165
Doyle, K.T. 158
Dubin, J.A. 21, 22, 165
Duggal, V.G. 25, 37, 40, 165

Edwards, R. 16
Efaw, F. 89, 121
Engberg, J. 88
Eskeland, G. 176, 195, 196

Fenton, R. 27
Fisher, B. 198
Folz, D.H. 21, 23, 24, 155, 165
Fraser, I. 108, 112
Friedland, S. 190, 197
Fullerton, D. 10, 11, 12, 13, 17, 23, 25, 26, 27, 34, 35, 36, 37, 38, 40, 42, 43, 75, 93, 105, 106, 107, 112, 121, 122, 125, 136, 139, 140, 144, 149, 151, 161, 162, 165, 172, 184, 187, 195, 196

Genereux, J. 15
Genereux, M. 15
Glen, J. 2, 3, 5, 7, 153, 160, 164, 165
Goldstein, N. 88, 122
Goulder, L.H. 168, 171
Gray, N. 153
Gupta, A. 189

Halstead, J.M. 8
Hanley, N. 23, 27, 156
Harrington, W. 183
Haveman, B. 102
Havlicek, J. 40, 89, 92, 138, 151
Heap, P. 88
Heinz, J. 49
Henstock, M.E. 105
Holthausen, D.M. 65, 108
Hong, S. 34, 35, 38, 39, 40, 41, 89, 105, 121, 122, 123, 138, 151
Huhtala, A. 24
Hupert, D.D. 166

Inchauste, G. 120

LIVERPOOL
JOHN MOORES UNIVERSITY
AVRIL ROBARTS LRC
TITHEBARN STREET
LIVERPOOL L2 2ER
TEL 0151 231 4022